D1172469

almost anywhere

almost anywhere

Road Trip Ruminations on Love, Nature, National Parks, and Nonsense

Krista Schlyer

Skyhorse Publishing

Memoirs, by definition, are written depictions of events in people's lives. They are memories. All the events in this story are as accurate and truthful as possible. Many names and places have been changed to protect the privacy of others. Mistakes, if any, are caused solely by the passage of time.

Skyhorse Publishing books may be purchased in bulk at special discounts for sales promotion, corporate gifts, fund-raising, or educational purposes. Special editions can also be created to specifications. For details, contact the Special Sales Department, Skyhorse Publishing, 307 West 36th Street, 11th Floor, New York, NY 10018 or info@skyhorsepublishing.com.

Visit our website at www.skyhorsepublishing.com.

10 9 8 7 6 5 4 3 2 1

Library of Congress Cataloging-in-Publication Data is available on file.

Cover design by Laura Klynstra
Cover photo credit by Krista Schlyer

Print ISBN: 978-1-63450-236-8
Ebook ISBN: 978-1-5107-0056-7

Printed in the United States of America

For Daniel, Bill, and Maggie

Acknowledgments

This book was fifteen years in the making and many people along the way have played a part in its becoming. First I have to thank my mom, Maureen Dowd, for her support in all things—and also because I forgot to thank her in the acknowledgements of my last book (huge oversight—sorry, Ma). Thanks also to my friends and family, in particular Nick and Rob and Penny, for all your support over the years through good times and bad.

I owe a great deal to Shannon Davies, who published my first book *Continental Divide: Wildlife, People and the Border Wall* for Texas A&M University Press and who generously encouraged me in the publication of *Almost Anywhere*.

The fate of the *Almost Anywhere* manuscript took a fortuitous turn when Shannon Hassan of the Marsal Lyon Literary Agency agreed to be my agent. Thank you, Shannon—your thoughtful guidance has helped me immensely through the publication process. My thanks to Nicole Frail, my editor, and the whole team at Skyhorse, for all the hard work and dedication you have given to the manuscript, design, and publishing of this book. To Cat Lazaroff and all the literary warriors of my writers group, my thanks—with special appreciation to Holliann Kim, for her copyediting help during her ninth month of pregnancy!

And finally to those who have shared in the events contained in this book, I will be forever grateful to all of you who lived this time with me. Especially Barbara DiTondo, I thank you for being a model of grace and kindness and a lifelong friend. Your son will always be a bright shining supernova in my life. Your support of this project has been essential. And finally, I would like to thank Bill Updike, my best friend and biggest supporter, without whom this book, and my life as I know it, would never have been written. My love and gratitude always Bill.[1]

[1]Also, please stop hogging the Pringles.

The only constant is change.

—Ancient Greek Proverb

You can't have life without dirt. You can't have dirt without death.
Dirt is death and life.
Dirt.

—Future Ancient American Proverb

1

Wisdom can be a sadistic, extortive prize. Sure, some people emerge from the womb dripping unearned wisdom from their newborn digits, floating through life making nothing but good choices and accepting the random cruelties of life with the grace of a fat, happy Buddha. Good for them.

The rest of us have to earn wisdom through exacting measures levied throughout our lives. As for me, I was lucky. I managed to live much of my life without it.

When I was a small child living a quasi-feral existence on a Kansas farm, I had little interest in wisdom, knowledge, or even books, for that matter. I preferred to spend my time running wild after my big brothers as they explored the endless acres of farmland and forest that surrounded our country home. I was a dirty-faced, crazy-haired tomboy with bruised knees, battle scars, and places to be, and I didn't have time for books. But one book in particular piqued my interest and insinuated itself into my earliest and most kitten-brained philosophies.

It was an old family bible that sat on a table planted in our thick, grass-green, shag-carpeted living room. It was ornate, as all things pertaining to godishness must be, and it was *huge*. The bible weighed fifteen pounds and measured about one foot by two feet. Had it been hollow, it could have housed a family of mice, a newborn goat, and the baby Jesus, all together, quite comfortably.[1]

---

[1]Not the freakish alien man-baby Christ child or obese cherubic Jesus in early artistic renditions, who looked like he'd been breastfed Coca-Cola. But a regular infant-sized baby Jesus would have fit just fine. It was the largest bible in the world. My oldest brother assured me the truth of this fact. This brother also confided in me that he, at age six, was one of only five people in the universe who could whistle the *Andy Griffith Show*'s theme song. A terrible burden for one so young.

The cover of the book was richly textured faux leather and the script of the title, which read, *The Holy Bible*, was shiny faux gold leaf. Celestially large and lavishly ornate, the book had a gravitational attraction for me and when I grew tall enough to reach it, and strong enough to pry open the cover, I would often do so in order to behold the gloriously dramatic painting of an old bearded grandpa clothed in a pristine white billowing robe lounging on a cloud, pointing at something. What was he pointing at? I often wondered. Maybe it was my five-year-old brother across the living room, wearing a silky brown shirt with an enormous collar, his blindingly white towhead bobbing around as he danced to the Bee Gees. That was funny and point-worthy, but bible-grandpa didn't look amused.

I never found an answer to that question, but what I did surmise from this painting was a very clear notion of the nature of a place called heaven. Heaven is . . . impeccably ordered; free of chaos; it is clean, without stain; deathless. Deathless. I didn't really grasp what that meant at the time, but I knew it was important. The chaos and disorder that permeate the fabric of earthly life had not yet touched my reality, but I understood that the illustration was depicting a place very different from the world where I lived. I had gathered ideas of this other, presumably better world everywhere. There was bible-grandpa, movie actors wearing clean white robes, angels glittering like starlight, and for me, there was my grandma, an angel in her own right, with soft white curls like a puff of cloud glued to her head and papery hands that smelled of bleach, who told me I would go to hell or get bitten by a poisonous spider if I didn't keep my room clean.

The idea of hell scared me, and my whole family was terrified of spiders, so I noodled quite a bit on this grandma warning. The clean=good=heaven equation sounded reasonable, if inconvenient, to my young self, and though I never adopted it in practice—as I said, I had places to be, things to do, brothers to follow, and no time for tidiness—it did permeate some of my foundational childhood philosophies. As did the inverse equation: dirty=bad=hell. Whenever I was alone and scared, if I closed my eyes I would see a jumbled dirty mess of brown chaos, like a hideous brown shag carpet made of barfed up spiders. And when, at age four, I would find this barfy image in my mind, I could calm myself only by conjuring a cloudy white image of a place called heaven.

Nowhere, in all of these visions or images of the perfect place I would hopefully go to after I died if I stopped being such a dirty slob, nowhere, was there ever even a speck of dirt.

Cornville

There's plenty of dirt in Cornville. Ergo, Cornville is not heaven. For a flitting moment in time though, it was just shy of paradise. This tiny town in the high desert in northern Arizona was home for Daniel and me, the last home we had before the very idea of home imploded.

At the time, Cornville consisted of a sprawling rural community and two main city center buildings—the Cornville Mercantile and Vince's Little Star Italian restaurant. Great restaurant. I can't speak to the relative greatness of the mercantile, as I have never been in another mercantile, before or since. It had a little bit of everything, from video rentals and propane tanks to potted meat and a four-foot-tall barrel of pickles.

We had moved to Cornville from Tucson so that I could start my first job out of journalism school at the *Verde Independent* newspaper, a small news organization based in nearby Cottonwood. It was an exciting moment: the first time I had ever made the decision to move in with another person and the beginning of my career as a journalist. And despite the fact that our new hometown was named Cornville and he didn't have a job lined up, Daniel was as excited to move to the middle of nowhere as I was.

We had found an adorable little cabin to live in, with walls of knotty pine and a sleeping porch where we could feel the crisp desert night air and watch the summer thunderstorms blow through.

Upon getting settled in, we found out just how close to nowhere we were living. There were exactly three things to do in Cornville: mountain biking, eating at Vince's, and stargazing. Well, four in our particular case; we spent a lot of time searching for my dog, Maggie, each time she tunneled under or climbed over the fence or snuck out the door. The little tramp always had someplace better to be. Where, exactly, I never really found out—she was openly scornful of my attempts to contain her movements and tight-lipped about her vagabonding.

Cornville sits a dozen or so miles from the nearest towns, Cottonwood and Sedona, neither of which are very large or well lit, so the night skies outside our house were spectacular. Daniel's mom had given him a telescope prior to our moving there, and almost every night he would take it outside and get acquainted with the universe. Generally, while he was doing that, I was getting acquainted with the backside of my eyelids. I was, in that era, an epic napper. I spent most of my free time stuffed inside my head, preoccupied by some existential malaise, which I had contracted a few years earlier from a mutant strain of thinking I encountered in college. The resulting sluggishness dragged on for years intermittently as the meaning-seeking bug worked its way through my system. It was exhausting, so I slept. And slept. And slept. It took me fifteen years and a twisted knife in my back to realize what Daniel seemed to know instinctively, that any meaning that need be found in this world is right there in the arms of Orion.

If I believed in regret, one of my biggest in life would be covering my head with my pillow and sinking farther into the couch when Daniel threw open the Cornville cabin door and yelled, "Come on! I found the Orion nebula!"

Siriusly

It wasn't like I always ignored Daniel's entreaties. Often I would grumble, wipe the sleep from my eyes, and follow him out into the starlit night. Once awakened by the chill air and endless amphitheater of sky, I would amuse him by misnaming stars, planets, constellations, our future progeny, and anything else I could think of.

"Mars!" I'd announce.

"What makes you say that, sweets?"

"It's red."

"Hmmm . . . Yeah, that's not Mars."

"Could be."

"No."

"Well, there's Saturn, I can see the rings."

"You can't see the rings of Saturn with your naked eye!"

He found this really funny.

"Yes, I can."

"Nooo, you can't," he would retort, while laughing the belly laugh he reserved for the most preposterous of ideas. It wasn't a mocking, sneering laugh, like, "Oh, please, moron, get yourself book-learned." It was more like, "Oh! You're delightful, the way you say such nonsense!"

Like a king being tickled by a court jester with an enormous feather.

Or like the impression Daniel did of his Sicilian grandmother, Gertie, who would grab Daniel's chin, shake it gently, and smile at him with love while saying, "*Que beeeedo.*" Daniel never understood his grandmother but assumed she was shaking his chin and saying, "Ooohhh, you so stooopid." When he told me this story he would laugh his laugh that made me forget the meaning of the word *meaning*.

I loved this laugh and worked constantly to provoke it.

"Look! There's Venus," I'd say smartly, pointing to the brightest thing I could see.

"No, that's Sirius, the eye of Canis Major," he'd correct, still chuckling but shifting into teaching mode.

"Oh. But it's so bright, I thought it was a planet."

"Looks like it. It's twice as large as the sun, and twenty-five times more luminous," Daniel would tell me. "But it's so much farther away, we can only see it when the sun is down."

I'd think on this for a moment, then say, "If we ever have a child, and he's a boy, we should name him Sirius."

Daniel would just look at me, only a faint scrunching of his eyebrows to suggest he was not enamored with the idea.

I'd nod my head quickly, "Good idea, right?"

"No."

"Why?"

"Because that's a terrible name," he'd say.

"No, it's a *great* name. When he introduced himself to people he could say, 'Hi, I'm Sirius.' And they would say, 'Whaaa?' and he could say, 'I'm serious, my name is Sirius.'"

Daniel would shake his head and say, "Seriously, that's a ridiculous name. Stop saying it."

"Make me."

Sigh.

"Can you think of a better one?" I'd challenge him.

"How about Sebastian?" Daniel would say, his eye peering into the telescope and out into the universe.

A sharp twinge of sadness would temper my humor as I followed his gaze to stare into the eternal glimmering dark.

"Yes," I'd say. "That is better."

Sebastian

Like many good parents, Sebastian was everything Daniel aspired to be and everything he struggled to overcome. He was intelligent, creative, strong, a success in business, a talented self-taught painter, a lover of music and wine and food, a gifted vocalist. Daniel wanted to make his dad proud, but he also wanted to be free of the need to live his life according to anyone else's plans or expectations. And shortly after he came into adulthood, as he was grappling with how to mold his life as something distinct but respectful of the life of his dad, he was suddenly faced with a very different quandary—how to envision a lifetime with a silent void where his father's voice once was.

Several months before Daniel and I met, Sebastian had died of cancer after a long and painful battle. Deciding to move to Arizona and live with me had been one of the hardest decisions Daniel had ever made—it meant leaving his mom, Barbara, for the first time since his dad's death.

During the year we lived in Cornville, Daniel spent countless hours gazing into that beautiful telescope his mom had given him. Occasionally, when I was supposed to be napping, I would look out the wall of windows near my perch on the couch and watch Daniel watching the sky. Often, I imagine, he was looking back in time, sifting through the infinite points of light in the endless darkness, searching for Sebastian.

Orion

It's hard to find anything or hold onto it for very long in a world that's always changing. Thus the allure of a static, clean, painless place called heaven. Here in the ol' Milky Way, time is the sworn enemy of stasis. Outside of time, permanence is possible. But within time, all things change eventually. No matter the strength of our vice-grip on the present, it cannot hold. May as well command the sun not to rise or your fingernails not to grow. Impermanence is rock solid; no, more solid than rock.

Mountains wear down, explode, and crumble. Continents drift. Even constellations shift over time. Not over time as we know it and perceive it, but in their own timeframes the cosmos are as restless as the rest of us. Lucky for us, we exist in a different strata of time and space and we will never witness a major transformation of our beloved night guardians. Cassiopeia will always look like a misshapen "w" sprawling in the sky, the Big Dipper will always seem to us an enormous ladle of soup, and Orion will always be standing beside his faithful dog Canis Major.

Orion, due to his great distance from Earth, will likely be one of the last constellations to drift beyond recognition for Earthly eyes. It's a good thing. I'm not sure what we'd do without Orion. For as long as civilization has existed, we have counted on him to be right where he is supposed to be every night, never failing us, never deserting. He is, we can say with great confidence, one of the very few elements in the world we know that will never abandon us.

2

As a periwinkle dawn shuffles across the sky, sleepy Lake Michigan laps against its shores with halfhearted persistence. The great lake seems distracted from its great-lakeness this August morning, as though it lacks the heart to rise with the sun or tussle with the wind.

Bill absentmindedly strolls the high water line, making the day's first footprints in rippled sand. He looks out across the lake toward Chicago, whose skyline floats as a dark amorphous crown on the southwestern horizon.

I vaguely watch Bill, then the waves at his feet, then the dull dawn light upon the lake. I drop to the sand and sit motionless while my mind spins, laboring to conjure a coherent recollection of how I came to be here, in this place, with this man in front of me.

We had awakened at Bill's mom's house in New Buffalo, Michigan. That much is simple enough. And by noon today we will have reached Ohio, also fairly simple. But then it all begins to unravel, 'til all I have in front of me is a tangled mess of knotted yarn. I grasp a loose end and trace the thread backward in my mind to six months ago and a city half a continent away. The gentle lapping of Michigan's waves becomes a rustling of gingko leaves and I'm lying on the floor, staring at some white curtains as they dance upon an early spring breeze pouring through the open window of a condo in the Adams Morgan neighborhood of Washington, DC. The tree outside sways and shivers in concert with the wind and curtains. I watch the scene impassively. I've been here for hours, it seems, and hours before, countless times, watching these curtains dance like a ghostly bridal veil caught in a puff of summer air. My mind floats weightlessly with the apparition.

Daniel and I had debated buying the curtains. He wanted blinds or shutters. I wanted something that would act as partner to sun and wind, not as dictator. I was persistent. I had, in fact, imagined them on a day exactly like today, when, weary of winter, I could watch spring blow in, accompanied by a premonition of summer, a light melody of leaves and an interpretive curtain dance. Only, I hadn't imagined any of the rest of this scene. Not the empty apartment. Not the bags of Daniel's clothes sitting by the door.

Not the tourniquet that binds me, pinning me to this floor, freezing the blood within my veins. My brain, heart, and limbs suffer the deprivation but they hold on, hoping I will find a pulse again.

Let them wait. The dancing drapes are enough for me now.

My curtain musings are interrupted by the phone. I let it ring, uninterested in the larger world outside the condo walls. But when I hear the voice on the answering machine, I haul myself off the floor to pick up.

"How are you?" says Bill when he hears my voice. Bill was Daniel's best friend, and mine. We spent most spare moments together the three of us, playing cards, hiking, eating, dancing. We had followed each other across the country and back again over the past ten years—with or without intention, we just ended up together.

"Watching the curtains," I answer.

"Hmmm," he says. "I've been staring at my computer screen . . . for maybe half an hour."

"Stuck."

"Yeah." He's quiet for a while, then continues. "We both need to get out of here. Way out."

He didn't elaborate but I knew what he meant. The idea had come up several times over the past year, but this time he really meant it. He worked for a magazine focused on the national park system. Every day he would sit for eight hours at a computer and write about a world of wild places he had never visited, smiling the smiles that are the obligation of office jobs, all while dealing with a personal despair that was too crippling to even express. He would see photos come across his desk, of places like Yosemite, Sequoia, and Great Smoky Mountain national parks, and he had a growing sense that there was a place to be both broken and whole at the same time. He thought we should go out on the road, to all those national parks and wild lands, as many as we could get to in as long as we could manage to stay away. We'd go by car, sleep in a tent, eat cheap noodles and canned beans, whatever it took.

The idea seemed foreign to me, impossible; and yet inevitable.

"How?" I asked.

"We'll figure it out," he said. "You need this. You're not making it here, and neither am I."

Memory washes over me as a rogue wave, the remnant violence of a faraway squall that shakes and batters, then spits me out on the Michigan sand, pinning me down, clogging my nose, mouth, lungs with a cold, gritty sludge. I collect myself, consider picking up that tortuous clump of yarn, and going back a little further into the past, but the idea of it renders me immobile. That won't do. Not today.

No, the rest is too much. Too much for the beach at dawn. Too much broken apart, corroded by chemicals, fallen away, lost. Need more than a morning, or a month, or a beach, or endless melancholy lake to contain it. Maybe a country will do and a year or more.

Bill walks over to me and holds out his hand.

"You ready?" he asks.

I grab his hand and allow myself to be pulled out of the sand.

"Yeah, let's get going."

We had walked to the edge of this listless lake to photograph ourselves before commencing a long languid drift across the North American landscape. We've come from Washington, DC. This morning we're in Michigan. Tomorrow we could be, well, almost anywhere.

Kleenex

After the photo, we gather the last of our stuff and Maggie the dog and load them into the maroon station wagon we bought for the trip. Our transformation into the Beverly Hillbillies is nearly complete: we have food, bedding, a tent, portable shower, our books, backpacks, clothes, water filter, a stove, computer, and camera gear packed inside or strapped atop the roof of the car.

Bill's mom is sure we've missed something. . . .

For a while she watches us pack up, wiping tears away as they fall. Then she disappears into her house momentarily and when she returns to the car, her arms are full of this and that, a mound of random things she has gathered from her cupboards and drawers. In appearance, the items are flashlights, pens, blankets, socks, and snacks. But by intension, they are talismans meant to keep us safe over long distances and in unknown spaces.

"Do you want this bag of pretzels?" she asks.

"I don't like pretzels," Bill responds, with a slight hint of impatience.

"How about some juice?"

"Mom, we don't have any room."

"Oh . . . How about some almonds . . . a pillow . . . this little packet of Kleenex?"

As she watches us stuff the car, she may be unconsciously cataloging the unannounced visits Death has paid to her family over the past few years and fighting with the urge to lock her twenty-nine-year-old son in the basement, where he would get little light but plenty of warmth and food and shelter from the infinite dangers that loiter this world. But she makes no outward sign of it. She has seen an ashen mask build on Bill's face over the past years and knows the tangle of pain that holds it there cannot be unraveled in a vault. Light is key. She lets him go.

And secretly hands me a packet of Kleenex and a bag of almonds.

Wham!

In keeping with our vow to avoid interstate highways, we point the station wagon east on US Highway 20. In the 1980s, though we knew nothing of each other then, Bill and I grew up about fifteen miles apart, in the space where Indiana meets Michigan. Locals call it Michiana. My parents had divorced when I was about seven and Bill's parents split when he was a toddler. He lived with his mom and two older sisters on the Michigan side of the Michiana line, and I with my mom and two older brothers on the Indiana side. We all lived in a world of low pay for single moms and pity parties on the nightly news for latchkey kids like us. Despite the difficulty of those days, the memories aren't all bad, and I flip through them as Bill drives us past the cornfields, movie theaters, and malls of my youth. I recall the intrigue and alliances of my group of girlfriends in eighth grade, quantifying who is BFF and who is just BF; the staggering heartbreak when my avowed best friend Molly[2] showed up to school on Monday wearing a matching neon Wham! T-shirt with another girl in our class, Lisa[3]; hiding on

---

[2]a.k.a. "the cheater"

[3]a.k.a. "the chisler"

the bottom of the pool in swim practice to get out of swimming laps; donning hag-wigs and wax teeth with my friend Denise and sauntering as uninvited contestants around the mall beauty pageant. First love and first sex, first adult freedom, joy, and heartache all happened within smellshot of the South Bend ethanol plant and in sight of Notre Dame's shimmering golden dome.

Awash in these memories, I recall for a moment: there was a me before Daniel and me.

3

Daniel and I met at Bill's mom's house in Niles, Michigan . . . sort of.

At the time, Bill and I were attending graduate school at the University of Arizona. We had been close friends, and briefly more than friends, since we first met while attending neighboring colleges in northern Indiana—he at Notre Dame and I at St. Mary's. Shortly after beginning graduate school, Bill invited a bunch of undergrad pals back to Notre Dame for a football game. We all met up at an Indian restaurant where we used to gorge ourselves before going out to the bars in college. Ever fashionable, in every sense of the word except how it is normally used, I arrived late. The last available seat was next to a tall guy with eyes like a sunny summer sky and a mop of dark curls springing from his head. He was one of the few people at the table I didn't know.

Most everyone ordered the same thing we ordered in college—the vegetarian platter—and most everyone shared this enormous meal with at least one other person. Most everyone except for me and the stranger sitting next to me. Three quarters of the way through the platter my belt started to cut uncomfortably into my belly. Rather than stop eating, I loosened that tiresome belt. A few bites later, rice expanding rapidly, my pants exerted themselves as a tyrannical container that refused to give another millimeter. I cursed and unbuttoned them and continued eating.

Daniel, who had already swept, mopped, and polished off his vegetarian platter, noticed my adjustments.

"You should do like I do and just wear pants a size or two larger than you need."

I like the cut of this guy's brain, I thought to myself, eyeing him over, making note of the baggy fit of his shorts. Which also made me notice that he was wearing shorts, in late October, in Indiana. Everyone else had worn pants, sweaters, jackets.

"You're not wearing pants," I declared.

"I don't like pants," he countered.

Hmmmm.

"And I'm from Buffalo," he added.

"Right," I said. Odd and adorable. Check and check, two of my favorite qualities.

And that was that. For the rest of the evening and on into the morning hours, Daniel and I gravitated to each other—like children to an oversized, sparkly bible.

Sometime past midnight, at a bar called Club 23, we were dancing, drinking, and singing when some dude took off all his clothes, jumped up on a table, and commenced a free-swinging dong-dance that was tragically stopped short by the hard hand of gravity. The table tipped, toppled over, and splayed the entertainment out in an unladylike fashion on the bar floor, wet, sticky, and filthy with decades of clumsy-drunk college-kid detritus. He wasn't down for long. Gotta dance! But by the time he clambered up and started gyrating again, management had taken him by the arm and escorted him out the door. No one bothered to toss his clothes out to him.

"And I thought shorts made for chilly attire," I commented to Daniel, then leaned my head against his shoulder and continued singing/shouting.

"Oh what a night! . . . late September back in dadada! What a lady, what a night!"

"Hey!" Daniel said, grabbing my arms and looking into my cross-eyed, drunk face. "We've met before."

I thought to myself, you don't need a line, baby, you had me at "get your pants a size too large!"

But I was looking to impress this guy, so I said, "Huh!?"

"You went to the Blues Traveler concert, senior year?"

"Yeah?"

"I had come from Buffalo to see the concert with Bill."

I was disinclined to say I didn't remember but I didn't remember. Binge drinking was kind of my social signature in college and it had its downsides.

"We were at the concert, all standing," Daniel said. "And you were walking on the folding chairs behind our row, leaning over and giving everyone noogies."

Sounds like me . . .

"You tried to give me one but I leaned out of the way. After the concert, we all came to this *exact* bar, were dancing, maybe even to this *exact* song, and you leaned your head against my shoulder, just like you did just now!"

As he grinned down at me, it all started coming back. I remembered a boy I had wanted to follow around that night but a good friend of mine was visiting from out of town. I didn't want to lose time with my friend but the man who had escaped my noogie had intrigued me, so every once in a while I would wander off toward Daniel and dance in his vicinity. I had forgotten all about it, had never heard from, or of, him since. I didn't even know his name. And two years had passed.

I looked at Daniel in disbelief, smiling at the strange truth of it, and we went on dancing.

This was a beginning.

What followed did not come without conflict. Bill and I had stopped dating not long before. I still had strong feelings for him and in fact had almost not come that weekend because of it. Bill was dating someone new, and though months had passed, I was not yet able to put my feelings aside. But something changed the moment I sat down across from Daniel at the Indian restaurant, and all throughout that weekend, life took a seismic turn.

Late at night, while everyone else was asleep on the floor of Bill's mom's house, Daniel and I sat among a dozen sleeping bodies and talked.

On the second night, having grown to trust me in a short time, Daniel told me the story of his hero, Tony Robbins.

"Who's that?"

"What?! You don't know who Tony Robbins is? He's only the greatest motivational speaker who ever lived!"

"I don't watch much TV," I said.

"Well you should, Tony Robbins could change your life."

"Yeah?"

"He has changed my life," Daniel said. "Well, he's changing it anyway."

"Oh?"

"Yes. He teaches you how to put mind over matter. He can actually walk on fire!"

"No!" I said. "No way."

"Yes, he can sleep on a bed of knives! And he has a program that can help you do it too."

"Wow, I could really use that," I said and began thinking of all the applications for this particular skill.

I asked Daniel, "So, can you?"

"Can I what?"

"Fall asleep on knives?"

"Noooo . . . no. I'm not Tony Robbins . . . not yet! But I'm working on it."

"Yeah?"

"Mmmmhmmm. I'm working my way up to knives. I started sleeping on a bed of steel wool."

"Wow."

"Soon I'm going to make a bed of straight pins . . ."

"Ooooh. Ouch . . ."

". . . laying flat, you know, not with the pointy side up. . . ."

". . . oh . . . but still, sounds uncomfortable."

"Yeah. Eventually I'll turn them point side up."

"Sure."

When the sun came up, everyone else was still asleep and we walked out to the St. Joe River, which meandered along the edge of Bill's mom's yard. For a while we sat and watched the water roll on by. Then, in the morning quiet, Daniel told me about his dad's illness and death earlier that year. Tears rolled down his cheeks. I reached for him and for the first time of many to come, I held him and the cavernous sadness that lived inside him and time stopped for a while.

When the others awoke, we headed back inside and ate breakfast with the rest of the group, as if nothing had changed since the night before. When time came for me to leave for the airport later that morning, I hugged Daniel goodbye. I was heading far west to Arizona, he to the east and New York. We didn't make plans to talk anytime soon.

A few days later, on his birthday, Daniel called. We talked for half an hour and before I hung up the phone he said, "See you soon." I'm the queen of saying the wrong thing at the wrong time,[4] so I didn't think anything of it.

Two days later I opened my front door in Tucson to find Daniel with a mischievous grin on his face and his white Honda behind him, which he had just driven from Buffalo.

---

[4]Person at airport check-in says, "Have a nice trip!" I respond, "You too!" Friend says, "Happy birthday!" I say, "Thanks, you too!"

4

In the heart of Indiana Amish country, near Shipshewana, Bill slows down to accommodate the many horse-drawn carriages ambling along the rough shoulder. A thick black canvas is all that protects the passengers from the deafening steel hurtling down the highway past them. The horses have no protection, unless you count the protection from reasonable fear that blinders provide. Buggies quake and horses jitter as semi trucks roar through their lives of deliberate living.

A basic tenet of the Amish belief system warns against making one's life too easy. The community avoids cars and electricity in order to outsmart the snare of privilege and ease. What a concept. What could possibly be wrong with unbridled comfort?

As Bill drives, I stare out the window upon fields of corn and soybeans and imagine finding a place for myself here, a space to sort the pieces my mind cannot contain or order. The bare fact of my life is this: I'm lost. The creamy, vanilla cloud image that soothed me in childhood cannot calm the chaos that has accumulated and condensed and now hovers as a mottled gray cloud that occludes all possible pathways in this labyrinthine life.

Simplicity is an attractive thought. I construct an image of the Amish Krista. I wear a plain black dress and a meshy white hat over a tight bun—the hairdo gives me a headache but I keep up appearances, happy to resemble the rest of my Amish kin bouncing along in the carriage over a gravel shoulder of Highway 20. Except for one thing. For every speeding driver that veers too close to the shoulder—without even acknowledging that his monster vehicle's proximity has just made everyone in my family soil their pants—I thrust my body halfway out the window and scream, "Slow down dickwad!"

An uncomfortable silence pervades the buggy thereafter.

I try to explain in a voice harsh from righteous epithet:

"I was just . . . you know . . . that goddamn asshole almost hit us! Right? Right!?"

Silence. Stares.

Clearly my search does not end here with the Amish. I will leave them to their imposed-upon peace minus my inevitable imposition. Simplicity in life will remain hostage to fossil fuel mentality and I will remain hostage to my fury.

Maggie

Speaking of hostages . . . there is a big-eared furry runt of a dog leaning against the back seat being lulled into drowsiness by the motion of the car.

Maggie has been with me for five years, longer than any other companion in my adult life. She is like a sister, and she's seen it all go down.

Like most siblings, we have some tension in our relationship, but as family, she sticks, no questions asked. So of course there was no question that she would be here with me now. Well, there was one question. She was one of those reasons I absolutely could not drift because I didn't want to leave her for a year and I didn't know how I could possibly bring her along. I figured that part out: I just put her and her small amount of baggage in the car and closed the door. It was that simple.

My other traveling companion took some issue with Maggie's inclusion. Bill's basic philosophy on dogs is that they all should be reintroduced into the wild. In the five years he has known the puppy-faced mutt Maggie—an indisputable mutt success story, cutest dog on the planet, cross between a corgi and a dachshund, an adorable, irresistible dorgi—she has not affected the slightest shift in Bill's theory of radical pet reintroduction. But, when pressed, he agreed that wandering around the country with Maggie would be better than not wandering at all.

There were stipulations of course: "I'm not *ever* picking up her poop," and "We have to put a blanket down to keep her hair and dirt off the car seats," and "Under no circumstances is she ever, *everrrr* sleeping in my tent." (It isn't just that he's a fussbudget. He remembers the time Maggie made a night deposit atop my sleeping bag in Daniel's tent.)

Maggie, for her part, expressed no concern over Bill's inclusion on the excursion. She would not care if he took a dump in the tent. She is, in fact, a charter member of the Bill Fan Club. I take no liberties, or indeed pleasure, in describing

Maggie's life priorities in this order: 1. Obtaining a lifetime supply of bacon and expensive cheese, 2. Catching a chipmunk, and 3. Winning Bill's affection.[5]

So there she sits on an old blanket covering the back seat, leaning dopily against the door, unencumbered by all the hard memories of the life we've shared together and with Daniel. She's fighting off highway hypnosis like a champ, her head jerking upright every time she realizes that she is starting to fall asleep. She looks around to see if anyone's noticed her nodding off.

Unfortunately for her, Bill has noticed.

"Look at Maggie!" he says, giggling and pointing at her flailing attempts to stay awake.

Dirt

Bill and I rouse Maggie in Pennsylvania's Allegheny National Forest and the three of us set out on a trail that leads to the Tidioute Lookout. The path splits in two directions: one leads to a vista of the Allegheny River, the other to a view of the town Tidioute. Both are shrouded and muffled in a misty silence. But above the town, voices echo up the hundreds of feet to the overlook, voices without face or physical form. The only sight to pin them to is the fog-fuzzy town, silhouetted rooftops poking through cottony ether.

"Tommy!" an irritated mom-voice echoes through the mist.

"What!" comes the equally annoyed young response.

"Get in here!"

Then fog-silence settles upon the tree-framed town.

At dawn we wake in the company of trees, and rise to stretch our tent-cramped legs on an Allegheny trail that winds through a stand of old growth forest. On a bridge over a narrow stream, mist lingers over spider webs woven in glistening light streaming through the forest canopy. In this island of life, spared the saw that felled almost the entirety of the eastern forests of the United States, the largest of the old are white pine, hemlock, and beech. In the deep moldering matter at the foot of their trunks and the flesh of their fallen family, are unimaginable fungi life forms, fed by the perpetual death of the forest: mushrooms growing out of downed trees like icing out of a woody wedding cake in layer

[5]Within her lifetime, Maggie attains only one of these goals.

after layer of creamy white chocolate fungus. You can feel the old breath of time here, in deep shadows that build beneath aged trees a sheltering canopy of connection with something enduring, almost eternal.

No . . . not almost . . . *exactly* eternal. Dirt is both aged and new: the product of cosmic processes that began as far back as the Big Bang and forever regenerating as creatures live and die and merge with the dust of a fourteen-billion-year-old explosion. Dirt is eternal. And in this forest I begin to understand the fatal flaw of the clean=good=heaven formula. This forest is full of filth and chaos and death, and it is also the very essence of life.

In the old growth forest floor is the consummation of life and death—a misty, moldy cradle of decay that nurtures the future with the decomposition of the past. From the pungent black earthen crypt on the forest floor grows an Indian pipe, bowing a delicate frosty-white bell head to the bittersweet cake of soil that reared it—ice sculptures melting in the rising day, as delicate and improbable, as ephemeral as life. If I stood here a few more hours, I could watch it transform from the bloom of birth into withering decay, one intense burst of perfect infancy, exquisite beauty, decrepit old age, and oblivion in a blink of time.

Well, not really oblivion. The Indian pipe's disappearance would be better described as a dramatic change of state. This plant takes energy from fungus in the soil to grow into one of the most unusual plants on the forest floor, seemingly constructed of frosted glass. But it soon withers to black and is consumed by the forest, becoming energy for insects and other creatures, as well as nourishment for the forest itself. It becomes dirt. And from dirt will transform into fragments of a thousand different creatures over eternity.

The Architect of *Yes!*

The morning hike has primed us for a prolonged escape from the car. Anxious to gain some distance from asphalt, we find a trail, stuff our backpacks, and begin a five-mile hike to the Allegheny Reservoir. Maggie falls immediately into ecstasy, as these woods are brimming with her favorite mammal—the chipmunk. Bill and I hike, each in our own universe of trees and birdsong; we exhale the stuffy air of the car and inhale the rich, cool breath of the forest. When we arrive at the reservoir, I sit to rest my grumbling bones and write. Bill works on dinner.

I am absorbed in documenting the details of the day when suddenly I hear a *yelp!* Expecting to see Maggie overrun by a horde of vengeful chipmunks, instead I see Bill spastically slapping his own face and beating on his arms.

"What are you doing?" I ask, rhetorically. I've seen this erratic behavior of Bill's before.

"Goddammit! Goddammit! I did it again!"

He set himself on fire while trying to light the camp stove. As often happens, a huge flame burst from the stove when he opened the valve on the white gas. Bill jerked his head and chest back to avoid serious damage, but the flame singed his eyebrows and arm hair into smelly brown hairballs. I know several people who have this same backpacker's stove and none of them have ever set themselves aflame. For Bill, it happens every time he uses the stove—and it never ceases to enrage him. And, almost unavoidably, it sets off a chain reaction of mishaps. So I stay alert for what he will do next.

"Aghhh . . . Gooodddddd . . . Aghh!"

He has stepped backward into our pan of water, the very last quart which we had set aside to make dinner.

He kicks at the now-empty pan, which emits a pained metallic *twang!* every time he strikes it. After a few hard blows he stops, hangs his head, stands frozen with his hands on his hips, and takes a few deep breaths to compose himself. One . . . two . . . three. He gathers himself and the battered pan and trudges down to the lake to filter more water so he can give dinner another try.

I consider him, wrestling with his temper and a temperamental water filter. He is both colossal and minute, granite hard and fragile as a hatchling bird, bald and wrinkled and guileless. He is what has kept me here.

Many nights, standing alone at the center of a bridge a hundred feet from the ground below or gazing out the open third floor window of my apartment, it was his sad face I saw. I could not cast further anguish upon it; I couldn't. No amount of pain would absolve the remorse that would shadow me through the dark quiet of death and any afterlife I might stumble upon.

You simply can't abandon your best friend.

Ten years ago in college, when I saw him for the first time, Bill was the architect of *yes!*, the embodiment of youth and life, dancing naked around the fire, the last to go to sleep, and the first to get up and construct some elaborate plan for the day. This was one of the reasons he and Daniel were such good friends. Whatever adventure or idea either of them thought up, the other would invariably find both brilliant and doable. Anything was possible.

"Week-long canoe trip in the Algonquin wilderness?"

"Sure!"

"We've never canoed before . . ."

"We don't even know which end of the canoe is which!"

"Sooo . . . when do we leave?"

There was no adventure too small and no obstacle too great. This was the way they worked. Invincible, undaunted, immortal.

Some lessons in life come too soon. And Bill has aged a lifetime in little more than a year. Today he struggles to muster enough energy to fill a second pan of water. I wonder as I watch him, can either of us ever really heal?

But he brought me this far and I know that boy is still alive inside of him somewhere.

I watch him kneel by the waterside and grumble as speedboats and pontoons dash a short-lived silence that had blanketed the reservoir. They dock near our camp, unloading a dozen people with coolers full of beer, forty-pound camp stoves, half a ground-up cow, and amazingly, an enormous green inflatable easy chair. I wait for the inflatable TV . . . no? Don't have that? What a shame. Disheartened by the noise and plastic furniture after hiking in search of some stillness, I've decided I'll head to bed early and reconsider my bid for acceptance by the Amish.

Dog Victory #1

I commence setting up the tent. We have only brought one tent on the trip in the interest of saving space in the car, weight on backpacking trips, and time setting up camp each night. There is one problem with this situation. Bill reveres his tent as a demigod. He tutors me on proper setup, take-down, and usage, and narrows his eyebrows if Maggie so much as looks toward the unzippered door. I'm assuming time will quell his tent anxiety, but for the time being, it causes some mild tension.

With the tent readied and inspected by Bill, I lie down for the night with Maggie snuggled on her blanket just outside, but not touching, the tent door. Sleep comes easily but somewhere deep in the night, Maggie awakens me with a continuous low growl from outside the tent.

"It's okay, Maggie . . . okay . . . go back to sleep now," I mumble wearily with little hope my disingenuous cooing will quiet her. She's exceptionally stubborn. I consider the option of ignoring her and try to fall back to sleep.

"*Grrrrrrumble. Grrrrrrrruuuuuumble. Gggrrrrrumble . . .*"

I've known Maggie for most of her life and have never heard her make this particular noise. It sounds as if she is disgruntled by an intrusion on her territory but too scared of the intruder to audibly protest.

Though barely twenty pounds, Maggie's general approach to life is a no-fear, take-no-prisoners mentality. To my knowledge, she has only one mortal enemy that provokes a visible fear reaction in her. I am, however, reasonably certain that there are no marble lion sculptures in the Allegheny National Forest. I begin to worry. What could this new dog-nemesis be?

Sitting up, I hear leaves crackling and sticks snapping. Something uncomfortably near and unquestionably large is prowling about. I hold my breath and listen while formulating theories about the source of the noise:

Threat Theory 1. It is a drunk motorboat camper who has mistaken our tent for an inflatable toilet.

Threat Theory 2. It is a hatchet-toting serial killer on the prowl.

Threat Theory 3. Bear!

I immediately dismiss the first two options, knowing Maggie would not fear a threat of the human variety. Meanwhile, Maggie continues to growl despite my halfhearted assurances as to our safety. I open the tent door. Pitiful. The dog is crouching at the tent threshold, quaking. After checking to make sure Bill is still asleep, I bring Maggie inside and set her on my sleeping bag. While trying to calm her, I grow increasingly alarmed myself. My mind homes in on Threat Theory 3, BEAR!, and the phrase "we're sitting ducks!" begins to overwhelm my reason. Certainly the creature has been licking potato chip crumbs and burger grease off the faces of our neighbors and has now come to see what we have to offer. What if it doesn't like Lipton Noodles & Sauce?!

I touch Bill's leg and try to wake him. Not surprisingly, he doesn't stir.

When Bill sleeps, his mind retreats to some unreachable planet. He could have an industrial fire alarm implanted in his ear and still not be easily roused. I can sleep that deeply for about ten minutes a night; for the other eight hours, plant respiration can wake me.

After a few more minutes and many more sticks snapped and leaves crushed around us, I shake Bill's leg harder and harder until he wakes. He immediately spots Maggie on my lap, narrows his eyes at me and says, "What the . . . !"

But then he hears the prowler, sits up, and in a few moments we are both frozen quiet, listening for information as to what is lurking outside our tent, surely ready to eat us quite painfully.

"I'll go out and see what it is," Bill offers.

"*No*," I protest, "what if it's a bear?"

"I'll stay right by the tent."

Oh. That's comforting.

He puts his headlamp on and steps out into the vestibule, shining the dim light around the tent. I watch through the blue nylon walls as the beam of light bounces around, darting here and there in search of the persistent noise.

"I can't see anything," Bill says.

In the dark moonless hour we wait, motionless, listening, expectant. What would we do if attacked? I, for one, would scream and ball up in my sleeping bag. I expect more from Bill.

Thankfully, the worst-case scenario does not play out. The noise begins to subside from a snapping/crunching to a distant rustling and eventually fades to silence.

When it seems clear our prowler has departed, I courageously poke my head out of the tent and say, "You know Maggie won't be able to stay quiet out there."

Bill looks down at me and then at Maggie, who is now sitting on his beloved sleeping bag, still shaking and ever-so-softly growling. Bill shakes his head slowly, sighs, and says with exhausted acquiescence, "I didn't figure it would last long."

He steps back into the tent and sits down, nudging the dog over so he can get his feet into his sleeping bag. I close the fly and lie back down, feeling calmer, figuring if it was a bear, even if it returns, there is nothing we can do one way or another. Bill stays sitting up for a while longer, listening and shining the light out onto the formless night.

As I fall off to sleep, I realize there will be many such encounters on this journey. Humanity's obsessive containment and control of nature, built over thousands of years, have made it possible for people to live a lifetime without ever stepping foot onto wild lands. Lessons of the wilderness from which we evolved have become almost entirely lost to modern human culture. I wonder as I drift toward unconsciousness, can I become accustomed to an environment not dominated by human devices?

Evangola

Despite the night's restlessness, we wake at 5:30 a.m. to the sound of owls in lively conversation and a ponderous moon gazing into the glassy Allegheny Reservoir. The moist hush of the woodland morning has yet to be disturbed by boaters, who remain moored in dreams of inflatable plastic lakes.

In the early darkness we depart and trek the five miles remaining on our hike through the sleepy woodlands of the Allegheny National Forest.

When we reach the car and jettison our backpacks, an edifying puff of air reminds Bill and me of the long days and miles that have passed since we last showered in Michigan. It's an unfortunate fact, whether you are hiking or driving, that miles traveled correlate directly to the degree of stank your body carries.

"What we need is a lake," Bill declares.

We scan the atlas for options and find Evangola State Park on Lake Erie, about twenty minutes south of Buffalo, New York.

Upon our arrival at Evangola, anticipation begins to fizzle. The parking lot for the beach is crowded and huge; the beach, a solid blanket of human bodies. I am immediately skeptical about this locale fitting into our aesthetic for this trip. We're looking for Yosemite and Yellowstone, and avoiding Disneyworld and Dollywood. Admittedly, Evangola is not Vegas, but neither is it the Everglades. It lies somewhere in the middle and seems to strive for the best of both worlds, while achieving the worst. But, we are in the East; our choices are few. And Bill is insistent.

"Come onnnnn!" he says as he heads toward the water.

I come onnnnn, recognizing the fact that I am truly too ripe to turn back. We meander through a lawn jammed with picnickers, partiers, and a priest leading his casual, tone-deaf flock in a round of "Then sings my soul, my savior god to thee-ee-ee."

I stand in a long line outside the bathroom, willing my ears to block out the discordant tuneage and sighing indiscriminately as I wait with the other sheep, sweating and rolling my eyes, perhaps talking to myself. After I don my suit, I emerge into a horror film from the 1950s—the beach has been overrun by a swarm of hundreds of small screaming *Homo sapiens*. In the water, they have been herded into a sort of swimming corral, which is fine, good idea to keep 'em contained, but all other access to the water is cut off. The lake is roped so that the only legal place to take a dip is a twenty by twenty yard square of Marcos and Polos, splashing wildly and indiscriminately and howling like they've just been released from solitary confinement at the federal pen. I watch Bill jump in with gleeful abandon and return to my sighing.

"I'm not going in there!" I yell to Bill.

"Okay!" he responds and plunges underwater.

I walk Maggie down the beach (she isn't allowed in the sapien area) where I see and smell a littering of dead fish like a post-industrial plague upon Erie's eastern shore. My mood has already reached a pinnacle of pissy but this nudges me toward a deeper sense of sad.

This Great Lake was declared ecologically dead in the 1960s. Human industry had dumped on the lake for years without giving it a thought until Erie's waters were a barren mess of heavy metals and invasive algae. Erie's death was so well-known that it made it into the line of a Dr. Seuss book, *The Lorax*.

You're glumping the pond where the Humming-Fish hummed!
No more can they hum, for their gills are all gummed.
So I'm sending them off. Oh their future is dreary . . .
I hear things are just as bad up in Lake Erie.

The United States and Canada signed an agreement in 1972 that required a reduction of pollutants entering the lake, and things have improved since—native plants are actually growing in parts of the lake. But the New York Department of Health continues to issue health advisory alerts about the number of fish people should eat from Lake Erie. Last time I checked, people were supposed to consume at most one fish per week, and women of childbearing age and children were instructed to eat no more than one a month. This surreal state of affairs knits my stomach in a sad-angry tangle of knots.

We would rather live with fewer meals of toxic fish than simply demand that corporations stop polluting our earth and pay to clean up their previous destruction. Or, to explain it to the kids who will inherit this mess:

Corporations polluted,
they had lots of gumption.

Did we tell them to stop?

No! We just lowered consumption!

I thus rule out a swim at Evangola. I'm fairly certain that I smell better than Erie's moldering fish and a shower is guaranteed at our next stop. So Maggie and I take a seat at the edge of the beach. When Bill emerges from the heavy metal bedlam, we ferret out a shady spot near a rocky stretch of lakefront. I take a moment to ponder my emotional nose-dive since our morning hike in the Alleghenies. Gazing out onto the lake, along Erie's southeastern shoreline, I immediately recognize an underlying source for my Evangola-irritation. Buffalo. It lies just across the lake from where I sit, rousing merciless memories that slumber in some deep, wary place. I turn from the lake toward the uncomplicated sky and lie down in search of forgetful rest.

Suddenly, one of our thousand neighbors plugs in a microphone, flips on a karaoke machine, and goes to town.

"Some say love . . . it is a flowerrrrr!"

"Jesus!" I say, less as a curse than as a plea for help.

Bill rolls his eyes dramatically.

We stand up and trudge farther down the beach, out of the range of the surprisingly powerful karaoke sound system.

Once liberated from the quasi-musical racket, my mood begins to ease. I then find that if not for the drone of speed boats belching fumes into the air and the fish carcasses and karaoke screamers, there would be a pleasantness to this place—a cool breeze coming off Lake Erie carrying birds dreamily aloft.

With this bit of optimism filling my head, I lie down on the grass for a nap, nodding off to the distant drone of "Marco!" "Polo." "Marco?" "Polo!"

I fall asleep and begin to dream of yanking "Polo" up by the scruff and stapling his shorts to a tree. But before long I am awakened by two girls standing above and behind me, whispering about Maggie, who lies at my side.

"It looks like a Chihuahua."

"Isn't it?"

"It is, I think . . ."

They are clearly willing me to sit up and turn around so they can pose the question.

I oblige them.

"What kind of dog is that?" they ask in unison.

I say she is a corgi/dachshund mix.

"She is sooo cute," they each say. Maggie mistrusts kids but she is being indulgent of these two slobbering admirers. Generally she is an unkempt scraggly mutt, but she has doe eyes and a puppy face that appeal to kids, and an impressive feathery tail.

"Our cat would like to play with her tail," says one of the girls.

"We had two cats but one died," the other chimes in matter-of-factly, and in the same breath they turn their backs and walk away.

I lie back down and drift off into the uncluttered blue of the cloudless sky.

5

Six months after moving to Cornville, Daniel and I found a runty gray tabby cat hanging on our screen door, meowing obnoxiously. We told her to scram. She ignored us. We ignored her. But after a few days of her ripping holes in our screens we gave in, opened the door, picked her up, and carted her off to the Humane Society.

The folks at the animal shelter said, "Well, you can leave her, but if no one claims her in three days we'll have to euthanize her."

We left her. But three days later we called the shelter to find she was still on death row.

A conversation commenced.

"We can't have a cat," I said.

"But they're going to kill her," Daniel replied.

"Better them than Maggie."

I didn't know how Maggie would respond to a cat. She wasn't by nature aggressive, per se. When I adopted her, the Humane Society gave me a report card filled out by her previous owners (who, by the way, had named her Buttsy, which right there should have undermined their credibility). The report stated that Maggie got along well with dogs, kids, and cats. As I became acquainted with Maggie, I learned quickly that the first two items on the report card list could be classified somewhere between a fabrication and a pile of horseshit. With cats, Maggie had not yet proven her previous owners wrong, but there was cause for worry.

Daniel and I asked the people at the shelter if we could return the cat to them if she and the dog didn't get along.

"No," they said without hesitation or explanation, which led us to believe they were quite serious when they said the cat would be euthanized the next day.

So Daniel and I took her home with us, hoping for the best.

For a couple of days we kept dog and cat in separate rooms. Maggie spent those days with her snout jammed as far into the crack of space between the door and the floor as she could possibly manage. When she stopped obsessively snorting under the door, we let the cat out.

Maggie tackled her.

The cat swiped at Maggie with her paw and the dog squealed, and squealed, and would not . . . stop . . . *squeeeeeeeeeaaling*!

Daniel and I investigated and surmised: the cat had gotten a claw stuck in Maggie's lip and neither party could shake loose of their entanglement. Every time Maggie would thrash her head, the cat attached to her face was yanked back and forth, back and forth, along with the claw and Maggie's unfortunate lip. The panicked cat's eyes were at maximum diameter and Maggie wailed louder and louder, her lip flapping wildly about like a spinnaker caught in a violent gale. We grabbed hold of the mess and unhooked cat claw from dog lip. Maggie fled and spent the next few hours hiding and whimpering. We named the cat Xena: Warrior Princess.

And we had ourselves a family.

When Daniel was accepted to Teach for America later that year, we packed up Xena: Warrior Princess, Maggie, and all our stuff and moved to Washington, DC, into an apartment just around the corner from Bill and his girlfriend Katie.

Many of our college friends for one reason or another wound up in DC so in addition to spending the majority of our evenings playing cards, watching movies, and eating dinner with Bill and Katie, we spent the summer and fall of that year as one long carefree reunion with old friends in a new city, starting a new era in our lives. I had gotten a job as a writer at *Congressional Quarterly*. Daniel was starting work as a teacher. We lived a short walk from many of our best friends in the world.

The city, even in the strangling humidity of summer or in an autumn downpour, seemed to me at that moment the most beautiful city in the world. We spent weekends at the Smithsonian galleries and museums; played Frisbee on the National Mall; kayaked on the Potomac; went to shows at the 9:30 Club on V Street. We watched Fourth of July fireworks lying on the grass under the Washington Monument. It was the closest I had ever come to the life-state: idyllic.

Fate is Not a Feral Cat

It's amazing how something that can change the very nature of your life can actually sneak up on you. It seems like a jarring twist of fate should, like any other predator, have to come with some warning—a growl; the sound of sticks snapping or leaves crunching; a loud, quick breath before pouncing. But fate is not a feral cat chasing a songbird. No, that's a bad analogy. Fate is more like a moving walkway. When the run of a walkway ends, you get off. Period.[6] But even a walkway gives a warning. For the sake of liability, cloaked in courtesy, at the end of the line you hear "*Ding!* The moving walkway is now ending. *Ding!* The moving walkway is now ending. *Ding!* The moving walkway is now ending." And only then does it toss you off.

Farragut Square

Looking back, maybe we were given a warning, but nothing as obvious as a *Ding!*

Daniel had a backache. We thought it was stress from his new job teaching fifth grade at a school in Washington, DC. There were two fifth grade teachers at his school that year; one would teach the higher functioning students and one would face a room full of behaviorally and academically challenged kids. Inexplicably, Daniel was assigned the at-risk fifth grade class. In part, Daniel had gotten into teaching to help these very kids. Since college he had worked with the Big Brothers Big Sisters program and as a social worker for teens who had been in trouble with the law. And he was good at it. Daniel was not an anxious person by nature but with the month or two of training that Teach for America provided, he didn't feel ready to handle the immense responsibility of teaching twenty young people who needed more help than he could realistically provide.

So a stress backache seemed a reasonable outcome. But then he started asking for my prescription pain medication in order to sleep.

"You need to go see a doctor," I told him one night.

"I know, but I haven't gotten the health insurance squared away at work yet."

"Please do it tomorrow."

"I will," he promised.

A few more weeks passed, the back pain did not.

One February day, Daniel and I had just finished signing the papers to buy our first home together: a beautiful, bright condo in the Adams Morgan

[6]Or walk backward, which gets you nowhere.

neighborhood. As we were walking out of the title company's office, Daniel felt a pang in his back. His face contorted.

"Let's go to urgent care," I said.

"We're supposed to be celebrating tonight," he said, a weak protest.

"Come on, there's one right around the corner."

There was a long wait to see a doctor, so we went next door to an Indian restaurant for dinner. In my mind, when we returned to see the doctor we would learn that Daniel had pulled a muscle or torn a ligament. He would need to go to physical therapy, put some ice on it, maybe take a week off of work. At worst he would have to have surgery. We ordered some wine and toasted to our new home. We began planning where our furniture would go, where we could set up Daniel's easel for painting, my piano, Maggie's bed, and Xena's litter box. We planned a party for when we moved in, talked about who we could invite, what we would serve, when it would be.

Looking back, if I could have seen the future, if I could have known, I would have slowed that moment down, made it last infinitely longer, made myself more conscious of its significance, videotaped it, written down every . . . last . . . word. It was important, that dinner, a singular span of time I could never relive. It was the last moment of untroubled joy we ever shared. And the last precious hours of my own sanguine youth.

When we returned to the urgent care office, Daniel went right in to see the doctor. I stayed in the waiting room. He emerged after what seemed like a very short time. As he walked down the white hallway toward me, I looked for a clue, but I couldn't read his face. I stood up, he took my arm, and we walked outside into an unseasonably warm winter day. Rain began to fall. Daniel stopped outside the building, looked down at me, and said, "The doctor thinks I have testicular cancer."

Ding! Your life as you know it is now ending. Your life as you know it is now ending. Your life as you know it is now ending.

No.

I protested. "How could the doctor know that? You were only in there for five minutes!"

Daniel's words didn't make sense to me.

We walked in the rain through Farragut Square Park.

"I'll have to have surgery, a biopsy to check for cancer."

I couldn't process this. "Maybe the doctor is wrong."

I became angry that he suggested cancer before they even did a biopsy and said that Daniel shouldn't worry yet, because it couldn't be . . .

And Daniel just said quietly, "Yes, Krista. It could."

Daniel had been through this before with his dad. He knew that fate could shift instantaneously—that the impossible and unforeseen hard angles of life were always possible, and, in fact, just waiting, out of sight. That no matter how cleanly and exactly you ordered your life, time could and would unravel it. Somehow he knew the doctor was right. He seemed to know, even then, that this often-curable form of cancer would take his life. His precious twenty-eight-year-old life. When we met, Daniel had pretended to be a pupil of Tony Robbins, studying the ability to survive on a bed of knives; it was good training, because we were about to live there.

We returned to our apartment, agreeing to just wait and see what the biopsy found, but already everything had changed. I could feel hairline fractures beginning to force a pathway through the substance of us.

We laid down in bed and for a long time I searched the white plane of the apartment ceiling, every edge of the window frame and each and every shadow cast upon the walls, looking for some bit of information or insight, some kernel of truth that we had missed that would negate everything that had happened in the past hours. I turned out the light, took hold of Daniel's hand, and searched further in the darkness, if not for the perfect answer to throw a wrench into the moving walkway, then at the very least the perfect words to calm the terrible fear and sadness that I could feel coursing through Daniel's mind. But I could not. I could not even find the words to ask him what he was thinking about. But before long his voice cut through the choking silence.

"How am I going to tell my mom?"

6

Just before dark Bill and Maggie and I drive through evening traffic into Buffalo. Sunset explodes across the sky in a cacophony of color. From the center, where the sun is sinking, pink fingers stretch in a longing, desperate grasp toward wisps of white in the darkening eastern sky. And the whole western sky, strewn with silhouettes of Buffalo's industrial skeletons, pulses in a radiant reflection of the sun's last whim, salmon ablaze.

This sublime drama over Daniel's hometown showers me with grief. I think of him standing at the easel I bought him for his twenty-fifth birthday, painting this absurdly beautiful sky.

Daniel brought me here many times during the five years we were together, but the last time he was here, he came alone. It was the Christmas before he died. Daniel had flown to Buffalo to see his mom, while I traveled to Arizona to spend the holiday with my mom. This wasn't normal; we usually stuck together wherever we went. But then, there are times when normal holds no meaning.

Daniel had recently recovered from a lung surgery meant to remove all the cancer that the chemo didn't get. The surgeon felt confident that this time, the cancer was gone. And, as I had several times since Daniel's ordeal began, I had again convinced myself that he was now going to be okay. Still, on Christmas Eve at my mom's house in Tucson, I sat alone on the living room floor and wept.

A few hours later I got a call from Daniel's mom, Barbara, who told me Daniel was in the hospital, paralyzed. He had woken up that morning unable to move his right arm and leg. He didn't want an ambulance but there was no way Barbara could carry him, so Daniel crawled and scooted and scrambled down the stairs and into the car. At the hospital he was told a tumor was crowding his brain, blocking the workings of his muscles. It had to come out, and soon.

I took the next flight to Buffalo. We spent Christmas and the week that followed in the hospital.

Now, for the first time since, I'm back in Buffalo.

Bill and I arrive at Daniel's childhood home on the northeastern outskirts of the city, just after dark. Barbara rushes out of her brick Cape Cod home to welcome us. She's a small woman, mid-sixties, of obvious Irish decent—pink cheeks, salt-and-pepper hair, bright eyes, and strong hug. She carries unimaginable pain with the poise of a queen and the serenity of a monk, and I wonder how she does it. Perhaps it has something to do with the way she papers her refrigerator with photos of Daniel and Sebastian and eats ice cream for dinner when she feels like it.

Daniel asked few things of me before he died. One was to stay close to his mom. He needed to know someone would be there on his behalf. Five years earlier he had been by Barbara's side when his dad died of cancer. He stayed with her for a year afterward, not wanting to leave her alone. Now he needed a proxy to hold a tissue over her hemorrhaging heart.

Mortality

At 2:00 a.m. I lie awake in bed in Daniel's childhood room, staring at the glow-in-the-dark constellations he carefully arranged on the ceiling long ago.

With my eyes transfixed by Orion's belt, my mind wanders and I begin thinking of the human psychological imperative to believe our life span is as infinite as the boundless night sky. We clutch a comforting delusion as each step of time ticks past us that the moment will extend into eternity, which makes the hurt of our losses escalate, and conversely, the intensity of our joy increase. If at every moment we comprehended our mortality, the meaning of that moment would shatter. A first kiss, graduation, a wedding day, a debut, a raise, a party—everything that inspires happiness would be disfigured by the unforgiving fog of time. But without a constant consciousness of death, our joy is untethered by time, free to float on the cushion of eternity. As Carl Sagan said, "We are like butterflies who flutter for a day and think it's forever."

On the other hand, believing that there is no end to my existence and knowing that I will never hear Daniel's laugh again creates a sense that my hurt will go on indefinitely. But it won't, because I won't. For certain I will someday pass through the same door that Daniel has disappeared behind.

In the darkness, staring up at the pale glow of the ceiling-universe Daniel arranged so long ago, I find deep comfort contemplating the finite nature of life.

All is as temporal as the moments we shared together in this bed. Just as morning marked the end of those moments, death will someday mark the end of all for me; sadly, all the joy, and mercifully, all the pain.

Surprise!

In the morning, Barbara drives us south of Buffalo, past pavement and utility wires, strip malls and suburbs, to the cornfields, forests, and hilly green near Ashford Hollow, New York. A riotous summer storm has just broken and the green fields glow with wet brilliance against the darkened sky. Barbara, Bill, and I are mesmerized by the moody dance of light on the land.

While utterly preoccupied by the emerald trance, I fail at first to notice the odd metal life forms that have begun to appear upon the fields before me. I say "life" forms because the sculptures that I finally focus upon are thirty feet high and seem to have some inward animation to them. The forms, some vaguely human, some animal, some abstract design, are planted sparsely, over a vast tract of what was once farmland. They seem frozen on a path of purposefulness. Some are walking, some pondering, some pursuing. Sculptures disappear into or emerge out of a thick stand of forest, or they trek across the high grasses of a field or hide in the shadow of trees. It seems as if, perhaps, time is structured differently for them—so much more slowly, that it only appears that they do not move, like constellations. And maybe conversely, that human time is moving so much more quickly that the sculptures cannot see us at all, as a camera using a slow shutter speed does not record a moving object. Something of a secret world, Griffis Sculpture Park is located in a place you either have to know is there or chance upon while touring the farmlands of western New York. Without a sign saying "here it is!" the effect of stumbling upon colossal metal sculptures milling about upon the isolated countryside is shock and wonderment. Deliberately subtle and consequently stunning, the sculpture park is a rare combination that defines the creative courage of the park's namesake and architect.

In the mid-twentieth century, Larry Griffis uprooted his wife and seven kids from Buffalo, leaving his successful niche in the women's hosiery boom that followed World War II, and moving to Italy to study sculpting. When he returned to Buffalo, Griffis had decided to create a marriage of the natural world and human creativity in a pastoral sculpture park that remains among the largest in the world.

Griffis and his wife and kids risked a great deal to establish the park and yet he apparently chose not to create an enormous amount of publicity about it. I had never heard of it before. There are very few signs and those that exist are small and blend in with the countryside. If there were more signs, the effect of this place would be totally different, just another museum though in a beautiful natural setting. It is instead a hidden treasure, a landscape of surprise.

There is no guide for the park mapping where each piece lies. Approximately ten miles of trails are marked to prevent visitors from getting lost but the sculptures are hiding everywhere, and around the bend, and over that hill. It is the subtlety in their placement that sets you up for the serendipity.

The park reminds me of a story in Annie Dillard's *Pilgrim at Tinker Creek*. In the chapter "Seeing," Dillard writes of a childhood game that involved hiding a penny and creating a map on the sidewalk that would lead an unassuming passerby to a "surprise." Dillard recalled her excitement over the course of the night as she thought about the unknown person finding her map and tracking down the penny. I have to believe this anticipation was one known to Griffis. What a thrill to plant beauty and mystery for others. It is like playing a trick on someone; only the trick is one that makes them feel amazed and delighted rather than foolish.

One has to keep in mind that Dillard was crafting her game in the 1950s or '60s, because frankly, I'd be pissed if I followed a bunch of signs to a "surprise" and all I found at the end of the trail was a fucking penny.

That reminds me.

I invented a childhood game too. It involved quietly following my older brothers to the bathroom, lying in wait behind a nearby corner, jumping out at them when they emerged, and watching them scream. I could do it several times a day (assuming they had to pee that often[7]), and they never failed to scream. Not very original, but let me just tell you, seriously funny. While it lasted. My mom made me stop when they started showing signs of PTSD.

---

[7]As insurance, I would offer my oldest brother, the world-famous *Andy Griffith Show* whistler, a "special glass of water," an enormous glass the size of a Super Big Gulp.

Grifter

In the early evening, Barbara, Bill, and I stand at the edge of Lake Erie watching the sun sink. The sky casts a coppery pink light on sailboats returning to their moorings upon the shimmering metallic lake.

As we are enjoying the scene, a young boy sidles up to me. Forgoing the formality of a "hello," he says, "I'm going home to watch TV . . . [dramatic pause] . . . but this is my favorite show right here," and his small arm gestures grandly toward the setting sun.

I smile and nod, amused and suspicious. Something about his tone makes me suspect a motive prompts his dashing approach. I wonder why he has chosen to talk to me rather than Bill or Barbara. I consider my appearance, wondering what has marked me as the sucker.

"I just got off the boat," he continues making conversation.

"That must have been nice," I say earnestly, for it is a beautiful night to be on the water, boat sails billowing like angsty clouds on a sky of silvery magenta. The boy stands quiet for a few moments, then turns to me with a shoddily engineered desperation, the smile in his eyes belying it, and says, "Oh man! I really need a quarter!"

I raise my eyebrows. Oh really?

"If I have a quarter I can get the pink bear for my little sister," the little prince continues.

"Hmmmm." Lucky little sister. I know my brothers never scammed money off strangers for a pink bear, and if they did, they would never have given it to the pigtailed she-demon whose comedic pastime gave them night terrors.

"I had a quarter, but I dropped it," he says, looking longingly out at the endless lake.

"Yeah, that's happened to me before," I say. I'm not trying to torture him, just giving him the opportunity to hone his scamming skills. Seriously, he's going to have to do a lot better if he wants my loose change.

The boy walks away a few paces. I assume he has abandoned his quest, but it's just the subtle approach he's hucked.

Rushing back to my side, he says (breathless though he was just a few yards away), "You haven't got a quarter, have you?"

"No, sorry," I reply, and scowl harshly to scare the beggar out of him.[8]

---

[8]No, not really. I smile at him 'cause he's a cute little booger. I had patted my pockets after the soft-sell and found them silent.

Satisfied he's given it his all, the little grifter turns and walks off. I watch him sit at a picnic table with a grandpa-looking character. The man hands him a hotdog and points at the fixin's bar,[9] where the boy avails himself of ketchup and relish, hold the onions. The youngster sits down and happily starts eating his dinner. I return to the sunset but before long I hear his voice one last time as he bounces past, his desperation forgotten.

"We're going home now. Bye!"

I say goodbye, glad he has not held a grudge about the quarter thing and wondering if the older man knows the little guy is honing his panhandling skills on grandpa's watch.

Daniel-Vintage

A miserably muggy-hot August-in-Buffalo day has us sitting inside Barbara's house, organizing ourselves for our impending departure. When the day has passed into evening, we sit down to dinner. At the table, Barbara produces and opens a bottle of 1971 Daniel-vintage.

When each of their three children was born, Barbara and Sebastian cellared a case of French wine from the kid's birth year. It was a way to mark a moment in time, to bottle the essence of indescribable joy to be savored at leisure over the decades. The bottles mean much more to Barbara than she and Sebastian could ever have anticipated thirty years ago, much more than their now quite-valuable substance. They are fruit and fermentation and time, all tied to birth and now to death.

For me it is like tasting a sip of the life Daniel lived before me; and it is a treasured gift from Barbara. Three lives were intimately tied to the life span of this one bottle—1971 being the birth year of Daniel and Bill and me—and all we have faced, together or alone, over the past thirty years. For Daniel, the bottle had reclined in a cellar from the moment he first took breath, to the last he would ever breathe; from an unlikely ultimate beginning, to an untimely infinite end in this world.

---

[9]Maybe that's what the bible-grandpa was pointing at too.

Barbara has shared several bottles of the '71 over the past two years, at moments that seemed to call for it. Our departure on this trip means something to her—a vicarious journey to find light and some new hope in silent places.

She lifts her glass and toasts the adventure of life and the road to anywhere. "May you both find healing and hope and much laughter."

We three casualties of life's offhanded cruelties lift our glasses as the complex crimson history of thirty years wafts upon the still Buffalo night.

7

New Yorkers call Letchworth State Park the Grand Canyon of the East. As I gaze into the golden riverbed cloaked in deep shadow by the setting sun, it occurs to me that perhaps New Yorkers have never seen the Grand Canyon. Or even heard much about it.

If you have seen the Grand Canyon, Letchworth will not likely remind you of it.[10] Except for the erosive manner in which they were formed, there are few similarities between the gorged lands of east and west. Still, it is the dissimilarities that make Letchworth something to see. The greenery and presence of trees softens the Letchworth landscape, allowing an easy intimacy with this eastern canyon that is difficult to establish with the visually startling, blunt-angled, incomprehensible riverbed of the Colorado River.

On a short hike Bill and I come to a railroad bridge that spans the canyon, passing high above Letchworth's upper waterfalls. Bill looks at me, steps between the two parallel steel tracks and begins to walk out onto the bridge.

"What are you doing?" I say, pointing to the sign that says, "Stay off bridge."

"Daniel brought me here once," Bill says. He and Daniel spent much of a summer together during college when Bill lived in Buffalo with his girlfriend at the time. They took several camping trips that summer, including one to Letchworth.

"Want to go out there with me?" Bill asks.

"Not s'pose to," I bray, like an enormous ass.

He turns away and walks out on the narrow train passage, seventy-five feet above the noisy determined water. I watch him as he totters out to the middle of the bridge, where he stares down into the rapids, lost in the thoughts of a younger man in an untroubled time.

---

[10] For this reason, you would be hard pressed to find an Arizonan who refers to the Grand Canyon as the Letchworth of the West.

The Battle of Ithaca

On down the road, in Ithaca, New York, Bill and I face off in a bagel shop over who is lord and master of our destiny.[11]

I have heard good things about Ithaca and want to stay for the night, which would mean paying for a hotel.

"Let's stay," I say. "This is a cool town. We should stop and explore it."

Ever mindful of budget and unimpressed with humanity, Bill wants to move on.

"We don't have enough money to stay in a hotel," he retorts.

"Yes. We do."

"Not if we want to travel for a year we don't. We can't sleep in a hotel every . . ."

"It's not *every* night," I interrupt, getting frustrated.

". . . Besides, I don't care about towns, I want to get away from people."

"I do too, but . . ."

"I want to get farther north to the Adirondacks."

"Jesus, just slow down! We'll get there!"

He turns his back and walks away.

I turn my back on his back and chew my bagel harder than it deserves.

Bill always wants to keep moving; action pulses in his blood. Lethargy snores in mine. It's hard to find stillness when we're always discussing the next locale, the next patch of sky under which we'll sleep. I know I will struggle all this year to slow us down long enough to look around. Bill will struggle to keep our momentum of the forward variety, fighting my tendency to want to hole up in a tree hollow and disappear. We will both enmesh our mulish selves in the conflict. That's how we work.

I've known Bill since our junior year in college. Our history defies my unraveling, like a ball of string dipped in gluey tree sap. We seem to have known each other long before we ever met, our pasts trudging an oddly similar trajectory—Midwestern upbringings, lacking a consistent father figure and any real financial stability. Both with two older siblings of the opposite sex.

We each found ways to find strength from within to survive the shaky ground that held us before our legs were stable enough to stand. This shared

---

[11]This episode is later reclassified as The Battle of Ithaca in the as-yet unresolved War of Attrition II.

experience draws us to one another, but also repels us with its stubborn baggage. Before I met Daniel, Bill and I dated for a brief, intense moment. Our jagged edges made for a puzzling, erratic closeness so we parted, still friends, still loving each other, but not in such close proximity.

Things change. Life's foulest winds have weathered our sharp corners and tossed us about. We've ended up on the low-side, clinging to lifelines over an ocean of despair. Really, from the beginning of Daniel and me, there was Daniel and Bill and me. The two had been friends for years before either of them met me. And Bill and I had been friends for years before I met Daniel.

I told Daniel the day after we met that I still had feelings for Bill.

He said, "That's okay, me too." Then he proceeded to build a nest in my heart for himself.

It didn't take long. Shortly after moving to Tucson, Daniel moved in with Bill and his girlfriend Katie and we all spent much of our waking hours together. A few years later when we all ended up in Washington, DC, we carried on in much the same manner until Daniel's diagnosis put us all in an airtight container and shook it violently, leaving us bloodied and disoriented. And while he was staggering from the beating, life took a few more kicks at Bill.

8

From the moment Daniel was diagnosed at the urgent care center, life began to spin out of control—though from the outside events proceeded along the orderly path prescribed by doctors. Scalpel goes in scrotum, testicle comes out. Chemicals go in veins, hair and food come out. The counterintuitive nature of cancer treatment set me on edge: Daniel is sick, so we need to cut him open and put poison in his veins? My grip on reality felt tenuous, though I clung to the one-day-at-a-time mantra that all in such situations must embrace. Daniel, weakened by pain and nausea, and more familiar with the wiles of cancer and the shortcomings of cancer treatment, oscillated between fear, resignation, and determination on a daily basis. From the beginning, his oncologist encouraged us to be hopeful because the overwhelming majority of men with testicular cancer were cured with chemotherapy.

But hope can be an elusive thing, especially when your body is assaulted with toxic chemicals and you spend most of your life within the four walls of a hospital room. But we, or at least I, remained optimistic.

And sure enough, several months after Daniel's first round of chemotherapy, his doctor pronounced the treatment a success. We gathered all our friends at a nearby Italian restaurant to celebrate. It almost seemed possible that night that things could return to normal, that the struggle was over, and for a short while it was. But at the same time, Bill's life took another unexpected turn. One night shortly after our celebratory dinner, we found out that Bill and Katie had broken up. Daniel and I walked over to Bill's apartment to see how he was doing.

He and Katie had been struggling for several months and in fact she had moved out a few weeks earlier. In some ways their parting seemed expected, so when Bill opened the door, I was surprised to see how shaken he looked. His eyes were red, face ashen.

"My mom just called," Bill told us.

We waited for more of an explanation, he was having trouble articulating his next thought.

"My dad has cancer. He has been sick for a long time but wouldn't go to a doctor. He's only got a few months to live."

Though neither of our fathers were a consistent presence in our childhoods, Bill's father had never been far away. Bill saw him several times a year and talked to him regularly. It wasn't that he didn't love Bill or Bill's mom, he just didn't know how to be there for them. He spent his life at the Chicago bar where he worked and at the racetrack where he gambled, and he could never quite separate himself from the alcoholism that had taken hold of him at an early age. Bill's mom, who never stopped loving his dad, left him so that Bill and his sisters could have a different life. She asked Bill's dad to leave Chicago and come with them to Michigan, to start over, but he was stuck, too mired in sadness to climb out of his stagnant world. His mother had died when he was young and he had determined to spend the rest of his life mourning her. Which didn't leave a lot of room for Bill. Still, there was a strong unspoken love that persisted despite everything. And there was always some hope that in time he would find the courage to step out of that world.

For Bill's graduation from graduate school, his dad took a flight to Tucson; the only graduation he ever attended, the only time he ever visited Bill as a man. Perhaps the only flight he ever took, other than to Las Vegas. It was a big gesture. It was also the only time I ever met Bill's dad. And it seems likely, looking back, that he was sick even then.

Bill was tired from the news, so Daniel and I left him alone to rest. We spoke very little on the walk up Eighteenth Street to our condo. Adams Morgan was crowded and noisy with bar traffic, people with smiles wider than this world could possibly justify. Within a year, Bill would lose his dad, his aunt, and his grandma. That year every family gathering was a funeral.

9

Perfect squares of perfectly mown grass quilted together with squares of level concrete. The concrete is just large enough for one happy car. The grass is just large enough for one tent and one picnic table. Ahh, nature as reengineered by the New York State park system. The park where Bill and I are camped for the night and whose name I cannot bear to utter here, was designed for cars, and I suspect, *by* cars. Some mutant car/person, maybe his name was Car-son, infiltrated the New York State parks design team and scratched this festering blister on the landscape. Camping for cars, by Carson™. I hope our station wagon is enjoying it.

Bill and I are not. We are situated in a ten by ten patch of grass about ten feet from a hundred or so other campers, nearly all of whom have built the compulsory bonfire on a warm summer's eve. A porridge of smoke surrounds us, bubbling from a forest of flaming felled trees. Screaming children, barking dogs, and raucous adults vie for dominance over the night's stillness. We may as well have camped at the Mall of America on the day after Thanksgiving.[12] Our dinner of butter-flavored Noodles & Sauce makes the perfect pairing for this facsimile of nature. If only we had some Tang,[13] a hunk of Velveeta, and an inflatable easy chair.

We sit at our picnic bench, enveloped by smoky chaos. Through the grimy fog Bill seems beaten in his heartbreaking soft-silent way—a mood of his I had never seen before his dad and Daniel died, but have witnessed all too frequently since. At these times he is a child lost in a supermarket, sitting silently in a safe

[12]Perhaps in some hilarious bureaucratic mix-up, New York confused the term "park" as in "park your car," with "park" as in "a nice island of green space where birds sing and trees . . . exist."

[13]No offense, Tang, I love you.

corner, fearing to call out for help, yearning to be found but lacking all hope that fate will oblige.

"Are you as unhappy as you look lately?" I ask him.

He just looks quietly at the picnic table, then up at me.

"You seem even more sad than in DC," I continue, hoping he will talk with me.

"I am," he says softly. "But I just need time to adjust."

I want there to be more for me to say, something that will spark a light in his hopeless eyes. But I know that only an altered past could change what he is feeling now. Helplessly, I leave him to his thoughts.

I wish he were free of this darkness but selfishly understand how alone I would be if he was. Even though I'd perhaps not have bothered to outlive Daniel if Bill had not been there to hoist me from the dark earth each time I sank to my knees, at times like these when Bill's sadness dissolves him to a nebulous inconsolable cloud, I wish he'd been around the world in some safe unreachable place.

And now he is trapped in a car with me and my dog, camping in a place that could not be more antithetical to the natural world unless it was shoved inside a Ziploc baggie filled with DDT. What are we doing here? What could we possibly hope to gain from this?

I try to retrace our steps, rebuild the decision to sell everything we owned and become vagabonds. This was not my first choice. I had done all I could to hold myself together before Daniel died. When he did, I gave up and the ensuing explosion scattered bits of me. Am I wandering out of some desperate hope that I can gather those pieces up, reorder them, and watch the disparate fragments of flesh and bone reknit themselves into a recognizable whole? Do I think that some of the pieces of my self ended up here, on a concrete slab in a New York State park?

Where did I get the notion that something as uncomfortable as living in a car would soothe me? It's true that I have an inability to visualize the negative aspects of the future and an overly romantic notion of adventure, but it was more than that. Experience has taught me that no matter the hardship, a change in perspective can be of incalculable value. I needed to be anywhere but DC, walking the streets lined with towering memories of every joy, heartache, and mundane moment I'd shared with Daniel. I needed to find myself in spaces I did not know and where no one knew me or what I had been through. Where I would never see someone who would ask, "How *are* you?" and have to come up with an answer. There was no answer to that question except, "I am not."

A friend once told me about the first day she was alone after her son died. She could not make herself go outside to get the mail. "What if somebody sees me?" she had thought. She decided she would have to wear a mask and gauze bandages from head to toe because she was bleeding all over her body.

This kind of pain, it seems, has no place in modern society, where we are all supposed to be happy all the time, where no one can see the places where we are broken apart or bleeding because we hide them down deep in unseen places where dark thoughts remain shielded from polite society. Why can't we be like elephants who have been known to return to the bones of their dead family every day for years, just to touch their trunks to what's left of their loved ones. We are expected to move on, speak little, be strong.

I could not. Not yet. And I could not reconstitute myself in a place where every corner, restaurant, and face was defined by who I was when I was the person who loved, lived with, and walked beside Daniel. The constellation of me had drifted beyond recognition. If I was Taurus before, with Daniel's death so many of the stars had suddenly ruptured that the remaining collection no longer even resembled an animal. It was maybe a pair of hooves at best. Or at worst, a collection of random quivering lights that resembled nothing, nothing. I am not.

Many people turn to God for answers about death. This was not an option for me. I studied religion in college and by the end of school my connection to the Judeo-Christian god I had been brought up with had been transformed. I saw the systems and stories that cultures create to demystify the universe as informative and important, as context for who we are and how we understand ourselves, but the idea of praying to a god in heaven was no longer possible for me. I also studied biology and the image of an afterlife in a clouded paradise devoid of dirt, chaos, and death no longer offered any reasonable solace.

Some people turn to friends and family to sort through this anguish. Also not possible for me. Not because I don't have friends and a loving family. But because I don't know how to connect with them, over *this*. Two people besides Daniel and I were present through the worst of his illness, Barbara and Bill. I could not burden Barbara further with all I was feeling, so I started with the friends I could be completely open with, Bill and Maggie. With them I could show my darkest, most unleashed anguish, my most impolite rage and self-pity;

I could be just exactly who I was or wasn't at any given moment and know they would not run away, get uncomfortable, or suggest I check in to a hospital and start taking meds. But I also needed someplace that if I wanted to howl with anger, the world around me would absorb it without unease or judgment. I imagined a forest of deep shadowed green or an ocean, noisome and fathomless. I believe Bill's motives were similar. It all made sense. But there was something about the amount of confusion and anguish simmering in our memories that was going to make it all much more complicated. In a way, Bill and I are not going on a trip together. Our agitated and unpredictable psyches are each going on a trip alone. In the same car. For a year.

Morning light coaxes us from our tent, our snuggly patch of concrete, our beloved mutant spawn of Carson™. We both begin feeling better as we drive away from the park and down the road to Montezuma National Wildlife Refuge, just north of Cayuga Lake. The refuge—established in 1938 to protect resting and nesting grounds for waterfowl and other migratory birds—got its name from a house nearby that a local doctor named after the Aztec Emperor Montezuma. Strange name. But the birds don't seem to care. And like the other 544 wildlife refuges around the country, you step onto the grounds of this quiet place and feel for a moment that all is not lost, that the wild lives and we can return, at least for a visit.

On this visit, in the misty blue dawn we set up our cameras and wait atop an observation tower for the sun's rays to bend toward the wetland horizon below. As we stand upon the platform waiting, our eyes adjust to the subtle movement of the grasses and three red foxes appear. They are far off, only visible through an observation scope, but are headed in our direction. Eventually the little slinkers come within fifteen feet of the tower, where they stop momentarily, peer up in our direction, then submerge again in the tall grass below. Their departure appears as a vibrating current on the surface of a pale green sea. From the tower island the sky swims around us in a kaleidoscope of fluttering monarchs, soaring bald eagles, and chattering redwing blackbirds.

The nightmare of the state park begins to dissolve in the quiet morning fog and once back on the road we determine to hold out for a place to sleep that resembles the natural world. We check four New York State parks on the edge of Lake Ontario—all worse than last night (smaller squares of mown grass, larger fields of gravel and concrete, fewer lonely trees, and no solitude). We are just about to acquiesce when we stumble onto a state park dream. There are trees! Our site is about as good as it comes in the East without backpacking. The sun will be setting in a few hours off the sandy shore of Ontario on which our tent sits. A gregarious breeze meanders about the lake, tickling the water into ebullient waves of white froth, and breathing life into the limbs of the trees that canopy our site.

It's perfect—for a time.

We build a fire to cook the corn Bill has hunted down (along with blueberries, cheese curds, and *real* butter) to supplement our painfully omnipresent dinner of Lipton Noodles & Sauce. For about fifteen hungry minutes the corn loiters cold on a grate above the fire pit because the wind is blowing our flames flat. Not to be outsmarted by the wind, we put the tent on the beach side of the fire to shield our heating source. We then congratulate ourselves on having bested the pesky foe and sit down at the picnic table to eat a first course of Noodles & Sauce. Bill is sitting with his back to the fire munching his hors d'oeuvres, when suddenly my eyes grow wide and my mouthful of noodles drops open. He turns in time to see the wind pick up the tent and toss it into the fire pit.

"Ohhhh shit!" he screams.

Bill clamors to rescue his beloved tent, our current home, while I sit by watching him grapple with the wind and the lively dome of nylon.

Now, I am an introspective person by nature and I've often wondered how I would react in a crisis situation. This apparently is what I'd do: sit, gape, and yell, "Get it!"

I'm always annoyed when characters in movies do this; it seems so unrealistic that someone would just sit there and yell when the shit's going down. But it turns out, these characters are very realistic, and just like me.

The tent bobbles once off the fire . . . "You got it!" I yell from the picnic bench . . . And once back on the fire. "Get it!" I command, before Bill manages to land it safely on the sandy beach. He inspects it for damage. I stride over and help with the inspection.

"Seems okay," Bill sighs.

Well, not perfectly fine. Fire has charred the tent and melted it in a few spots but it remains surprisingly intact. We stake it down out of harm's way and return to our noodles. Bill begins eating, but after a moment he stops chewing, looks up, and fixes his gaze on me.

I avoid eye contact.

"Thanks for the help out there," he says.

I shrug my shoulders and stick my face back in the pan of noodles.

•

Forever Wild

Stillness hangs heavily, almost eerily, in the air surrounding Cascade Lake. At the edge of the water, where our tent now rests, we cannot even hear the lake lapping against its shores. Except for the lonely call of several loons deep in the morning darkness and a strange owl/coyote call we never do identify, there are *no* sounds—no birdsong or rodent crunching leaves beneath feet. Silence encapsulates the lake and surrounding wooded hills so thoroughly, it echoes in my ears in a muffled trill. We did not see another soul through the night. There are no screaming children, no smoke haze or concrete slabs. No karaoke machines or Marcos or Polos, no motor boats or semi trucks. There is only silence, deep, grateful silence.

At dawn, a thick fog loiters upon the lake, deepening the stillness of sound by muting vision. No sound, no sight, only a diffuse and calming light that holds the power to suspend time for a while. Just a little while. As the sun climbs higher it goads the morning from its repose and the mist begins to move, rising and encircling the high green hills. With the fog lifted, I can see a stream that feeds the lake cast ripples upon the water. This solitary movement breaks the trance, rouses the sleeping world, and reanimates the anxious step of time.

I sit at the water's edge and watch the quiet morning unfold. We are here, I think to myself. Though hard to define, easy to recognize—this is the place we were looking for when we began this journey.

We have arrived at Adirondack State Park, the largest state park in the country, encapsulating more than six million acres of land. It is not entirely public land—about three million acres remain privately owned. But the state manages a tricky balance here between private landowners and public interests. By monitoring development and setting aside wild spaces, the park provides a rare gift to the northeastern United States. New York established the park more than a century ago following several decades of ruminating and ranting by conservationists. Those enviro antics worked and in 1892 the state created what has become the jewel of New York and a respite destination for much of the East.[14]

---

[14]Suck it, Carson™.

Today, about 130,000 residents live in small villages inside the park's boundaries. The local economy is fueled by about seven million annual tourists seeking out the shelter of great expanses of forest, New York's tallest mountain peaks, thousands of miles of hiking trails, and the calming blue waters of thousands of lakes and thousands of miles of streams and rivers.

Upon which, we are about to set out.

From Cascade Lake we drive to Little Tupper Lake to embark on a three-day canoeing trip. Little Tupper, as a designated wilderness, has the rare distinction of being one of the few lakes in the East that is not surrounded by houses or churned by the angry-loud blades of motorboats.

The wilderness is an oddity born from capitalist excess. New York State purchased the lake and surrounding land (approximately 15,000 acres) from the William C. Whitney family in the late 1990s. Whitney and family at one time owned 68,000 acres of lake and virgin forest in the area of Little Tupper. During his ownership of the land, Whitney logged the forest (which is now mostly second growth) and built several houses for a family retreat. But very little else was done to change the landscape.

The forest will not return to what it was before the Whitneys cut it down, certainly not for a very long time. But now that forest once again covers the land surrounding the lake, a semblance of balance has returned. If the Whitneys had not been so filthy stinking rich, this land would likely have been sold off to hundreds of mildly malodorous rich folk who would have littered its shores with vacation homes. So, in the ironic end, the people of New York and all those who come to visit can thank the Whitneys for using their extreme privilege to amass immense tracts of private property. By hoarding their great big piece of the pie, they thwarted others from developing their many hundreds of little pieces, and open-space-starved public land lovers were the ultimate beneficiaries. Though a much deeper debt is owed the conservationists and state government that ultimately set this land aside as a public trust and wilderness. The same type of visionaries that created Yellowstone and Yosemite saved this space for future generations, including a very thankful me.

There are so few places like this anymore.

People are drawn to water naturally. But once they acquire private rights to build on it, they bulldoze the greater part of the splendor they were first drawn to. You don't notice the difference until you see the inverse. Absent the clutter of metal and plastic and groaning engines, lakes become a cluster of lily pads lively with the ridiculous beady eyes of leaf-green frogs, the wail of a loon that fills your ears and travels through your mind settling into the cavernous reaches where all is echoes, the feel of wind-driven waves as they slap, slap, slap-slap against the bow of your canoe.

Also at the bow of the canoe . . . Maggie the dog. Though never schooled in the ethics of sportsmanship, Maggie is a right good sport. She carries a backpack when we are hiking. The headstrong little dog hates it and walks with the air of an overburdened pack mule when I first fasten it around her back—limping and stumbling even though she is only carrying about a pound of dog food and some snackies. At the first chipmunk sighting, however, she jettisons her martyr routine and bounds into the chase.

Her drama is not always affectation though. Yesterday on the trail to Cascade Lake I fitted her backpack too tight and it chafed her underarm raw. And though Maggie stayed up all night licking, infiltrating my dreams with dog-parent shame, she stayed quiet and lying down on her first canoe trip ever today. Of course, she was threatened repeatedly. If she had tried to jump ship, we would very likely have tipped and our home and belongings would have rested for eternity on the bottom of Little Tupper.[15]

Instead, we arrive without incident at our destination, a small, forested island at the western end of the lake. We three are alone on the small spit of land and perhaps the entire lake, as we have seen no other paddlers. Given the wide-open tent real estate, we meander a while before settling on a primo spot atop a low hill, beneath a grove of sheltering trees on the western edge of the island. While I erect the tent and furnish it with cushy sleeping bags, pads, and pillows, Bill prepares a dinner of rice-n-sauce, or shall I say, rice with a delicate briny glaze of domesticated, desiccated mushrooms.[16] Maggie does her customary scan of the camp perimeter—noting concentrations of chipmunk poo that she can keep monitored for activity—then she returns to watch Bill prepare dinner.

---

[15]Had Maggie realized her backpack was in the canoe, she may have chosen sabotage and a long doggie-paddle to a new life in the Whitney wilderness.

[16]Everything tastes better when you're backcountry camping.

The five-mile paddle has worn us out, so we retire to the tent after dinner. I lie awake for a long while, listening to the leaves whispering in friendly response to the lazy breeze. I feel contentment here, despite the accompanying sadness. This place was special to Daniel; he often spoke of showing me the park, hiking its mountains, paddling its lakes. But we never got the chance.

As the night deepens, loons begin to call into the darkness of Little Tupper. My heartbeat quickens at their every utterance. Loon voices seem to come from a faraway place of grief and madness and profound beauty and they saturate my mind with their mysterious longing. Something in the sad thin wail urges me to seek them out, as if the sight of the singer alone can break the spell of the song. Their lyrical entreaties form the soundscape of my dreams through the night and in the morning I wake disoriented by a vague memory of ancient voices and a sense that I dreamt something important.

Bill is already awake, consulting our map in preparation for a paddle.

"You okay?" he asks, looking down at me and smiling at the confusion on my face.

"Huh?"

"You look a little fuzzy."

"Yes. I think I had weird dreams, but I can't remember."

"Hmmm. Maybe it will come to you while we paddle."

A gentle subtext underlies his suggestion: Get your ass up, I've been waiting to get on the water.

I shake off my sleepiness and we grab some power bars for breakfast and hop in the canoe, setting out on a narrow water trail that winds through a lush wetland toward Rock Pond. At the trail entrance, off to the right, a beaver rests afloat with its head just above the surface, eyeballing our canoe suspiciously. We paddle as far left as possible, knowing these guys can be grumpy if their space is invaded, but we pause briefly to admire the beaver's lodge, adorned by a thick stand of purple wildflowers.

We see more beaver handiwork further along the trail, a series of dams that staccato the waterway to Rock Pond. Most are low and easy to portage but one necessitates a carry of almost a mile. By the time we reach Rock Pond, we are exhausted and cursing the industriousness of beavers. We beeline the boat to an island that sits in the center of the pond and there we find a sizeable, sun-drenched rock where we settle in for a bit of lounging and a lunch. While Maggie inspects the island, Bill and I vegetate, watching sparse, cottony clouds float by and listening to a wilderness of birdsong. As the daylight wanes, we begin the paddle back toward our camp on Little Tupper.

Along the way our path intersects with that of three otters and a great blue heron, which we float within a few yards of before its great wings lift it from the water. For a moment, it hovers so close I can hear and feel the air displaced by the force of its flight.

We have heard loons sporadically throughout the day and each time I have felt a nagging dream-memory gnawing at me. But we don't catch sight of any until just before sundown. As we leave the water trail and paddle the last stretch to our island home, a black-and-white tuxedoed swimmer pops up alongside our canoe.

This is my first close-up experience with a loon—such a striking bird, every delicate feature seems carved of polished ebony with bright ivory inlay. These creatures belong to a classification all their own and though they resemble ducks, they are more closely related to penguins. Their genus has existed for perhaps fifty million years, making them among the oldest of bird species. They have been around hundreds of times longer than my species, and perhaps my human ears sense they sing of something I need to know. But loons have not survived this long by accident; they are wary apparitions whose voices float in disembodied waves upon the lake.

Still, occasionally they make mistakes. The loon in front of us takes rapid stock of its situation as its eyes say, "Ratfarts!" and it plunges hastily back under the water.

Bill looks at me with eyes wide and he grins happily.

Suddenly I remember my dream.

I was snorkeling somewhere in aquiline waters, following a school of shimmering silver fish, when Daniel appeared in the water before me. My first reaction was fear, a terrorizing pulse of understanding that he was dying, or dead. But then I saw very clearly a calm in his eyes and I watched a wide, peaceful grin fill his gentle face. A glitter of mischievousness flashed within his eyes before he darted off with the quicksilver motion of the glimmering fish. I tried to call to him through the water but he was gone.

A momentary joy accompanied the dream-memory as I looked into the space where the loon had been, the ripples of its departure still dancing on the water.

Transfixed, Bill and I float the final yards to the island in a dusky half-light. We throw together some Noodles & Sauce, then retire to the tent. Silence settles over the wilderness. Even the loons stifle their cries until the early dawn hours. I wake and gratefully listen as the darkness subsides.

When the sun has fully risen, Bill and I pack up our home, load the canoe, and paddle back towards the car on the opposite end of the lake. It's time to leave the embrace of wilderness, and return to the world where my demons were born.

10

In the surgical wing of Georgetown Hospital, Barbara, Bill, and I waited for Daniel to emerge from brain surgery. How long had we been there? It is impossible to gauge time accurately at such moments. Clocks lie, their mechanisms failing in an electromagnetic chaos charged by the fear and anxiety swimming in the minds of waiting family and friends. What appears to be two hours on the clock is really two months.

When the doctor finally appeared in the waiting room, our initial anxieties were eased. Daniel was fine. They got the tumor. We could see him shortly.

But when we entered the recovery room, something was wrong. His jaw was tight, his face contorted.

"It hurts," was all he could manage to say through clenched teeth.

We alerted the nurses, who said they would increase his morphine dosage. But fifteen minutes later, nothing had changed. Daniel gripped the bed, his eyes were cold with panic. We asked them again, this time with more of an edge, and thus began a torturous pattern that lasted for three hours, by the clock's accounting.

It seemed impossible that the hospital, which surely had a good supply of morphine, could not fix this. I imagined the doctors were performing some sort of study on us, giving Daniel placebos and waiting to see how much he and we could take before we broke. By the end of the night, Daniel, Barbara, Bill, and I were broken.

Barbara and I generally took turns staying with Daniel and that night Barbara stayed at the hospital. We said goodbye in a fog, as if the morphine that finally took effect for a now-sleeping Daniel had permeated all of our brains. Dazed, Bill and I took a cab to our neighborhood.

Back at Daniel's and my condo, Bill sat with me for a while listening to music. I put on Sarah McLachlan's album *Surfacing*. We tried to imagine a different tomorrow than the one we knew awaited.

11

At my insistence, Bill and I have stopped for a while at a warm coffee house in the Olympic-Games-famed town of Lake Placid. I expect this will be a much-needed, though brief, respite from the road. Instead, while sitting comfy in a cozy chair, sipping my coffee, Sarah McLachlan comes over the café radio singing "Full of Grace." And immediately some inner fault lines shift and a geyser of grief erupts. Tears burst forth as time and space bend backward, as if I'm not sitting in this warm dry café but instead I'm sitting on my couch late one night after taking an immersion course in the language of agony.

Bill has grabbed a handful of napkins for my face sloppy with tears and running nose. He wipes my cheeks. I try to explain what has come over me so suddenly.

"I'm really afraid nothing will ever be right for me again. This trip was a drastic last grasp, but I'm just the same!"

"No," Bill assures me. "You've come so far in the past year. I can see it even if you can't."

Time, right?

I have to believe Bill that I am making progress but it scares me, how little I am able to accept watching Daniel suffer for so long and then finally, after all of that horror, losing him. My notions of justice gnaw at me. If you're good, bad things aren't supposed to happen. That tired simplistic fallacy—one of humanity's greatest cruelties to the human mind, right up there with that goddamn pointy bible-grandpa in his pristine paradise.

I cry angry, messy tears into a sopping paper napkin, and then another.

"Krista, you are never going to be the same," Bill says softly, almost apologetically.

I cry harder at this, knowing he is right but stubbornly refusing to quiet my rail against unacceptable reality, no matter how exhausted I am by the fight against this unbeatable foe.

"Life is never going to be the same," he says. "And this trip was never going to change that. Darkness on the inside doesn't leave because you find some brightness on the outside. It just means new harshness is not being added to a crowded mess of pain. And maybe by adding more beauty, the balance will shift at some point."

I manage to calm myself a bit and say, "I just feel so numb, like what beauty there is—and there is so much I've seen in the past few weeks—I barely see."

Like the light can only dimly penetrate the gray crust of film over my eyes. I strain to feel the intensity of what I see but fail in frustration.

Time, right.

Time

Well, what is time anyway? We live for the most part inside the limited confines of our own minds and memories. Outside of this is a reality quite different than what we perceive. We look to the night sky and see Orion, Sirius, and infinite other points of light hurtling through the darkness. We call them stars, understand them to be some tangible thing, something that if we could only get close enough, we could touch, even as we can bend down and touch the soil of the earth. But that is reality only as our eyes perceive it. In fact, many of the billions of stars we see are not objects at all but rather memories of objects projected through time and space. Ghost trails. Beautiful luminous ghost trails.

Stars, like people, are dying all the time. But they are so far away from us that we continue to see their light long after the star itself has dimmed to darkness. When a star lying 50,000 light years away from us dies, it takes 50,000 years for the last bit of its light to reach us, for it to die in our eyes.

What we see in the sky is real in the sense that history is real, but you can't grasp on to it any more than you can hold a beam of light in your hand. Our night sky is like a home movie of what the universe looked like at some distant time in the past or, rather, what the universe looked like at various infinite points of time in the past. In this way the past and present exist simultaneously—some light reaches our eyes as the continuing vibrancy of a distant living source of energy, while some is remnant radiance of a long-dead celestial body. Our eyes don't distinguish. We can never really know what the reality of the universe is at any given time, only what we perceive it to be based on our position within it, with life and death, light and darkness and our own understanding of time fabricating a relative sense of what is real. As small creatures of limited life spans, we are conscripted to incoherence, we are the wide-eyed children of an incomprehensible and sublime mystery.

Lingering Light

Barbara has a photograph on her refrigerator taken long ago, of Sebastian, his sister, and Daniel as a boy. All have since died of cancer: husband, son, and sister-in-law. But the photo remains, a lingering record of the pathways light took after it bounced off their smiling faces. This record of light and shadow maintains, in some small but important way, the universe of Barbara's life, the essential stars in her constellation, even though they have long ago dimmed to darkness.

12

Before setting out on the road, Bill and I thought long on a mode of transportation. We needed space for four seasons of clothing, gear, and cameras, reasonable storage room for food, and a place to sleep if the weather became nasty. But we were also concerned about the amount of gas we'd be using and our impact on the environment. So we looked for a station wagon, and looked and looked and looked. Most car companies had discontinued their wagon models and replaced them with gas-guzzling sport utility vehicles. We finally found a used Saturn wagon, with just enough cargo space and 35 mpg on the highway. At the dealership we asked the salesperson to open the back so we could lie down and check out the sleeping arrangements. Bill's head touched the back of the front seat and his feet touched the hatchback. It was tight, but given our parameters, it worked.

Well, an empty car at a dealership seems downright palatial compared to a jam-packed car on a dark dirt road in a rainstorm with two uncomfortable humans and wet dog. But tonight we try to make the best of things.

We have both accepted that we will not find a legitimate place to camp for the night and Mr. Budget Pants won't assent to staying in a hotel.[17] So we find a quiet dirt road where we hope no one will notice us and we park for the night. In an attempt to make room for sleeping, we rearrange all our stuff to one side of the folded-flat rear-end of the station wagon, leaving just enough room for two vacuum-packed humans and one small-but-sprawling dog.

I make Maggie's dinner, a seemingly small chore that consists of pouring her food in a bowl and topping it with Cheez Doodles. Seeeeeemingly small chore, which grows larger after I flip the cheese snack bowl over and broadcast

---

[17]He also has simultaneously declared that we should henceforth only purchase generic Noodles & Sauce, rather than the overpriced Lipton brand, except on special occasions.

powdery cheddar-parmesan nuggets over the two front seats and floor and every nook and cranny in between.

Maggie's eyes widen as she sees the mouth-watering doodles depart out of her reach.[18]

My eyes narrow on the extra sharp cheddar mess I'm going to have to clean up.

Bill's eyes remain in their regular state but his jaw tightens as he commences grumbling, ". . . never find them all . . . rodents . . . stinky cheese . . . *urgrumblegrumble.*"

As I gather what I can of the cheese-doodle wreckage, I think to myself, *Rodents? We live in a car, not tenement housing, for Chrissake. Of all the ratzen, fratzen, mother-scratchin' things he has ever said . . . I can't believe . . . umblegrumblegrrr . . .*

And the walls of the car close in as I toss the salvaged doodle-carfunk-detritus atop Maggie's dinner, then lie down while she crunches and munches and snarfs it all down.

Making myself as small as possible, I toil to find some sleep as the rain marches down through the darkness of the mud-slopped side road make-shift rest stop.

When morning comes, I take a baby-wipe shower, change clothes, and brush my teeth in the morning's mist of rain. We reorganize the car for the tenth time in fourteen days and hit the road again.

Hardest Hue

The Robert Frost Interpretive Trail in Green Mountain National Forest winds through the Vermont woods where Frost walked and lived for much of his latter life. Frost was a person well-acquainted with grief. He lost both of his parents before the age of twenty-five; four of his six children died young, including one who committed suicide; and his beloved wife died of heart failure in 1938. Afterward, though born and raised in the city, Frost turned to the woods. I read his poems in school, like most American students do. But they are new to me now.

---

[18] She will be pondering the fate of those snacks, which she can now smell but not see, for the duration of our life in the car.

Nature's first green is gold,
Her hardest hue to hold.
Her early leaf's a flower,
But only so an hour.
Then leaf subsides to leaf,
So Eden sank to grief.
So dawn goes down to day.
Nothing gold can stay.

Frost's time in the woods coupled with a lifetime of loss helped him express one of life's most important and painful truths. Beauty is ephemeral.

Why do I torture myself by clinging to it so desperately? I want to carve it in stone, write it on paper, put it in chains so it can never leave. But it always will. If I cage beauty, it will wither before my pleading eyes. If I don't, it will drift away like a butterfly on a warm August breeze. Death and ephemerality are not just elements of life and beauty, they are part of the essential nature of reality. They are the features in the face of existence. Everything ends.

This is why I love photography. With a camera, I can freeze an image of the sublime, one that is often invisible or fleeting in the relentless progression of seconds, minutes, hours. I cannot capture and prolong a moment in time—can't freeze a sunset or resuscitate a dying flower. But I can hold a fraction of the idea of the experience and record it like the lingering light projecting from a dying star. Just as a star's death does not consume its light, a projection of a moment in time can be suspended in a photograph. For a while. As residual starlight eventually fades, so will the photograph.

Nothing gold can stay.

13

Like a scratchy broken record, stuckstuckstuckstuck . . . on a topic, Bill and I debate the relative merits of staying in a hotel for the night.

"We haven't stayed indoors for almost ten days," I say.

"No, but we don't really need to and maybe we should save the money for when we need it."

"At what point do we *need* to stay in a hotel?" I inquire.

"I guess we don't ever need to. Good point."

Grrrrr.

"I had prunes and coffee for breakfast, with a side of laxative!"[19]

"Whose fault is that?"

"Just give me this one," I plead. "I need a little indoor time, a bed, plumbing, an incentive to brush my teeth . . ."

"Fine."

Haha! I win!

Bill and I begin scouring the town of Burlington for budget accommodations, which doesn't seem like a difficult request until we have looked under every . . . single . . . cheapo . . . rock in town and found nothing. Even the shabbiest motel is seventy dollars and that place has no phone service and is run by a surly, gravely-voiced, terrycloth-robed woman with a flaking pancake makeup face, a towel on her head, and a cigarette dangling from her lips dusting her pink terrycloth with ash. She's hanging her pantyhose on a clothesline in the main hotel courtyard when we arrive.

Not that there's anything wrong with that. At twenty dollars a night, I would have helped her hang her underpants. At seventy a night, she must become the object of my deepest ire. I won't go so far as to categorize her as evil, but she

---

[19]I'm not sure where I was going with this line of argument, threatening to poop my pants maybe . . . or to soil Bill's precious tent.

is clearly a cruel and heartless approximation of a human and she will get no laundry help from me.

We head to the woods and I sulk while Bill sets up the tent at the Moosalamoo campground in Green Mountain National Forest. Then I sulk some more in the privy (that bit about the prunes was true, unfortunately). Then I close myself in the tent and commence throwing myself a doozy of a pity party. I want to stay asleep all day and through the night but when I see Bill getting food for Maggie and sitting on the picnic bench alone, I get up and face a few more days without a shower like a big girl.

And I am rewarded for my bravery.

On a morning run for groceries in Middlebury, we spot a black bear scurrying into the forest growth. I'd not have seen that at a shitty motel in Burlington.

The Princess (Warrior)

Contractually, I am obligated once every two weeks to call my mom and let her know I'm alive. We don't have a cell phone or an itinerary, so the moms asked that we alternate calling one of them per week. So once each week we find a pay phone and make the mom-call.

This week it's my turn so I ring my mom, and while I'm telling her about the Adirondacks canoe trip she interrupts and says, "You sound better than you have in a long while."

This stops the conversation for a moment. I've been having some bad days, but telling her about the things we are seeing must have sparked a light in my voice. Perhaps I'm doing better than I realized.

"How is Xena doing?" I ask Mom. "Or, more importantly, how is Granny doing with Xena?"

When I asked her a few months ago, Mom readily agreed to take Xena: Warrior Princess while we were traveling this year. She also managed a very unenthusiastic agreement from Granny, who had just moved from Kansas to live with Mom in Arizona. Granny would do almost anything and most generously for her family, but she has had a complicated history with cats. When Granny was young, she was told by her dad that if she wanted to have a cat, she was responsible for getting rid of any feline offspring. Spaying was not an option in the early 1900s on a Kansas farm and neither was feeding more than one cat. So when the cat had kittens, it was Granny's responsibility to take them by the tail and euthanize them against the trunk of a tree. The scars of youth fade slowly, or never, and Granny's relationship to cats remains complicated at eighty-seven years old. Still, she agreed for my mom and for me, that Xena could stay with them.

"She has been jumping on Grandma's lap," Mom says.

"Ohhhh . . . Uh-oh. Well, Granny can just push her off. Sorry, Mom," I say sheepishly.

"No, no. She won't admit it, but I think Mom likes the company while I'm at work."

"Oh good."

"Actually, the other day, I saw Xena go to her bowl and start meowing, meowing, meowing until Mom went and put some ice in her water."

"Jesus."

"Well it *is* pretty hot here still," Mom says in defense of the cat's demands.

Granite State

Bill and I arrive at The Basin in White Mountain National Forest in the early dawn hours when the rush of water over rock and wind bustling through treetops are the only audible sounds the world makes. We rarely speak at these moments but instead listen to the voices that created this sculpted granite landscape—the water, the wind, they hum softly as they work. Like Granny does when she's making cookies.

A thick curtain of morning clouds shifts and separates over New Hampshire, making a path for the sun to fall upon this unusual landscape forged long ago by a restless glacier trapped between two mountains. As the glacier paced the confines of its imprisonment over many years, it scraped a U-shaped hollowing in camel-colored rock, then smoothed the depression to the polish of bone. The path leading to The Basin follows a stream that has weathered its granite bed to the appearance of a fabricated zoo habitat for polar bears. At the end of the trail, the spirited stream bursts through a cracked opening in the east side of the Basin's churning bowl of water. The location is earth-sculpture, water-art, loud with the creative energy that over eons formed it.

Presiding over the work of the world's elements is the weathered face of the Old Man in the Mountain, New Hampshire's state icon.

"He looks grumpy," says Bill of the haggard granite profile emerging from a lush green mountain peak.

"He watched these forests grow from seeds, be hewn down, and grow back again," I say. "That fucker's O-L-D. Of course he's cranky."[20]

Rather than dawdling with the Old Man, Bill and I travel onward in search of a campground, because as usual we don't have a place to stay for the night. If all else fails we can sleep (or at least spend the night) in the car.

Right?

Before we commence scavenging for a place to stay, Bill and I stop at the Woodstock Public Library to check email. Maggie, of course, has to stay in the car.[21] When I go out to give her some water and a chance to stretch her legs, I notice two boys, around age eleven, climbing on their bikes nearby. I try to quickly secret Maggie back into the car, but before I can get her hidden the smaller of the two boys spies her and says to his friend, "Hey! Look at the puppy!" and then to me, "Hey! Can we pet her!?"

"Errrr . . . . yes?" I say. She has been cooped up in the car and is known for being grouchy around strange kids, especially enthusiastic boys who speak only in exclamation points. To my relief Maggie humors them. She is just happy to be out of the car and it makes no difference to her if the boys stick around awhile, petting and fawning all over her.

"She's sooooo soft!"

"Heheheh," I fake-laugh nervously, silently willing them to leave before Maggie starts showing her harder side. My prayers are answered shortly when they walk away and start to climb on their bikes. But before they ride off, the smaller boy again speaks for them.

"We love dogs and we always will!" he barks at me, as if he senses some unspoken doubt of their dog devotion. And then, to emphasize the infallibility of his declaration, he calls for confirmation from the other half of his "we."

"Right?!"

"Right!" The heretofore silent sidekick testifies with a surprising gusto.

---

[20]Plus his face was about to fall off.

[21]I don't trust her with an email account.

Having settled the situation for all times, they pedal off down the sidewalk.

I look at Maggie and shrug.

When Bill emerges from the library I tell him about the boys, a mistake I regret almost immediately, and for a very long time after.

We climb into the car and head toward a nearby campground. In hopes of going to a restaurant for dinner, I raise the subject of food.

"What do you want to eat tonight?" I say.

"We're having rice-n-sauce for dinner and we always will!" Bill replies.

He looks at me expectantly. I turn my head toward my window and curse my lack of foresight.

"Right?!"

"Right," I grumble.

The Battle of New Hampshire

In hopes of delaying dinner (the hungrier I am, the tastier the gruel), I suggest we take some sunset photos before setting up the tent and making food.

Big mistake.

Bill is pleasantly distracted while taking his photos but when he finishes, he turns his attention on me.

"How many shots have you taken?" he asks.

I ignore him because I know where he is going with this fatherly line of inquiry. Our cameras are film cameras, not digital. Film costs money, we don't have much of that elusive green substance, therefore, if I want this trip to last through the year, I should stop clicking the shutter.

"Krista?"

"Not that many," I say.

"How many? Is that your second roll?"

"No, it's not. Now leave me alone, I'm almost finished."

"You have to stop using so much film. It's not a very good shot anyway."

Oh now that's it . . . !

Rather than finish that thought aloud, I refuse to talk to him for an indefinite period.

He's been having a tough day and I am tired, not a good combination. After a long tense silence he approaches me.

"I'm sorry I have been difficult to be around the whole trip," he says with a soft, strained voice and tears in his eyes.

"It's only sometimes and I shouldn't be so impatient," I say to him. "But what's wrong?" I know the answer, but I ask anyway. It's anger, just anger, the corrosive residue of pain.

"Just everything," he says. "Plus I'm hungry."

Bill is like a parking meter: if you don't feed him every few hours, he goes on tilt, which for him involves fainting, melting, barking, biting. He has a blood sugar condition that renders normal intervals of food consumption insufficient. In the ten years I have known him, he has had some frightening responses to low blood sugar, the most memorable being when he ate a trail map to revive himself from a blackout in the Arizona desert during a mountain biking expedition.

Well, the White Mountains trail maps are fifteen dollars, so I tell him he will have to settle for noodles and grilled cheese.

Dog Victory #2

I wake at 3:30 a.m. to the sound of Bill murmuring to Maggie, "Come over here, Mags."

Cute. I turn over and go back to sleep.

I wake at 4:00 and 4:30 to the same thing.

At 4:45 a.m. Bill whispers, "Krista?"

"Mmm?" I mumble.

"Maggie has been shaking all night. I put her in my bag but she's still shaking. Do you think she's cold still, or scared?"

"I don't know," I say, moving closer to the bag Bill is now sharing with the dog. I question whether she is playing us for suckers.[22] Is that a muffled dog-chuckle I hear coming from inside Bill's sleeping bag? But when I uncover her head she looks so pitiful I mentally lash myself for dragging her around the country and place my hand on her vibrating head to try and calm her. She settles in and seems content in Bill's embrace, so I fall back asleep and into dream visions of her big dark eyes looking at me sadly. Ohhhh she's good.

---

[22]Well, Bill mostly, which doesn't really bother me that much.

When the sun rises, Maggie is still curled inside Bill's bag, his arm draped protectively over her. She has stopped shaking, but the moment Bill pulls his bag away she starts again to quiver. He gives me a worried look as he covers her again quickly and pulls her closer. An almost imperceptible, self-satisfied dog-smile spreads across Maggie's face.

The little dog warms up as soon as she bolts from the tent and by the time we reach Passaconaway Historic Site she is her old self. The historic site consists of an old pre-Civil War cemetery and homestead. I stroll through rows of graves and come upon one that marks the burial of a young man named Orrin who died at the age of twenty-eight years and seven months. I count the months past Daniel's twenty-eighth birthday before he died, not quite five. I find myself wondering if there are people who live in short bursts, over and over. And I imagine, if I looked hard and long enough, I could find those lives Daniel lived before this one—as a magician, artist, medicine man, explorer, or astronomer. And perhaps if I studied them, I could predict where and when he would start his next one. I could find him and say all the things I wished I had.

Lost

Looking for a grand view of Mount Washington, Bill and I make a slow ascent up the steep rocky trail to Glen Boulder, an enormous rock poised precariously on the side of a Presidential Range slope. We cover only seven miles but the trail trudges straight up and straight down, all rock, from river rock to granite boulders. My heart is cursing me as I am cursing Bill and Maggie—many seemingly effortless steps ahead of me—as Bill is cursing a man in shorts and a tank top who jogs past us both and quickly disappears into the vertical distance.

We swallow our curses as we clear the tree line and round the soft green of the bald alpine landscape, peppered with jade lichen and deep russet grasses. I stop a moment to rest and reflect on the alpine world. Survivors of wind and deep freeze, lichen cling to life with a tenacity required of few others. They actually crush rock, breaking it down into a substance suitable for other plants to grow in. In this world, there are consumers of resources, chief among which is my species; then there are the producers of resources, those such as lichen who set the groundwork for life and creation. Humans have arrived here as heavy baggage on the backs of the soil makers and oxygen producer species like lichen: the unassuming mighty, the miniscule Hercules of the natural world. As such, they possess a grace reserved for the elite, for those life forms who have to struggle endlessly just to preserve their beneficial presence in an inhospitable world.

The sight of their stoic refinement shames and quiets my whining body for a while—a short while, and probably just because I'm momentarily standing on level ground. We meander the colorful, wind-swept mountaintop and gaze up at the towering Mount Washington, which, at 6,288 feet, ranks as the highest point in the northeastern United States.

When our tumble down the rockslide/descent trail begins, I whimper all the way. After about a half mile, I sit down on the blasted scree and kvetch.

"We're lost," I declare.

Bill just sits and rubs his knees, laughs at me, and then continues on down the path.

Another half mile down the mountain, I stop again, hoping to convince Bill our situation is dire.

"This can't be the trail. There's no sane forest ranger who would map a trail on this terrain."

"You might be right . . . this trail is terrible."

"It can't be the trail," I insist.

"Yes, you said that already," Bill replies.

"Yeah, well . . . it can't."

After the fourth or fifth time we stop to give our knees a rest, I think I've almost persuaded him to start panicking, but then the trail starts to level and we meet some spirited hikers heading up the trail who say we are on the right path to the waterfalls at Pinkham Notch. Bill jogs ahead of me (perhaps redeeming his pride, wounded by the accursed jogger) to gather the car which we had left at a trailhead a mile down the road. I stop with Maggie at Pinkham Notch, resting my knees and letting my mind wander as I listen to the thunder of water stampeding rock.

Perhaps it's something in the musicality of the waterfall that sends my mind back to the 9:30 Club in Washington, DC. The last time I went there it was to see Daniel's favorite band, Moxy Früvous. Daniel was sick, in the throes of chemotherapy, and though he wanted to see the show, he feared he didn't have the energy to stand in the crowd. So Bill called ahead and convinced the club to put a chair in the balcony for Daniel. Revisiting that moment, it occurs to me, Bill must have had to explain to the management at the 9:30 Club about Daniel's cancer therapy. A sharp pain begins to lodge in my throat and chest. My inability to protect Daniel continues to gnaw at me, an irrational but irresistible mouse that frays my spirit and shits on my memory. I fight with the urge to weep as a group of hikers march behind me on the trail.

How I wish Daniel was here with us, hiking through the White Mountains. He too would have found that trail contemptible but prized even more the life we encountered and the wild blueberries we plucked in the low growth of the rocky mountain highlands.

I return to the present when Bill arrives. We rest awhile more, then head up the road toward Baxter State Park, home of Mount Katahdin, the northern terminus of the Appalachian Trail, on the eighteenth-month anniversary of Daniel's death.

14

Driving through the darkness of a rough, deserted gravel road on the northwestern edge of Maine, Bill and I are wishing we were stowed in our sleeping bags rather than foraging for a campground, when suddenly out of the darkness charges an awkwardly enormous brown beast.

"Oh shiiiiiitt!" I gasp as I rear back in my seat. The whole episode lasts about fifteen seconds but my mind perceives it in super slow-mo: enormous brown blur galloping toward me, putting on the foot-break Flintstone style, smoke coming from the friction between hoof and road, beast rearing his front legs trying to block his view of the impending impact, me throwing my hands in front of my face to hide the horror, and at last . . . silence. Exhale. When it becomes clear that I will not have a broken window and a moose in my lap, there is a brief euphoric moment of pause, the creature's face only feet from mine, behind the car glass. Our eyes meet, both excessively wide and fearful. I can't claim to know what the moose is thinking at this moment, but the one thought that occurs to me is: *massive*.

Maybe fatigue has skewed my perception but the moose seems to tower over the station wagon and weigh nearly as much; surely if it landed on us the car would crumple like aluminum foil and my bones would crunch like an overcooked chicken wing. The beast apparently had a similar perception of our relatively smaller size because it nearly overlooked our ton of moving steel and plastic and humans and dog and junk as it galloped across the countryside.

After regaining its balance the moose backs away a few feet, then walks in front of the car, across the road, and out of sight.

"Whoa," Bill says. And that just about covers it.

Moose sightings are not rare around here but more so than they used to be. The moose population in New England declined as a result of the explosion of the deer population, a result of the decline of predator populations, thanks to the increase in human populations. The resulting ecological imbalance bolstered the prevalence of a tiny organism that lives quite happily and harmlessly in the brain of deer, but lethally invades the brain matter of moose. With climate change, long-term survival for the moose takes on an added set of challenges. Its habitat is warming, which is good for ticks and other parasites that live off the moose, bad for the moose and its forested home.

Thébaby

Bill and I have contracted a brain malady of a less serious nature. Life on the road does strange things to the human mind. The road-trip worm, which feeds on car boredom, has commenced boring into Bill's brain. He has taken to calling Maggie "The baby," and like an impressionable sidekick, I have copycatted. She's the hairiest, smelliest baby ever to gnaw on sticks and chase rodents. Occasionally, when he's feeling fancy, Bill adds a French twist to Maggie's new name that comes out "Thébaby." Maggie's bored looks at these inventions make me think she is beginning to resent our tomfoolery. I feel bad but still try to copy Bill's pronunciation because I like the way it sounds. And really, the hours in the car must be passed. And if she doesn't like it, well, she's just got to learn to stick up for herself.

Our socialization skills are slipping, slipping—from being too tired to brush our teeth at night, to being too persnickety to take the only shower available, an outdoor one. We will be passing by Kennebunk, Maine, and Bill said we should go to Tom's of Maine and propose we be their spokespeople. Our testimonial: "We never brush our teeth but a couple of weeks ago when we did, we used Tom's of Maine." It would work for their full line of healthy hygiene products: soap, deodorant, mouthwash, etc.

Baxter

Tom's will just have to make do without our endorsement because instead of Kennebunk, we head to Baxter State Park. This Maine park, one of the largest collections of wild lands in the East, owes its existence largely to the vision and generosity of one man, the former governor of Maine, Percival Baxter.

In 1911, prior to Baxter's governorship, a bill came before the US Congress to make the area—much of which was owned by a paper company—a national park. (That plan, which has been revived several times over the past century, has never taken off.) As governor in the 1920s, Baxter tried to get Mount Katahdin and its surrounding mountains and lakelands protected. In a 1921 speech, he said:

> Maine is famous for its twenty-five hundred miles of seacoast, with its countless islands; for its myriad lakes and ponds; and for its forests and rivers. But Mount Katahdin Park will be the state's crowning glory, a worthy memorial to commemorate the end of the first and the beginning of the second century of Maine's statehood. This park will prove a blessing to those who follow us, and they will see that we built for them more wisely than our forefathers did for us.

The state legislature was disinclined to build more wisely than their forefathers, and Baxter's Katahdin quest fell short.

Instead of giving up, after leaving office Baxter endeavored to create his park as a private citizen. After the crash of the stock market in 1929, the paper company agreed to sell 6,000 acres of land surrounding Katahdin to Baxter for $25,000. From that core parcel of land, Baxter added continually to the park until his death in the 1960s and eventually put more than 200,000 acres in public trust. When Baxter died in 1969, his ashes were scattered over the park, its quiet lakes, deep forests, and jagged peaks, including what is now called Baxter Peak, the northern terminus of the Appalachian Trail.

15

In 1996, a few months after his surprise arrival at my doorstep in Tucson, Daniel flew to Georgia to begin a months-long trek along the entirety of the Appalachian Trail. He had been planning the trip since his dad's death the year before he met me, hoping the long days of feeling his boots upon the ancient ground of the Appalachians would help connect him to the past and his dad and also to a future that had been eluding him. Daniel had made all the many preparations required for a successful thru-hike: buying provisions, organizing packages of supplies for his mom to mail to him at different points along the way, trying out equipment, training, etc.

Saying goodbye to him in Tucson was hard, but the journey was important. When he set out on the trail at Springer Mountain, I expected not to hear his voice for a month or more. After about ten days, my phone rang and on the other end of the line was Daniel.

"Everything okay?" I asked. "Where are you?"

"I'm in a bed and breakfast near the Georgia-North Carolina border."

"Oh. Taking a rest?"

"No. I'm waiting for a bus."

"Are you alright?"

"Yes, I am. I really am. That's why I'm catching a bus to Washington, DC, then a flight to Tucson. I don't need to walk this trail anymore to know where I belong. And now that I know where my life is going, I want to start it right away. I miss you. I miss Bill and Katie. I'm coming home."

"Yes, home," I said, liking the sound of the word.

I had only known Daniel a few months when he made the decision to leave the trail. I wonder now, if he had stayed, would his fate have been altered? Maybe we would not have started a life together, but maybe he would have been stronger and more able to fight the cancer that eventually stole his life. Daniel and I were like that Barenaked Ladies song: "She's like a baby, I'm like a cat, when we are happy we both get fat." So the physical effect of our togetherness was a general, shall we say, softening. Would he have lived without knowing me? I wonder. And if I knew that he would have survived if his path had been different, could I go back and make the choice to never have known him? Could I return to that weekend at Bill's mom's house in 1995 and when I first gazed into his gentle blue eyes and laughed at his ridiculous stories and danced with my head on his shoulder, could I look away and never back, knowing he would live a long life because of it?

Perhaps nothing would have altered the power of the cancer but I fear I will never stop wondering.

Though he gave up the idea of a thru-hike, Daniel always planned to return to the Appalachian Trail, to hike it piecemeal, and without question to hike the northern terminus at Katahdin.

Tomorrow I will hike it without him.

16

The Knife's Edge trail to Baxter Peak consists of a rock pathway about three feet wide with a thousand-foot drop-off on either side. Percival Baxter led a group of legislators along this trail eighty years ago in hopes of gaining their support for his Katahdin park. It was a good choice, even though Baxter did not then attain his desired result. In the upper elevations, clouds envelope the trail in a capsule of obscurity that shrouds the mountain and the earth beyond. The path seems to float in silent suspension outside of time and the world beyond.

As I inch along the Knife's Edge, I behold nothing more than a foggy silhouetted Bill ahead, an ethereal dampness around and above, and an infinite vaporous void beneath the rock ledge on which I tread. The insubstantiality of it all unnerves me, yet a part of me desires to embrace the damp misty nothingness, to free-fall within the clouds. My fondest wish and most frequent dream as a child was to lie about on cloudbeds in the sky. These notions occupied me long before I understood how fleeting and insubstantial clouds are, and long after my teachers upbraided me for drifting in daydreams. Of course the clouds wouldn't hold me; they have all the substance of dreams and, like dreams, are ever shifting at the slightest urging of the wind. Still, right now, right here on the Knife's Edge, the clouds hold me fast.

And I hold them. In a way, a person actually becomes a part of the clouds when walking this high within them. Each fine hair on your body becomes a carrier of the surrounding cloud, which settles upon you in minuscule beads of water. On eyelashes, silvery cloud-mist collects in a glittering arc that frames the misty world around. Not the same magic I dreamed of as a child, but magic just the same.

Bill stops and looks at my cloud-covered face. He smiles a smile of wonder, framed by a glimmering cloud-wet beard haloed by a far-off sun. His eyelashes and eyebrows glisten with cloud clothing.

But life in the clouds is harder than I imagined as a child, longer and harder to attain, and requiring much more effort than one involves in fantasies. This enchanted trail seems endless. Each summit reached disappoints and discourages, as an even higher peak rises in the mist ahead. After three hours of hiking, I am sure each time the vertical climb intensifies we are nearing the pinnacle of Katahdin. But each time we round a jagged peak we find the climb we just completed inconsequential in comparison to the one that rises before us. After several deceptions from the foggy landscape, I begin to fear I will not attain the culmination of this journey. I need to get there for Daniel, but fear I cannot make another summit.

Inwardly, I begin to fret. I fear we have been lost in some sort of Katahdin Triangle—a place where all paths are endless, pain-filled, and obscured by a confusing, nebulous haze. I've been here before many times, in life, in memory and in grief-addled imagery that comes in the night. The dreamy veil of clouds that drape the landscape makes my fantastical fears seem all the more plausible.

But I trudge on, as I have no real choice. There are places in life where no matter how frightening the path ahead may be, there is no viable alternative. The path behind is gone, as if it dissolved immediately upon the passage of your feet. Katahdin is one of those places and I continue on, because a descent upon the Knife's Edge is unthinkable.

Finally we labor to the top of a peak whose rounded plateau reveals not another higher peak in the distance but an enormous cairn that towers above our heads into the mist.

Undoubtedly this is Baxter Peak, crowned by a rock memorial constructed piecemeal and communally by decades of Appalachian Trail thru-hikers. The cairn looks as if each hiker added a bit of the climax he or she had reached, so I add a rock for myself, and one for Daniel. Bill does the same. Then he and I sit among the clouds eating trail mix under that colossal monument to pain, endurance, and tortuous journeys ended.

17

Lazy puffs of cloud sail the pacific blue sky above Baxter's Grand Lake Matagamon. In the distance between lake and sky, an osprey paces, intently observing the goings-on in the water below. A gust of wind lifts a leaf from the ground and carries it to the height of the osprey (from my perspective laying down on the earth) and then abandons it to flutter and float to the rippled surface of the lake. As far as I can tell, or care to tell, there is nothing happening on the entire earth aside from the osprey, the leaf, and the listless wandering of clouds.

But enough of this idle musing. Bill and I have business to attend to. It's been three or four days[23] since our last shower, so we set up our Sunshower[24] and hope the clouds will dissipate, allowing the sun to TCB. While the waterbag is awaiting solar attention, I write in my journal by the lakeside. Bill sits next to me reading.

After about a half an hour Bill says, "What does the shower gauge say?"

I look at the plastic multi-colored gauge on the glorified water bag. "Sixty-five degrees."

"That won't work for me," Bill declares.

"Me neither," I say.

Another half-hour passes and Bill again inquires about the shower water.

"A watched bag never warms," I caution him. "It's at sixty-seven."

"Impossible!"

He taps his finger on his book impatiently then says, "Can I use the pen?"

"No, I'm using it."

"I think that's actually my pen," he says, with an insinuating tone.

"I packed it in."

"Oh *wow*, you carried a pen in your backpack. So now I'm not allowed to use it?"

"No, I'm just saying, I'm not finished. Wait your turn."

---

[23]Whatever, who's counting?

[24]Plastic bag of water with a shower nozzle and fancy name.

He hesitates a minute and I go back to writing, thinking I've made the situation clear.

"I want to write a letter. Give me the pen."

I relinquish the pen, chucking it as hard as I can down the beach. "Down the beach" may be slightly misleading. As usual when I throw things in frustration, "hard as I can," equates to about five feet. But it makes a nice smacking sound on the pebbly ground, so I am mildly satisfied with the gesture. Bill chortles at my throw, retrieves the pen, sits down next to me, smugly, and begins to contentedly write a letter on his Gumby stationary.

In this way the day begins to pass away. We see a few loons, an osprey, a large troupe of merganser, and various rodents and birds, but no moose, and no 80 degrees on the Sunshower gauge. Finally we give up on a warm shower. We have long ago finished our other business for the day—fighting over who got to use the pen (check), cooking a lunch of cheddar potatoes with the (toxic?) desiccant packet included (check), throwing ruined lunch into our garbage sack (check), cooking a second lunch of corn without the desiccant packet (check).

We reluctantly decide to go ahead with our showers.

The water has actually become quite warm despite the misinformed gauge and the shower feels great, even though the lake water we use resembles Earl Grey and has at least one leech in it.

Roosevelt-Campobello

Upon reluctantly leaving Baxter State Park, we drive as far east as possible. As we meander through the quiet countryside I feel an unparalleled sense of freedom—from the expectations of normal life, a job, society, and from time and space in some strange way. I can be anywhere, almost, at any time I'd like. Turn left, go straight, sit still for minutes, hours, days. There are of course negotiations with passengers two and three, but at the moment we are all aligned as to where we might like to go next. There is a red dot on our *National Geographic Atlas*, in the watery blue space between the United States and Canada, and it is calling our names. And so, somewhere along the far northeastern edge of Maine, we leave the United States and cross the border into New Brunswick. There we beeline to our beckoning red dot—Roosevelt-Campobello International Park.

The park is a historic site memorializing the island on the Bay of Fundy where Franklin Delano Roosevelt spent summers as a kid and where he and

Eleanor summered with their children before economic depression, drought, and war overtook their lives. The location was a remote family refuge for the Roosevelts before a fateful moment in 1921 set the course of world history on the wobbly head of a straight pin.

In the 1920 presidential elections, Roosevelt had been the vice-presidential candidate on the losing Democratic ticket. In the summer following that election loss the Roosevelt family retreated to their vacation home on Campobello Island in New Brunswick. One evening, following a typical day of boating and swimming, Roosevelt took ill with a severe fever that precipitated into loss of urinary and bowel function and partial paralysis. It was the beginnings of a debilitating illness that eventually left Franklin Roosevelt paralyzed from the waist down for the rest of his life. The illness placed Roosevelt at a crossroads. The turn he took here would be the fulcrum for a monumental shift in the path of history. Everything from World War II to the Civilian Conservation Corps to Social Security would have been affected by this one moment of what must have been agonizing deliberation. Roosevelt had long wanted to follow in the political footsteps of his distant cousin President Theodore Roosevelt. But after his paralysis, his mother, a major figure in his life, counseled and nearly had him convinced that the crippling disease marked the end of his life as a political leader. Eleanor, who reportedly rarely stood against Roosevelt's powerful mother, persuaded him to defy his mother's council and continue public life.

The tides of fate and a protective mom cannot be denied their persuasive power. But, the power of personal will holds its own sway over the ultimate direction of destiny.[25, 26]

The Tides

On down the road from Campobello, tidal energy is illustrated with a bit more literal force. In the Bay of Fundy the tides rise higher and fall farther than any

[25]Note to self: This significant chapter in history underscores an important truth in life. Fate can run you over and leave you broken, and in general there is nothing you can do to avoid it. But the decisions you make while lying in a mangled heap of human hamburger upon the insidious off-ramp of destiny, those decisions are all your own.

[26]Note to reader: Please do not assume for one minute that the lessons of FDR's courage and fortitude have permeated my skull at this point in the journey.

other place on earth. Here the variation between high and low tide can be as much as fifty feet when 115 billion tons of water fills and empties from the bay twice each day. This epic movement of ocean water churns up nutrients, making the bay a summer haven for fifteen species of whales, including minke, orca, and the rare North Atlantic right whale.

The shape and location of the bay provide for these immense tidal extremes, ten to fifteen times greater than in most places where sea meets land. And in St. John, New Brunswick, where I sit, they create the Reversing Falls, a waterfall at the mouth of the St. John River that reverses the direction of its flow throughout the course of the day depending on the direction of the tide. Tide coming in, the waterfall flows upstream. Tide going out, it falls downstream.

This phenomenon illustrates the often-invisible interchange between every particle tied to this earth—from water molecules to the water bladder of molecules we call human beings[27]—and the cosmos. The major players are sun, moon, earth; we are nothing more than miniscule flecks of energy caught up in their magnetic dance. The earth, with its gargantuan gravitational pull holds our feet to the ground and keeps water in its basin, but it cannot keep the oceans still when the moon begins to beckon. The great seas stir when called and rise up on the land until the moon has paced further afield in its orbit of the earth. Only then can the water again retreat in peace to the earth's embrace.

Our concrete society has separated us pretty thoroughly from nature, but there are places in the world where connections are made so clear that we cannot fail to understand our place within it all, the space we began to occupy when our ancestors first stood on two legs on the savannas of Africa. In one sense, the spectacular show of cosmic power at the Bay of Fundy dwarfs even those people on Earth that seem almost celestial in their massive roles in the course of world events—people like Eleanor and FDR. The most momentous acts of the brightest objects in the constellations of humanity are reduced to the substance of a grain of sand tossed about in the game of magnets and mirrors played by the sun, earth, and moon. But in another way, these forces and their seemingly eternal power elevate us simply by association. Eleanor and FDR and all of us in each tragedy and triumph are a part of this universe-system. And we each have our own gravitational forces to employ in our own orbits within the cosmos.

---

[27]Sunshowers with legs and no fancy/faulty temperature gauge

18

Cadillac Mountain is said to be one of the greatest vistas in the world. It is the highest point on the East Coast and therefore the first spot in the United States where you can greet the rising sun.

In late 1998, Daniel and Bill and I began plotting a visit to Cadillac Mountain. We had for years discussed where we should go to mark the 2000 millennium, a once in a lifetime transition in time. There was a lot of early enthusiasm for reenacting the *Empire Strikes Back* at midnight while temple-top at Tikal. But as the millennium approached, Cadillac Mountain seemed more realistic. It was easy enough to get to that we could ask all of our friends and family to meet us there, and we could watch the new millennium rise with everyone we loved.

It was a good plan. But like so many of the plans we made, it became lost when an altogether different future unfolded. We spent the eve of 2000 together, and with many of our closest friends, but we were inside Daniel's and my condo in DC .When midnight struck, the sounds of celebration exploded from the city, filtering through our walls and windows. Fireworks, screams of revelry, champagne corks, applause. I listened to them not so much with envy, but rather with an angry disgust.

The evening could have been worse. Daniel had spent Christmas that year having surgery on the tumor in his brain that had caused partial paralysis. The doctors had wanted to keep him in the hospital over New Year's, but we managed to convince them that he really was better off at home. This was a major victory for us. When you are a part of the healthcare system, you lose control over the most basic aspects of self-determination; when you will come and go, how long you will wait, where you will spend holidays, etc.

That evening Daniel lay on our couch with his feet in my lap. Maggie was on the floor beside him, and Xena on the couch cushion behind him. Barbara, Bill, and a few other friends were with us. We talked, watched the coverage of Times Square, we even had party hats and noisemakers. But aside from the feel of Daniel's feet on my legs, and my hand on his feet, I felt distant from the entire experience. There was little more than cold fear in my mind. As a year, 1999 had been the worst I'd ever lived through. And though a part of me always believed Daniel would get better, that night my mind could not imagine that the year 2000 would hold anything but unimaginable pain for everyone in that room.

19

Bill and Maggie and I drive the winding road up Cadillac Mountain in Acadia National Park for a sunset hike. Of the places I've been in the world, this rounded mountain fringed with colorful sub-alpine plants strikes me as uniquely beautiful. It would have been a wonderful place to recognize the passing of a millennium.

The trail we hike affords an unobstructed view of the Atlantic to the east, set in the red glow of a fading sun in the west. We walk quietly, then sit looking out at the ocean, each lost in our own memories of a millennium that never came.

Solitude

At Acadia's Eagle Lake, Bill and I laze about for much of the day reading and writing and napping. With few people about the wildlife is active and unguarded. A group of red-headed mergansers feeding in a grassy cove become so absorbed in their business that they seem not to notice Bill and me watching them. The birds meander the cove, eyes focused upon the water, sometimes plopping their heads in to get a closer look. Then suddenly, they flip a switch and plow through the surface for ten or fifteen feet, throwing out waves and leaving a wake like a herd of tiny jet skis. They are running on the water. It's impossibly hilarious. Then they just stop, kick it down a notch, and paddle as before.

The mergansers cheer Bill momentarily, but before long he goes back to the grim mood that has held him through the day. His face, which had lit for a moment upon our sighting of the crazy birds, has fallen again into indifference.

"How about we go into Bar Harbor now," I say, hoping to jar him from his darkness. "We could get dinner or just some beers or go to a movie." I was sure he'd go for this; he loves movies.

"No, I just want to go lay down."

"Well, why don't we at least go get a shower? It will make us feel better," I suggest.

He just shakes his head and we return to camp where Bill lies down for another nap. I read for a while, but soon find the temptation too great and lie my head down too.

At about 6:00 p.m. we wake, grumble at each other, I get out of the tent, and Bill follows sadly. We have missed most of the sunset, but still climb a nearby hilltop to watch some pink clouds linger in the gray haze of dusk.

After sunset we make our way to the coin-operated shower. With our grime lifted, Bill's spirits rise slightly, but not enough to want to explore and I have lost my inclination to press him. So we return to camp for a dinner of peanut butter and jelly on bread for Bill and peanut butter and chocolate on a knife for me, then retire to the tent for an extended and altogether unpleasant night's sleep on a bed of pinecones.

In the morning, we are determined to find a quiet trail, something we have done little of in crowded Acadia. As national parks go, though beautiful, Acadia is a bit of a T.G.I. Friday's. We decide to hike to The Bowl, a pond sunk into an amphitheater of mountains. Bill and I take separate trails because Maggie cannot scale the boulders on the trail Bill wants to take. The divergent paths are a benefit to us both. When I arrive at The Bowl, I find myself, for a moment, utterly alone. I peer into the clear shallow pond, at the plants living out their lives on the other side of a watery window to another world. The quiet of the moment absorbs me.

I begin to realize, if we are going to make it through this year, I need more of this. Though I love Bill's company and I probably would not have come without him, solitude is essential. Sometimes I need it so badly I go sit in the bathroom for much longer than necessary, just because I know nobody will talk to me while sitting in a toilet stall. A quiet pond is better though; there's no stink. And the frogs and birds almost always leave me alone.[28]

A half-hour later Bill arrives from his hike wearing a long-absent smile on his face, no doubt cajoled by the rocky Maine landscape. Everything has changed about him in an instant.

---

[28]Maybe to their eyes I'm always sitting on a toilet. They look and me and say, "Oh, don't bother her, she's taking care of business."

With this revived energy, we set to breaking camp. As we are taking the tent down, we have to remove a spider who had set up its own camp between the tent and the rain fly.

More precisely, Bill has to remove the spider due to my multi-generational family arachnophobia. When I was young, every time I would leave my clothes on the floor, Granny would tell me the story of her sister, The Slob.[29] One time, a shirt The Slob had left on the ground became residence for a spider, and when The Slob put it on, the spider bit her. Granny described The Slob's neck swelling up until she couldn't breathe, and, as Granny told it, she almost died. In the telling of this story, you might expect my grandma to express a sigh of relief that her sister had survived. Instead there was generally a twinge of satisfaction in her expression, as if, yep, she had it comin'.

I imagine my eyes growing wide when my granny told an eight-year-old me of this near-fatal spider experience in my very own family. And I imagine my mom, who is even more afraid of spiders than I am, cowering in the face of The Slob/spider-bite parable. Ultimately, as our lives played out, the impact of the spider story was not as Granny would have hoped. My mom is very messy and I still leave my clothes on the floor. What we retained from the cleanliness lesson was that all spiders are deadly poisonous and are forever trying to sneak into your clothes to kill you.

Anyway, the spider on the tent appears to be dead. I noticed it earlier in the week from the inside and kept a wary eye on it in case it tried to gain more comfortable quarters inside my shirt.

Now that I'm truly safe and the spider has been pronounced dead, I take a moment to be amazed: we come to a place for a few days, a small portion of this year and a smaller portion of our lives, and this creature may have lived its entire life span on the temporary shelter we set up for ourselves. This whole life can be lived on the temporary shelter we set up for ourselves—an entire life lived in a blink of time, all purposes fulfilled. Or none, no matter.

Still, I keep an eye on Bill as he removes the critter. Spiders may play dead to give their prey a false sense of security and I want that bastard gone.

---

[29]Granny has alternate names for all her female relatives. There is The Pretty One, The Smart One, The Drunk, and the aforementioned, The Slob. Her parables to me are most often cautionary tales about The Slob.

20

Bill and I made a pact this year that we would not listen to news. We are journeying to find some distance from the turmoil of the human world and gain some connection to the world of nature. But, occasionally we listen to music on the radio when we can find a station. So as we are nearing the Boston metropolitan area, Bill turns on the radio and starts searching for tunes. He lands for a brief moment on National Public Radio and hastily turns the dial in search of some music.

"Hold on," I say. "Go back."

"I thought we weren't going to listen to news this year," he protests.

"Something is wrong," I say. "Listen to the reporter's voice."

Something, though I could only hear a few words, sounded different—real, effected, rather than affected.

"He sounds strange. We should listen for a few seconds."

When Bill tunes back to NPR we hear, "A plane crashed into one of the World Trade Center towers a few minutes ago . . ."

"Is this a joke?" Bill asks.

The shock and fatigue in the reporter's voice suggest otherwise.

". . . We are hearing now that a second plane has hit the towers," the reporter continues in his weary tone.

Bill and I look at each other in disbelief. I have a hard time visualizing what is happening.

"It is confirmed, the towers have collapsed," the report goes on.

"Is it the buildings that have collapsed or just the radio towers that tall buildings sometimes have?" I ask Bill.

I can't picture the World Trade Center.

". . . many are dead or trapped in the rubble. . ."

"It's the buildings themselves," Bill says.

My mind turns to my brother Nick who works in Manhattan. I don't know the city, don't know how far he is from the World Trade Center.

"We have to call Nick."

Bill points out a gas station and we pull over to a pay phone.

My brother's phone just rings and rings.

I try my mom at work.

"Thank goodness you've called!" she says. "I didn't know where you were, if you'd gone to the city, or what. . ."

". . . I'm fine. We're in Boston. But what about Nick?"

"Nick called after the first plane hit," she says. "He had been working in a building about a block from the towers. But . . . he hasn't called since the second plane hit."

"I'm sure he's okay, Mom. I'm sure he got out of the area," I tell her.

Actually, I'm not sure. I can imagine him going to the building to try and help, getting there before the second plane. I can imagine a lot of things. I try him again. No answer.

To distract myself from the uncertainty, I speculate about what has happened. It is fairly certain that this is an act of terrorism, but of a type none of us could have imagined here. Not here. But isn't that part of the issue? Our ability to feel so safe and secure is part of why something like this is inevitable. Despite the role that our nation plays in global history and culture, for good or ill, we are insulated from the troubles that many other nations face. Famine in Somalia, violence in Israel, these are things that we see on TV. Even when we are at war, most Americans are spectators of chaos living privileged lives a very safe distance away—so far away that many of us spare little of our conscious lives contemplating the misery behind the glass and plastic of our television sets. Our access to food and clean water are secure, our children continue to go to school, our greatest dangers are self-imposed—obesity, heart disease, car accidents.

We are safe. We are comfortable. It is . . . expected.

More news comes in by the minute, both towers of the Trade Center have fully collapsed, four planes were downed in New York, Washington, and Pennsylvania.

The air has become poisoned with shock, disbelief, and foreboding.

I am having no luck contacting Nick so we leave the pay phone and continue driving to the John Adams National Historic Site, where we had been heading when the news of the attack came. When we arrive, a police officer parked near the entrance informs us that all the national parks are closed due to the terrorist activity. He is a stout, middle-aged man with a heavy Boston accent. He asks where we are from and we tell him about our trip, which peaks his interest and sparks a list of suggested local attractions.

"You should go see the whales off Cape Cod. It's amazing! You are almost sure to see some," he tells us. His manner is so casual, familial almost, like we have known him for years. How does one come to be a person like that? And what if everyone treated strangers as if they were family?

His smile fades as he points to the building across the street from where we stand.

"A flight attendant from one of the planes that crashed into the World Trade Center lived there."

We all gaze at the brick apartment building where several local television news vans have gathered. Conversation falls to silence.

I need to hear my brother's voice.

We say goodbye to the policeman and head to the nearest gas station pay phone. Still no answer, so I try Mom again.

"He called back, honey, Nick is safe," Mom tells me. He called again after the initial chaos had subsided in Manhattan. "But I'm still worried," she continues. "What if there are more? You are all too close to all of this."

"You shouldn't worry about Bill and Maggie and me," I tell her. "We are going to wilderness, or as close as we can get in the east." The unpopulated areas that draw me are not likely terrorist targets. The attacks seem calculated to communicate a message, one related to the financial and military dominance the United States exerts upon the world. I spend my time with trees and animals, who seem a world apart from this deadly language of human ire.

I try to console Mom, but am feeling low this morning myself, especially after hearing more news about the collapsed World Trade Center buildings, about the people trapped inside, firefighters and rescue workers who died on the job because they arrived after the first plane hit but before the second one, before the buildings collapsed.

Grief and fear brood as a smothering cloud of anxiety above the destruction in New York, DC, and Pennsylvania. I recognize this moment, the realization of death's victory over life. But mine is the enraged wail of one while theirs rises in chaotic symphony, echoing through crumbling canyons of metal and glass, ash and bone. It gathers and forms a front of dark storms that scatter and rain a corrosive emptiness that saturates the land.

Of all the things I may have expected this year, this was not one. We tried to leave the darkness of human society behind for a while, but we would have to have been on the moon not to know about this new shadowy wrinkle in the world of men. What happens now, I wonder, both in a personal sense and for the world at large? Can Bill and I escape the pall this moment has cast upon the country? And more worrisome, what does this portend for the nation, for the world? In the grip of fear and grief, people have but a few choices: rise above the tragedy and use it for achieving something good, or wallow in it and let it destroy you. Terror has a unique way of burrowing under your skin and finding a home, parasitizing you silently, while you actually believe you are acting out of strength and courage.

It has only been a few days since the attack and today Congress gave the president nearly unlimited authority to wage war and the Battle Hymn of the Republic was sung at the 9/11 memorial service in the National Cathedral.

Mine eyes have seen the glory of the coming of the lord. He is trampling out the vintage where the grapes of wrath are stored. He hath loosed the fateful lightning of his terrible swift sword . . .

Childhood

In Provincetown I sit on a beach with Maggie curled up at my feet while Bill lounges next to us with a book on his lap. He doesn't read. Instead he watches the surfers riding the waves offshore and makes commentary ("I wonder who invented the wet suit?").

The last time I sat upon these warm sands I was a child visiting my grandparents. The smells and sights of this arm into the Atlantic have gotten me thinking of my grandpa. He died long ago and I was so young that I do not often have memories of him, but Cape Cod conjures images of that white-haired, red-nosed Irishman, and all of the summers of my childhood spent here with him and my granny.

Many people associate the word "childhood" with a sense of security, when concepts of money for clothes and rent and food are fodder for make-believe, not concrete fears. But because my youth was weighted by those fears, along with anxieties of abandonment and rejection that accompany the child of an absent father and an at-times despondent mother, the term "childhood" for me refers not to life's early years, but to moments of time within those early years. Summers with my mom's parents on Cape Cod are among those moments. Granny and Grandpa provided sanctuary, their trailer home became a habitat that inspired release from the everyday concerns that gripped my mom and vicariously my brothers and me. They couldn't really relieve my mom of the burden of an uncertain future and the responsibility of providing for three small helpless humans on a teacher's salary. But they did create a stable environment for those three small humans for the weeks we were with them.

Granny and Grandpa took care of us, left worrying for another time. We played cards and sang along to Bobby Vinton and Johnny Cash ("How High's the Water, Mama?") on the 8-track while Granny stirred cauldrons of seafood in her tiny trailer kitchen. Grandpa brought donuts every morning on his way home from mass, talked trash about Republicans, and carted us to the beach where we built castles for our make-believe kingdoms on the Atlantic.

My grandparents had a friend named Bobby Denton, and in the seventies people still talked often about Bobby Kennedy, who, to my seven-year-old mind, was still alive and well. And since I had never met any of the Bobbies face to face, Denton, Kennedy, or Vinton, they became for me the same person. I thought my grandparents were near royalty, being personal friends of the legendary Kennedy with the silky voice on the 8-track tape in the trailer home on Cape Cod.

"She wore blueooooh velvet . . ."

I have told Bill how Grandpa used to pass the time with us on long car rides. Three elements were constant: every time we would see a decrepit barn on the side of the road Grandpa would yell, "Burn it!" or "Torch it!" and my brothers and I would yell along with him; every time we saw the sign that declared we had passed into a new state, we would all shout, "You are now entering the great state of _______!"; and every time we saw a white horse along the road, my brothers and I would compete for who could be the first to lick one hand and smack it on the other (Grandpa would give the victor a fifty-cent piece).

Since I told him these things, Bill and I have gotten into several fights about whether a horse is white or not, who saw it first, and how much money each of us owes the other.

I wish Grandpa was here to settle it. As his only granddaughter he often took my side regardless of whether I was right. I'd be rich, and vindicated.

Embodied Wild

Here on the densely populated rim of the eastern seaboard it is impossible to escape the cultural aftermath of the terrorist attacks, the socio-psychological chaos and desperate search for a sense of safety and order. Everybody has American flags now. Flags on poles—half-mast; on cars—half antennae; in hands—half popsicle stick. The United States' past, present, and future, specifically in relation to the Middle East, is so much more complicated than stars and stripes on a wooden pole.

In order to disengage from this complexity for a while, Bill and I take the suggestion of our friend on the Boston police force. With wilderness unattainable, we seek out an embodiment of the wild and board a clumsy watercraft chugging out of the Provincetown harbor in search of humpback whales.

These cetaceans measure up to fifty feet in length and 80,000 pounds, so we are to humpbacks what tiny tree frogs are to us. And as we are often curious about our smallish amphibian neighbors, whales can exhibit curiosity about humans when we wander into their spaces.

When the first whales approach our boat, grown people begin shouting and squealing and bouncing around on deck. I see adult men struggling with the urge to push children aside in order to attain a better view of the breaching humpbacks. I observe myself jumping up and down and clapping my hands like a kid at a magic show, as the whales leap from the water and transform the glassy blue to boiling white froth on reentry. What exactly is the value of spontaneous joy, connection, and wonder? Incalculable. And infinitely more than we once imagined.

Not long ago, humpbacks had been hunted to the brink of extinction, largely due to the demand for oil produced from whale blubber. But since commercial hunting was declared illegal in 1966, humpbacks have greatly recovered and now number perhaps 30,000, or about a third of their historical population. What we found, as the species began to recover, is that people would pay as much, and eventually much more, to cast eyes upon a live whale as they would to oil their lamps with a dead one.

Though I can't express precisely, in quantitative terms, what the value of whales or any wild species is to humans, the value is no less real. One whale-watching cruise is evidence enough. The very sight of them is transformative at an almost cellular level, as if their presence inspires our every last electron to dance a jig.

After several hours of near constant whale companionship, the boat returns to its Provincetown dock. As we disembark I chew on the memory of the creatures gliding three abreast upon an endless watery field with the waning sun glittering upon their backs. My boat-mates must be doing the same, if the stupefied looks on their faces are an accurate indicator.

I begin to wonder: Is it a curse to be human? These beasts are naturally endowed with a grace and beauty that only the most talented human after years of training can approach. We have no real natural beauty of movement. A dancer has to struggle half a lifetime to become graceful like a flower bending in the wind. Everything we have, we must labor to learn: eating, walking, talking, reading, thinking, dancing . . . relating. . . .

21

In Rhode Island, Bill and I come to an enormous fork in the road. World events seem to have swamped our already wavering energy and the question becomes unavoidable: Can packing two wounded animals inside a small automobile result in anything but further bloodshed? On one hand, I don't know anyone aside from Bill who would drop everything in his life to travel around the country and live in a tent. On the other hand, maybe the similarity in character and experience that has brought us to this road, also drives this persistent tension between us. We are both struggling to stay afloat, to find reasons to continue living in a world that often seems dark beyond vision. We have been roughed up by life, and some days that makes us docile, others it makes us prickly and disagreeable. On the days when I am feeling better, Bill is often feeling down, and vice versa. We are like two poor swimmers trying to save each other in a station wagon-sized toilet, mid-flush. For weeks we've intermittently argued about where to go next, how long to stay, how much money we are spending, and who is more childish and annoying.

Today I blow up at him about something too inane to remember and we sit in the car arguing heatedly until Bill stops talking and hangs his head. Maggie, the only unbroken animal among us, watches with concern from the back seat. Neither of us speak for a long while, until Bill finally says, "I think you should take me to an airport in Boston. I'll fly back to Michigan and you can continue on alone."

Continue on alone?

This is an unexpected notion and I reel in anguished confusion. I turn Bill's phrase over and over again in my mind and begin to assess myself as I am—a tattered patchwork, the holes in my life that Daniel left, filled now by questions, doubts, sadness, and a queasy debilitating despair. I see before me the fraying threads that tie me loosely to this world, most of which lead back to Bill. For a fleeting moment I understand with unforgiving clarity what my life would look like without him. And in the car, parked outside the New Bedford

Whaling National Historic Site, my tears and ever accompanying nose-run begin to stream down the crook of Bill's arm, which I have grabbed onto, and upon the atlas, whose pastel pages display Massachusetts's Taconic Range, near the borders of New York and Vermont. In this moment I recognize that the promise of this journey, my hope of finding a future in a world without Daniel, comes hand-in-hand with the peril of losing my best friend. The idea of traveling on alone terrifies me, but it pales beside the idea of losing Bill forever.

After a while, I calm down a little, and say, "I think we should either continue with a new focus on getting along or separate before we destroy our friendship."

Bill answers in a small tired voice, "I want to try to continue."

It's what I'd hoped he would say but didn't feel I had a right to ask for.

"So do I."

We sit quietly for a while, then Bill starts the car and drives us out of New Bedford and non-stop though Connecticut, hastening westward toward our next destination, Catskill Park in New York.

The Devil's Kitchen

Near Woodstock, New York, a Buddhist temple marks the beginning of a trail into the Catskills. In the early morning, Bill and I shoulder our backpacks and corral Maggie long enough to attach her little pack, and we depart for a multi-day trek in the backcountry. We are all grateful to be heading into the woods on foot, and because the hike is only about four miles, the time passes quickly. When we have nearly reached our destination, Echo Lake, an entirely wacked young fellow, gangly dude in his early twenties, stops us on the trail to declare that he has left a fire burning at the lean-to, "figuring someone would come along and appreciate it."

We do not express appreciation. And I restrain myself from mentioning that it could have been days before anyone else came along, and if so he would have gained the distinction of being the dipshit who burned down the Catskills. When we arrive at the lean-to we find a mostly finished bottle of Smirnoff lying by a blazing fire. Apparently, he also left the remainder of his liquor (figuring someone else would come along and appreciate it), along with an unopened can of baked beans smoldering in the fire pit. The kid mentioned he had been camping there for a while with a group of people, and though they have apparently all departed, a substantial residue of their presence remains.

The campsite beside Echo Lake has become a landfill. Half-eaten jars of peanut butter heaped upon rusty tin cans, upon plastic sheets upon beer cans and broken bottles . . . depressing and dangerous. If the bears don't attack us here, they never will. There is plenty of food for them, but they might just go postal over the mess humans have made of their home.

And what a home it is. Towering oaks send a steady shower of acorns down all around us. One ricochets off a rock and clips Bill on the leg. Maggie receives a loud *pop!* on the noggin. I laugh at them. Then I walk around hunched over anticipating the inevitable karmic pelt on the cranium. It never comes and I laugh some more but then my neck becomes sore from all the hunching.

The lake is small and quiet, surrounded by low hills blanketed with trees that are near ready to give up the green and blaze their red and yellow farewell for the winter. One tree in particular seems to have false-started in the autumn race for red and gold. But the tree's leaves are a browning red and the nakedness of its white birch bark against the verdant forest canopy suggests the lone tree is sick, dying. In the golden last glow of the sun, the tree's image dances boldly on the water of Echo Lake. The vision holds my soul in awe of the dry crackle of rosy death on bones of alabaster—the courage to wither as the world around spins in green growth and golden light.

After a quick dinner we settle into the tent and I fall quickly to sleep with the pleasant exhaustion of a day of backpacking. Upon waking, we hike away from our rubbish-covered paradise to a lean-to at Devil's Kitchen. The Kitchen is a very quiet spot, much more so than Echo Lake, which buzzed with chipmunks enjoying a rainstorm of acorns, toads leaping through tall grasses, and fish jumping to surprise insects on the still water. Here the faint shooshing of leaves far above mingles with the tinkling of a tiny brook, which sounds like a dripping tub. The trees seem asleep except for the occasional light updraft that sets their lightest branches to dance a floating dreamer's dance.

The Devil's Kitchen displays a noticeable lack of garbage lying around. This surprises me. After beholding the state of the Echo Lake lean-to I expected all of the camping sites in this area to be trashed. Also, no one in my family would expect a campsite called "Echo Lake" to be filthy in comparison to the "Devil's Kitchen." My granny considers herself something of an expert on the character of the devil versus the divine and she believes firmly in the "cleanliness is next to godliness" axiom. A few years ago, in one of her many well-intentioned but fruitless clean=good=heaven lectures, she used the term "immoral" to describe the act of leaving a wet washcloth on top of a dry towel.[30] So, if she is right, then it would stand to reason that the Devil's Kitchen would be the stinkiest garbage dump this side of the Devil's Bathroom. Wherever that is, I'm sure there are fields of towel racks with sour, moldy washcloths hanging atop dry towels.

Dean 'O' '85

After one night camping in Devil's Kitchen, Bill and I pack up our home and hike a trail to a couple of overlook points that float above the Hudson River Valley. We eat a breakfast of trail mix on a flat rocky perch above the foggy green valley. The rock on which we sit bears carved inscriptions that span a century of Catskill mountain pilgrimages. DEAN 'O' '85 and DWIGHT JENKINS 4-'68 and even C.S.T. 1913 are among the many names and dates. As I gaze at the inscribed rock's record of the many strangers who have rested here, I imagine that a faint ghost of them remains with the names they left behind. And I consider the inclination of people to declare, "*I was here.*"

It's a natural impulse, to announce ourselves to the ages. We tag walls with graffiti, carve initials into trees, rocks, and other things of permanence. The act quells our sense of insignificance by joining us with elements of the earth we know will outlast us. On top of that, maybe the sweeping vistas from mountain tops suggest eternity to the human mind and cause us to feel especially insignificant. We carve our reality into the mountain rock to give it substance, to imbue our blood with a permanence that we know our fragile veins do not carry.

---

[30]Little-known fact, there were actually eleven commandments carved by the finger of God upon the stone tablets on Mount Sinai but "Thou Shalt Not Leave a Wet Washcloth Atop a Dry Towel" was rubbed out by Moses, a Messy Marvin who fancied round numbers.

Unraveling

I call Mom to check in and when she hears my hello says in return, "Hi Krista, is Bill with you?"

I think that is kind of a silly question since Bill is pretty much always with me these days, but I hear something strange in her voice so I just say, "Yes."

"I've got some bad news," Mom says, really bad it seems from her subdued tone. I think of my brother Nick in NYC and wait for her to continue.

"Xena was hit by a car. She's dead," Mom says.

I have no immediate understanding of what happens next, the torrent of tears seem all out of proportion to the moment and incongruent with the setting. But I cannot stop the heaving expulsion of emotion. Bill puts an arm around me in the Interstate 87 rest stop south of New Paltz, New York. I watch tears spill onto the open yellow-paged phone book, soaking the flimsy paper pages, and onto the floor below where they mingle sloppily with the grime of life. Around us New York's tired travelers mill about and the greasy smell of French fries fills the air.

"I'm so sorry, Krista," I hear Mom say on the far-off other end of the phone line.

After we adopted Xena, Daniel treated her like any five-year-old child would have: picking her up, making her dance with him, zooming her around like an airplane through the house, basically everything but dressing her up in doll's clothes (we didn't have any).

Daniel would say, "It's time to be the baby," and Xena would accept her fate, go limp, and be held like an infant for as long as Daniel had the notion. Daniel was a large man, over six feet and solidly built, which made it all the greater a spectacle when he would pick up the runty gray tabby cat and make her dance with him to Johnny Cash's "Ring of Fire." I have done that once or twice since Daniel died, and many times it has been time for Xena to be the baby, but now no more.

I wonder as I walk back out to the car, is my life with Daniel going to unravel entirely? String by string. There were but a few tattered threads left after he died, now another is gone.

22

After a restless night of sleep in the car at the toll way rest stop, we seek shelter from the rain in the Cragsmoor Public Library. I check my email and find several from Mom, one before the terrorist attacks, one after the attacks, and one after she and Granny found Xena dead in the street outside her house. Life can change tremendously in the span of three emails.

In addition to being dry, this library is small and warm and comforting, with a mezzanine second floor, many paintings and bright windows, and a friendly young librarian. All is very quiet; I can hear only the clack-tapping of Bill at the computer next to me and the soft stacking and book covers flapping as the librarian sorts her charges. I wish I did not feel so down and could talk to the librarian more. She took out a bunch of historical photos and told us a general history of the town—an artists' colony at the turn of the last century. I did not even ask her name.

I want to be different, but apathy saturates me and stills all expression. The muscles of my face feel indifferent equally to smile or cringe, frown or delight. My tired mind holds my body uncomfortably immobile, uninterested equally in where I stand and any potential place I could stand. I desire no change, but am unsatisfied.

Several hours later, though clouds continue releasing their gloom, we drive to the ice caves at Sam's Point Preserve, a nature preserve cooperatively managed by the Nature Conservancy and the Open Space Institute. In addition to the ice caves, the area boasts a globally unique dwarf pine community, with more than thirty rare species of plants and animals.

Soft, steady rain gives me reason to stay in the car while Bill explores, but when we arrive, my indifference toward staying in the car is equal to my indifference toward hiking three miles in the rain. Bill will not hike unless I do, so I go.

The ice caves are deep fissures in the bedrock that remain frozen through much of the summer. Coming here in the heat of summer, the ice caves would be a welcome surprise. Today, though, they are just an extension of the cool, damp day. But even so, the underground labyrinth that arose when the earth buckled here a few hundred million years ago boggles the mind and begs for exploration—a maze of gargantuan rock descending into darkness, and the wet, shimmering green of a misty landscape. Bill would like to explore for many hours more, but I call a halt to our adventure. I can't do it today.

As we are walking back to the car, the soft rain turns hard and hasty. Maggie trudges along in front of us, dripping with wet-dog misery. Bill and I are drenched too, except for the area under our raincoats and boots. I don't mind the rain, a bonus of my exceptional indifference. In the city, Bill dislikes the rain as much as Maggie and opens an umbrella at the slightest sprinkle. But it's different out here. For him, every step into the world of tree and rock and earth is one of contentment; the rain is just another emotion of the enchantment that overcomes him.

As we walk, I look down to see Bill's dripping fingers reach out from his sleeve toward me. Maybe it's the rain, or the unfathomable ice caves, or its just the clarity of calm that follows a storm, but in those soggy reaching fingers I see, perhaps for the first time since Daniel died, that I am not alone. You'd think I would have recognized this before. I hadn't been *alone* for months, but I had felt alone, drained of faith that there could again be a moment when life would be okay. I think I imagined that as close as Bill and I are, he would soon realize that I am far too broken to fully mend and he would understandably find reason to walk a different path. Well, he may yet. We have many miles before us, and based on the past few months I cannot begin to predict what will transpire on the journey ahead. But for the moment he is here, and we are soaked, walking out of a magical place in the shadow of ancient mountains. I take his hand.

There is a shift in my mind and for a moment, we are both at peace—with being alive, in this world, and together on a road with no definable purpose or end. We walk hand in wet hand as the sky falls in wet chunks and we trek the remaining muddy miles back to the car.

Victorious Bill

In the morning we head south through Pennsylvania.

Somewhere on the long drive, lost in the vastness of Pennsylvania farmland, we pass a house all alone on a distant grassy hill, completely isolated, with no other human settlement in sight. On their own little island of space, surrounded by forest and farmland for many miles, the owners of the house have achieved a remarkable isolation in the crowded East. I think to myself: these people really want some distance from the rest of the human world.

I say to Bill, "Those folks hate people as much as you do."

"No chance. I hate all people *plus* those people," Bill replies confidently.

"They hate all people plus you."

"But I hate all people, plus them, plus me."

"Alright, you win Bukowski."[31]

Simple Chronic Assitosis

In the asphalt meadow of a rest stop on Interstate 81, Bill and I pull out our sleeping bags and recline our seats, preparing for whatever sleep we can collect here. This is the fourth night in a row we are interstate camping and neither of us is pleased with the situation, but respectable campgrounds have been eluding us.

Just as we are zipping up our bags, preparing to nod off, a violent awareness stirs us both bolt upright. I spin my head towards Bill. He stares wildly at me, grimacing with visceral disgust.

"You smmeellll that?!" I ask.

Bill's contorted face manages a nod.

"What in the moldering hell!" I say.

It can only be one thing. It's the same unmistakable smell that pervaded the storage space in my condo building after the exterminator came to poison the rats. The same smell that simmered up from roadkill in DC alleys.

Bill and I exit our sleeping bags, get out of the car, and begin looking for the source of the odor. We first assume we have parked over, or near, a festering raccoon or possum, but a cursory scan of the surrounding ground proves the theory wrong.

"It's in the car!" Bill declares with cold fear in his eyes. "Something died *in* the car!"

A frantic search begins. We take everything, including Maggie, out of the back and lay it down in the parking lot. We open the hood and sniff around the

---

[31]Bill doesn't really hate people, he just feels better when they're not around.

engine. We move the blankets, look under the front seats. We rip the back seat cushions from the car, down to the bare metal. Nothing!

The odor seems to be shifting intensity and location. It begins to drive us mad as we rifle through the contents of the car now scattered in the parking lot. Travelers stare at us quizzically as they walk past on their way to the rest stop bathrooms near where we have parked. We don't really notice them because we are systematically dismantling every loose element of the station wagon, checking every surface to see if it is removable, either by design or brute force. Bill retrieves his flashlight from a storage bin and shines it into the small crack between the floor molding and the floor. He starts to poke his finger under the molding but jerks it back quick, terrified. He thinks he has heard a noise under the floorboards, perhaps some rancid-smelling, shape-shifting predator that eats fingers.

That man is ridiculous, I think to myself. But just in case, I pull a fork out of our kitchen stuff and try to pry the molding up from the floor. I can't get it up so I stick my nose into the crack and take a big whiff. All of the expected car aromas identify themselves . . . wet dog, unwashed human, carpet fiber and cheddar-parmesan Cheez Doodles, all mildly offensive but not noxious and rotten. Bill crouches beside me, staring hopelessly into the reeking car.

"What the hell!?" Bill declares, throwing his hands up and taking a seat on the asphalt a safe distance from the vehicle. I join him and we sit amid our small mountain of belongings, gazing quizzically at our home. It occurs to us both, we cannot get back in that car. We may just have to leave it here and continue on foot. Maggie is going to have to carry a lot more in her pack.

We are thinking and guzzling some fresh oxygen, when suddenly we taste putrid in the air again. Our four eyes look down, then narrow on Maggie, who has just sidled up to us.

Her eyes say, "What's up, guys?"

Bill and I take a good long look at the dog and ponder, "What *is* up?" She manages to appear nonchalant, uncomfortable, and guilty at the same time, so we lean in closer and sniff.

Gag reflex sends us reeling back onto the pavement.

"*Oooohhhhh*!" we both sputter. The unholy stank from hell is Maggie—she's been possessed by the ghost of a decomposing rat sealed in a smell-tight vault for three weeks. We then sit in the parking lot on a pile of our stuff sniffing every inch of Maggie. Our examination bears fruit, extremely ripe fruit. We determine after a couple of courageous sniffs that the odor is coming from both her mouth and her hind quarters, but that based on all the licking she is doing in the ass area, that is probably the source of the trouble.

"We definitely don't have a mouse—that's the smell of simple atomic halitosis," I say as we sit exhausted on the cold pavement.

"Assitosis," Bill clarifies.

"It's the worst prolonged smell I've ever been subjected to. At least if it's a dead mouse you give it a nice burial or pick it up by the tail and toss it in the woods . . ."

". . . Done. Gone." Bill finishes my thought.

As we reassemble the seats and pack all our crud back in the car, I consider whether I ought to be alarmed over Maggie's odiferous condition. She is eating fine, has good energy, and aside from her odd reek does not seem any different from her normal self. Even in the best of health, she is generally inclined toward grumbling at the slightest perturbation but has not expressed any discomfort despite the fact that she has a shrieking stinking poltergeist nestled in her colon.

I pick her up and force myself to cuddle her adorable but offensive little self. Then I settle her back into the car and Bill and I discuss the situation.

"We need to head to DC and take Mags to a vet," I say.

We had planned on going to DC but not for at least a week.

"Let's shorten our trip to West Virginia. If she starts feeling bad, we can be in DC in a few hours," Bill suggests.

"Okay," I agree. "In the meantime, we'll need to keep Maggie in open air as much as possible."

"How bout we cut a hole in our roof rack bin and have her ride up there?" Bill suggests.

"That's using your thinking cap. But we can't *do* that. We don't have a saw."

We take the more viable option and plan to do more hiking and keep the windows down, despite the ubiquitous rain, and give Maggie extra treats to help her forget the humiliation of the Pennsylvania rest stop.

The John Brown Question

In Harpers Ferry, West Virginia, the Shenandoah and Potomac Rivers merge at the midpoint of the Appalachian Trail and the site of a somewhat obscure but significant historic event in 1859 that helped ignite the US Civil War.

Sites commemorating the war dapple the mid-Atlantic region—detailing every battleground, turning point, and strategically significant location from here to Richmond and beyond. But most of these seem to offer little more than a play-by-play of how the Union won the war—like the post-game show after a Super Bowl. Harpers Ferry offers something more. It was here that abolitionist John Brown attempted to wrest control of the federal armory and distribute weapons to slaves for a full-scale revolt. Even now, 150 years after his improbable plan failed and Brown was hanged, the essence of courage and unyielding idealism colors the cobblestone streets of Harpers Ferry.

Some consider Brown a terrorist; to others, he was a revolutionary, a hero who refused to accept a slow, democratic death for the immoral institution of slavery. Perhaps he was both, or neither. Prior to his attack on the Harpers Ferry armory, Brown had been a central figure in a bloody dispute in Kansas, as the territory battled over whether it would enter the union as a free or slave state. Brown's Machiavellian actions raise a quizzical conundrum: Are there situations in which righteous ends could justify massacre? Are there institutions so evil that slow deliberate democratic solutions are as evil as the institutions themselves?

The term *terrorist* has become omnipresent in the past weeks. Harpers Ferry holds an apt lesson in the history of this bloody endeavor, on the types of people who are willing to engage in such methods, on the precipitants of rage and violence, and on the perceptions of the public depending on which side of the moral argument they sit. I don't believe that terrorism is ever justified, whether it be a radical Christian bombing an abortion clinic or a radical Muslim flying a plane into the World Trade Center. But John Brown gives me pause, and pause is a wonderful thing in a world disfigured by rash violence and self-righteousness.

Brown's actions were memorialized in a song that Union soldiers sung while marching into battle, a song that was a precursor and inspiration to Julia Ward Howe's *Battle Hymn of the Republic*. Howe's lyrics do not expressly mention Brown, but she and her husband Samuel were active in the anti-slavery movement. In fact, Samuel was a member of the Secret Six, a group of wealthy abolitionists who funded John Brown's work.

Still, the original *John Brown's Song* was a bit more effusive of Brown than Howe's *Battle Hymn*:

Old John Brown's body lies a-mouldering in the grave,
While weep the sons of bondage whom he ventured all to save;
But though he lost his life in struggling for the slave,
His truth is marching on.

The *Battle Hymn* has since become a symbol of patriotism and nationalism, but in reality it was an ode to a man who was convicted of treason and ultimately gave his very life, as well as the lives of two of his sons, in resistance to his wayward nation, and to the national sickness of slavery.

23

On the slow winding drive to Seneca Rocks National Recreation Area in West Virginia I inch Bill a little closer to madness with my octogenarian approach to piloting the horseless carriage.

Bill says, "You know the speed limit here is 55 miles per hour, right?"

I respond, a la Sammy Haggar, "I can't drive . . . 55!" And continue driving 50 miles per hour.

"Pull over so I can drive!"

"As you wish."

Once behind the wheel and speeding down the road, Bill soon finds himself trapped behind an aged, rusty pickup truck puttering along on a winding two-lane road. The truck looks like it may have been the very first truck model ever designed, and the white-haired, bent-backed man behind the wheel might have been the original owner. Bill grumbles about my driving doppelganger for a long stretch of no passing zone. Finally we come to a passing lane on a steep stretch of road.

"I'm gonna have to drop the hammah on this motah scootah!" Bill declares loudly, to no one in particular.

He pulls into the left lane, drops the Saturn into second gear, puts his foot to the floor and . . . and . . . er . . . uh . . . nothing. Nada. If anything, we slow slightly.

The truck ahead sputters on defiantly, exactly the same distance in front of us that it had been before. Deflated, Bill pulls the shiny new Saturn back to the right lane, behind Henry Ford.

When we arrive at our Monongahela National Forest campsite home for the night, I call my mom while Bill prepares camp and dinner. Mom and I are talking about the news and about Xena, when a scrawny blond feral cat comes over and starts rubbing against my leg, meowing loudly. I tell Mom about the friendly feline.

"You should take her with you!" Mom says excitedly.

I imagine me, Bill, Maggie, Maggie's ass, and a flea-bitten, mange-riddled, stray cat living in the Saturn. The idea lacks merit.

"I don't think so, Mom," I say.

When I finish with my bi-weekly call, Bill has finished preparing dinner. As we eat I tell him Mom's idea about the cat and insinuate that I am entertaining the idea, just for fun.

"No! We're not doing that. I'm serious, Krista. I'm drawing the line here."

When I have finished my inner-snickering at Bill's expense, it has grown late and stars begin to appear in the dark West Virginia sky above the amphitheater of mountain walls that surround us. Bill and I consult Daniel's field guide to the night sky and track down the Pleiades, Cassiopeia, the dippers, Orion, and Canis Major. I recall times in Cornville when Daniel could get me off my couch-ass and out of my book to come look with him at the Arizona night sky, a maze of mesmerizing bursts of brilliance in an endless black sea. The memory simultaneously comforts and erodes me—how lucky I am to hold such a moment in my mind; how foolish that my lethargy kept me from having more of them.

Riiiiight!

Negativity. Negatives. I hold these troubling thoughts to the light and turn them over and over, adjusting my eyes to gauge the contrast, to find a correlating positive to balance my mood. Such endeavors demand my full attention and make external conversation impossible. Thus, many times in the car I reach my limit for human companionship—not gradually, like a slow drip that is ever building toward an overflow. My threshold is breached suddenly, like a dam breaking into a reservoir the size of a thimble. I am a very solitary person, especially since Daniel's death. I daydream a lot. I create stories or have debates with myself or some imaginary person—anyone who is not in the car. It may be strange, and possibly insane. I've always done it to some extent and, especially now, it helps me cope.

So when Bill starts to make idle conversation and interrupts my thoughts, it frustrates me. I have started ignoring the comments he makes that do not, in my mind, require an answer.

We will be driving along and I will be enjoying the silence and creating some philosophy or drama in my head and Bill will say, "It's a good idea to have a tent pad," or "The Alleghenies kick the Poconos' ass."

I hold no official position on either of these declarations, so I say nothing and try to hold my place in whatever world I am creating in my head.

"Right?" he says.

No response, I point my face further out the window.

Bill does not notice, or decides to reject, my subtle suggestion that he ought to leave me alone. He just wants me to respond sooooooo badly. He persists with "Right?. . . . . Riiiiiiight?. . . . . *Right!*?" becoming increasingly louder with every "right?" I do not respond to. I never should have told him about those boys at the library in New Hampshire.

If I still don't respond, he says, "Hellohellohellohellohellohellohellohello. . ." and continues until I give him some sort of recognition, whether it be yelling at him or laughing hysterically or banging my head on the dashboard until Maggie starts barking in alarm.

Sometimes, within fifteen minutes of an outburst like this, after I have begged him to let me think in peace, Bill will say, "Wachu thinking 'bout, woman?"

The Drummer Boy

I'm thinkin' 'bout gittin' me a T-shirt that says, "I heart West Virginia." Beautiful, beautiful state, the leaves of cherry red, salmon, and gold mingle with the blanket of green that covers these mountainous lands. Sheer rock bursts out of rounded hills without reason or warning. A field of squat ponies or leisurely cows laze here and there. Waters falling and rushing over and through the deep Appalachian green. West Virginia is a land all its own in the mid-Atlantic. Here the rush of highways, the self-important hum of the machine of government, industry, and finance, it all fades away in the stoic, ageless mountains.

Unfortunately, we have been driving a lot again today because, like yesterday, the rain has been an ever-present nag. Unlike yesterday, the nag walks hand in bony hand with a menacing cold wind. Fortunately, Maggie's assitosis has subsided somewhat, or perhaps our initial exposure to the stench cauterized our nose-neurons. Either way, neither dog nor humans are suffering at the moment.

We drive to the Green Hills array of radio telescopes. The clouds break momentarily while we're there, so we stroll around the enormous listening devices and I daydream of Carl Sagan's *Contact*, one of Daniel's favorite books. When my daydream is finished and we are back in the car I get bored and start singing "Under the Boardwalk" over and over, until Bill cranks up the bad country radio station he had avoided earlier in the day. My melody silenced, I find other ways to occupy myself. I find a twist tie loitering about between the front seats and use it to tie back a piece of my hair. When it falls out, I tie it to a lock of Bill's closely cropped hair. I have to work at it, but eventually I get it to stay put.

Later, when we stop for gas, Bill has forgotten all about the twist tie in his hair. I snicker quietly as he steps out of the car, pumps the gas, and strolls into the station to pay and go to the bathroom. I walk in to the mini-mart after him, just to be there when he finally becomes aware of the foreign object on his head. When he sees me, he calls my name loudly and waves me over, white twist tie still jutting up from the top of his head like a tiny antenna.

As I approach him through the potato chip aisle he asks, "Want to get some junk to help keep us awake?"

"Sure," I say, smiling a bit bigger than the invitation to potato chips calls for.

"Why are you smiling?" Bill inquires.

"Have you looked in the mirror?" I ask him.

"Why?"

My eyes drift to the twist tie.

Bill feels his head and finds the piece of metal, then doubles over with laughter.

Sufficiently awakened, we decide to make the thirty-minute drive to Cranberry Glades Botanical Area. As entertainment on the way, Bill and I try to sing "The Little Drummer Boy," but cannot come up with the words. For twenty minutes we sing a loop of: "So, they told me, parumpapumpum, a new born king to see, parumpapumpum, da da da da da da, parumpapumpum, rumpapumpum."

When we arrive at the Cranberry Glades, we step out into a misting rain for a short hike. Bill sets Maggie in the back while he rummages around looking for her leash and a plastic bag to pick up any droppings Maggie might make along the way. I hear him singing to her as he searches, "You get to walk with us, parumpapumpum."

Maggie's ears perk up and she cranes her neck to look up at Bill.

"I'll get a bag for you, parumpapumpum."

Maggie's alert eyes say, "Yes, yes, go on . . . I'm listening."

"We'll put your shit in it, parumpapumpum, rumpapumpum rumpapumpum."

Maggie's tail goes wild.[32]

When Bill has Maggie all squared away, we set out for a walk on the boardwalk that passes over a rare remnant of bog formed ten thousand years ago when glaciers marched over West Virginia. In most places this far south, this ecosystem could not have gained a foothold. But here, nestled in a cool wet crook of the Appalachian Mountains the cranberry bog took root. Cranberries, one of the few fruit species native to North America, were a staple for the land's earliest human inhabitants. The plant itself can live for a hundred years and generations upon generations of its ancestors have amassed as a spongy platform of peat upon which rests the current blanket of bog plants.

In this place, the death of a thousand years of plant life rests in peace just below the surface of the landscape and forms a springy carpet that cushions the current generation of vegetative, but *not* vegetarian, life. Because the land is acidic and nutrient poor, some plants must rely on predatory prowess to survive. The sundew attracts insects with sweet secretions along the length of its tentacle-like stalks. When the insect takes the bait, it becomes stuck in the sticky liquid and begins to struggle for freedom. Alert to this movement, the plant contracts to more fully envelop the insect and then secretes enzymes to digest the hapless creature.

In similarly sneaky fashion, the pitcher plant lures insects into its funnel-shaped leaf. When prey falls inside, it becomes trapped in a sort of stomach soup of enzymes.

Carnivorous plants hold a special fascination for us humans. We think of plants as benign, sedentary, guileless. But members of the "other" kingdom have special niches and strategies for survival just like we do in the animal kingdom. We are all looking for ways to hold on, enraptured by life in all its cruel kindness. The infinite ways that we manage to do that, conjured up by countless forms of life, offer an eternity of lessons in living. And the pitcher plant in particular presents a perfect symbol: It represents a form of life that has by necessity adapted

---

[32]She has clearly enjoyed this musical overture to her walk, but more importantly Maggie realizes it is finally time to place a triumphant checkmark next to one of her life's goals. She has won Bill's affection.

itself through the ages of the earth into a creature stunning in its beauty and brutality.

As I observe pitcher plants sprouting out of the boggy ground in the Cranberry Glades, I recall a reflection by Janisse Ray in her book *Ecology of a Cracker Childhood*.

She writes, "The pitcher plant taught me to love rain . . . Its carnivory taught me the sinlessness of predation, and its columns of dead insects the glory of purpose no matter how small. In that plant I was looking for a manera de ser, a way of being—no, not for a way of being, but of being able to be. I was looking for a patch of ground that supported the survival of a rare, precious and endangered biota within my own heart."

Back to Eden

From the Cranberry Glades, Bill and I set our minds to finding dinner. We page through our guidebook to vegetarian restaurants around the United States, and in a stroke of great fortune, we find a restaurant located in a nearby town—one of three vegetarian restaurants in the whole state of West Virginia. We're so shocked that a small town in this particular state would have a vegetarian population, and the name of the restaurant is so enticing, we have to make a stop at the place called Back to Eden.

. . . Turns out our guide to vegetarian restaurants is slightly outdated. We find the spot where Back to Eden used to be, even go in and find the women who owned Back to Eden. But the sign outside the restaurant now reads Back to Eatin' and the only thing on the menu for a vegetarian is a grilled cheese sandwich. The owner tells us she tried the vegetarian thing but nobody in town was interested, so she had to change the menu, and the name.

We are too disappointed to settle for grilled cheese, so we drive back to our campground. But by then we are too hungry and tired to cook, so we stop in a little diner nearby. I order a grilled cheese.

Having done finished with my eatin', I begin to reflect on the idea of Eden. Though apparently not so salable in West Virginia, much of Western culture seems tied to this concept of a perfect place where we were once in harmony with nature. Our separation from paradise—as described by the sparkly, pointy-grampa-in-the-sky bible—was caused by eating some forbidden smart-food procured by a naked woman, for which we were booted from paradise and became acquainted with death and pain.

I will go to hell for saying this, I know because this is what Sister Marcellia told me when I was a kid—but the Genesis writers got the story just slightly wrong.[33] We didn't come to know death because we got dejected from paradise; we *abandoned* paradise because it included, by its very nature, death and pain. Give me a moment to explain, Sister Marcellia.

Though I was brought up Catholic I have, over the past years, been stumbling upon a more secular exegesis of the Genesis bible story. The writers of those ancient texts tapped into the very kernel of the human predicament: our severance from Eden by the evolution of human consciousness and a revolution in human adaptation.

Sometime in the past hundred thousand years advanced language and conscious thought vaulted humanity on a trajectory at odds with the rest of the natural world. The Genesis story elucidated the genesis of this shift in perfect metaphor. Consider the bible scene, juxtaposed with the historical reality. Here was a moment in time where humans learned how to go from a natural existence, constrained by natural laws—as hunter-gatherers, whose population was intimately tied to what the natural landscape could provide—to a species that cultivated and stored its own food. Agriculture was the greatest of revolutions. It meant we didn't have to rely on what Eden provided, we didn't have to live by her rules, we could increase our population far beyond the bounds of a hunter-gatherer society or any other natural species. It also meant we could live longer, have better nutrition, a more developed brain, and leisure time to use that brain. Everything shifted the moment we plucked that fruit from the tree. When Eve accepted the fruit from the (let's face it, phallic) snake, she accepted a sort of boundless fertility—freedom from natural laws. But everything has its cost, and freedom isn't free. Earth's creatures were meant to have boundaries so that they could live in balance within a fragile system of limited space and resources. With the onset of agriculture, the path to modern consciousness was born, but something else happened at the same time, something insidious and almost certainly imperceptible.

[33]Or possibly something was lost in translation from the Aramaic.

In the moment (or eons) when this revolutionary transition occurred, our relationship to the natural world mutated violently, so that we were no longer at home in this earthly paradise, but were, rather, strangers observing this land and flora and fauna that lie before us—and the death that was inexorably tied to it.

In the Genesis story, the idea of exile from Eden takes on a powerful symbolic substance: We were forced to depart from paradise, not physically, as a footstep beyond a forbidden border. But rather, though we continued to walk among the same trees and animals, we became isolated from our environment *mentally*, by an unforgiving byproduct of evolution and cultural revolution that left us suddenly alone and stranded in our own consciousness and at odds with the natural world. And in that brain of ours, we became confronted with the one assurance we have in life: death. It was unacceptable. So therefore nature and our Eden were intrinsically unacceptable.

Ever since, we have been looking for a way around this ultimate conundrum, and the terror that knowledge of it engenders. We created religions where one of the central tenets was the victory over death. We found drugs that would help us forget. We jerry-rigged boobs with silicon so they wouldn't look old. We created separate, forgotten spaces for old people so we wouldn't have to be confronted by them. We even created a way to freeze our bodies, to await the day when technology would conquer death. We'll never win that war. And we also can't really go back to the relationship we had with our earthly paradise before we began to reject it. We can't unfall, unlearn, or easily reconfigure what we are. And now that we know, nothing will ever be the same for humanity—no matter how many cultural lobotomies we create to distance ourselves from the reality of death.

Likewise, I will never be the same. A consciousness of death has been a part of me since the day my purple ass was spanked and my lungs first filled. But when Daniel died, death as an abstract concept suddenly became death, my constant companion. Now, I can never go back to Eden. Only toward it.

24

One day, not long after Daniel's brain surgery, I came home from work to find him sitting at his easel in our living room, staring at a blank canvas. Usually when I walked in the door at the end of the day, a smile brightened his face; often he got up and walked to the door and gave me a hug. That day he did neither. He looked briefly in the direction of the door, then turned back to the canvas. I walked over to him and bent down to give him a hug. He was shaking.

"What's wrong?" I asked, quietly alarmed.

"I can't paint anymore," he said in a voice drained of emotion.

I didn't understand what he meant until he held his hand, which was holding a paint brush dipped in a charcoal colored oil paint, up to the canvas. It was shaking so hard he could not control it. Erratic strokes of dark paint blemished the white canvas.

"It may be temporary, sweets," I offered. "We can call the surgeon and see what he thinks."

"It's not temporary," he said.

I was as yet unprepared to accept the enduring essence of this nightmare we were living. But I retained enough of a grasp of reality to understand the depth of the pain he was feeling and my helplessness to lessen it. He sat at that canvas for another hour, while I worked on making a dinner I knew neither one of us would have an appetite for. In the middle of chopping some celery I was startled to hear him cry out in anger as he stabbed at the canvas with the brush, leaving more erratic paint slashes on the white cloth. I left dinner sitting on the counter and pulled Daniel over to the couch where we stayed for the rest of that night, the violent emptiness of the canvas keeping us in cruel company. It was the last Daniel ever painted.

In my mind the walls of our condo have crumbled under the weight of the anguish that paced those halls, carpeted those floors, colored those walls. But it was an old building, and well built, the site of a century of the lives and deaths of a thousand tenants. It was, I'm sure, able to absorb our anger and fear and eventually my solitary, violent grief.

25

Though only a couple of hours by car, DC is a world away from the West Virginia mountains. And for me, a lifetime.

Sitting alone in Tryst, my favorite coffee shop in DC, two blocks from the home I no longer have, I settle into memories of the city I fled. On my walk to the café, I avoided the block where Daniel and I lived, fearing the sight of it would bring me to my knees.

I order a cup of coffee from a hipster waiter. I know most of the people who work here by sight but not by name, and the same is probably true for them. I also know a group of faces of the regular patrons here, people who I never spoke to but would recognize as Tryst regulars when I saw them in other neighborhoods around the city.

While I'm sipping my gargantuan bowl of coffee, my friend Jeff walks through the door and I wave him over.

When I called Jeff a few days ago, he offered Bill and Maggie and me a room in his flat where he said we could stay as long as we liked. I met Jeff four years ago at a dog park when we had both recently moved to DC. I rarely talked to people at the dog park because, in addition to being an introvert, I feared the occasional dogophile who would talk through their dog, to Maggie, through me. Saying things like: "Can we meet? Dooo we feel like meeting today?"

What do I say to that? I rarely had to wonder for very long, because Maggie would soon lunge menacingly at the person's dog, which would then be ushered away in horror. But when Maggie started growling at Jeff's dog Cody and chasing him around the park with all the other dogs, Jeff thought it was hilarious and we started talking. I soon learned that he had just moved to DC and within days, had picked up a roommate at a bar and had already made more friends than my whole family has made in three generations. As I talked with Jeff, I found myself suspecting a weakness in my granny's theorem that any man you meet at a park has a 99.9 percent chance of carrying the serial killer gene. (Although, come to think of it, Jeff could just be the .1 percent.) So convinced was I of the discovery refuting Granny's theorem, that I walked to Jeff's apartment with him and *even* went in to get a drink of water. Later, when I told different people about meeting Jeff (like my mom and Daniel and Bill—I wouldn't dare tell my granny), they each said something along the lines of, "You have to be more careful than that," or "You're in the city now. You don't just go to a stranger's house alone," or "He could have been a serial killer!"[34]

Then, when each of the people eventually met Jeff, they immediately said, "What a great guy," or "That's the nicest guy I've ever met," or "He's like an angel. Is he single?"[35]

When we arrived at Jeff's apartment last night, he and his roommates Steve and Ria helped get our bags into Ria's room, which she has vacated for our stay. Steve helped me get our stuff to the laundry room and gave me quarters to get everything started. Jeff helped Bill find a parking place, an ominous task in Jeff's Kalorama Heights neighborhood. Maybe I've come to associate staying indoors with the understated hospitality of cheap hotels, where no one is particularly excited to see you but openly enthusiastic about your departure. I was actually amazed that my friends seemed to feel quite the opposite.

We talked until late in the evening about where Bill, Maggie, and I have been and where all we will go.

As he was heading off to bed, Jeff said to me with a squeeze of my shoulders, "It is so good to see you! You look so alive!"

And right then, despite all the other sadness and conflict that resides within me, I felt just as he perceived me.

The Compliment Man

In the morning, I drag Maggie kicking and screaming to her least favorite place on Earth. The veterinarian quickly surmises that Maggie has a putrid whale of an infection in her booty glands and prescribes some antibiotics that should quickly bring relief to dog and humans alike. He also suggests a small dose of Dramamine could help her with car sickness, and finally, he kindly hands

---

[34]Mom. The apple doesn't fall far from the tree.

[35]Bill. No, kidding, that was Mom, too.

Maggie a dog biscuit for her trouble, which she spits onto the floor and then walks away.

I take Mags back to Jeff's house, where she can hang out[36] with Jeff's dog Cody, then I head out again and walk alone for a few miles through the small city of DC. I end up in Freedom Plaza, between the White House and the Capitol where thousands are gathered to protest the US war in Afghanistan.

The rally draws a colorful cross-section of Americans, from angsty anarchistic youth wearing all black (from facemask bandannas to combat boots), to elderly folks leaning on canes, to people marching in wheelchairs and in strollers.

I meander the crowded plaza, taking it all in. At one point I listen to my tired feet and sit down on some stairs to rest. An agitator (calling himself a pro-war protester) is trawling through the crowd, shouting, "We want war not peace!" He is an odd sort with a military haircut but a much sloppier body than most military personnel could get away with. He dresses like a Friday casual banker, with jeans and a tie and a yellow button-down sweater, which in his zeal to protest the protest, he has failed to button properly so his sweater sits slightly askew. The man resembles a squashed, angry doppelganger for Fred Rogers (a.k.a. Mr.). Come to think of it, this could make for some great television. He even has a silent, supportive sidekick—a nondescript guy with a ready smirk, who would make a great puppet-neighbor.[37]

An equally odd woman next to me takes notice of Angry Rogers and starts shouting, "You ignoramus! You ignoramus! Fucking war monger Republican!"

Mr. Rogers responds with an uncomfortable sarcasm, and seems slightly scared of this feral woman who has taken his bait. "Yes, we want war, blah blah," he tries to sound unaffected, as it becomes frighteningly obvious he's hooked a whale of a fish, someone who's here not just to express dissatisfaction with policy, but with actual people, perhaps anyone who comes along, but most especially to protest the protest's protesters.

---

[36]This generally involves Maggie continuing her quest to achieve dominance over Cody by taking his bones and lounging on his bed, while Cody ignores Maggie. Cody is Maggie's best friend, in fact only friend, in the dog world. But I'm not sure he knows she exists.

[37]His only line would be, "Right!"

She yells him into a wide-open corner and his provocative statements grow quieter as his face grows redder and he begins to back away from her. I sit directly beneath the yelling woman, slightly concerned for my safety but too intrigued to flee as most of the sensible people around me have done. As the man and his buddy walk away, this white woman, who is fifty years old or more, starts yelling at her antagonist, "Fucking faggot! I'll destroy you! I'm a rock-and-roll nigger!"

The pro-war agitator forces an uncomfortable laugh, backs away further still, then grabs the elbow of a TV reporter and tells her he wants to be interviewed. She ignores him but the ploy gains him further distance from his nemesis. After achieving a safe distance from the screaming demon standing next to me, the man has his adrenaline back and is ready to start some fights. He pats his silent buddy on the arm and says with gusto, "Come on, let's go over here!"

I remain seated at the foot of the woman who had become so agitated by the agitator. Having, fortunately, and rather quickly, calmed herself, she looks down at me and says, "Here, you want these? They're good." And she hands me a half-eaten bag of chips.

I am very hungry but I have a policy against taking food from *stranger*s. Plus, the bag of chips looks as though it has sat in the center of a putrid heap of garbage for about three days. You know, it's all crinkled and the coloring of the bag is worn at the crinkles. But she rather insists. I do not want to risk offending her, not only because she scares me, but because I am near phobic about offending anyone, especially those who have the daily insult of having to find food out of garbage cans. So I take the bag and start eating. After all, I really am hungry.

The woman leaves me with my lunch and disappears into the crowd.

Shortly thereafter, a different but equally disheveled woman sidles up to me.

"Do you have any spare change?" she asks.

Had she noticed I was eating chips that obviously came out of a garbage can, she might have passed me over for a more financially promising individual. Then again, perhaps she did notice because next she tries to hand me a sandwich.

"I got this out of the garbage but I don't want it," she says.[38]

---

[38]Now, I realize that I have been living on the road for a while, and my clothes are not (ever) the current fashion, but I did shower and put on clean underwear this morning. What gives?

I do *not* hold out my hand. Second only to the fear of spiders, my ancestral phobia of spoiled mayonnaise overrides my obsession with politeness. The words *rancid* and *death* and *mayo* are common compatriots in my granny's lexicon. My stomach begins to quiver as the woman thrusts the sandwich closer to my cringing face.

"You can just throw it away," she says, still holding out the sandwich.

I shake my head and try to look like I'm not hungry. I give her the remainder of the bag of chips that I have been given, which also came from the garbage, twice removed.[39]

I also give her some money after she tells me: "This man said I could suck his cock for money, but I don't want to have to do that."

DC can deliver a caustic dose of reality, leaving your back bent and shoulders hunched after a day of absorbing the latest information on the human condition—it's one of the reasons I needed to get away from here, and I will be glad to be moving on again tomorrow.

But the city also has its beacons.

One such inspiration, we call the Compliment Man. I have not seen him during this short visit, but when I lived here I saw him several times a week without fail. Each time, the tall, lithe man with threadbare attire and milk-chocolate colored skin would say "I like your hair," or "You've got a great smile," or, if I was looking especially disheveled, "I like your shoes," or "I like your hat" (whether or not I was wearing one). As I walked away I would hear him showering the next passerby, regardless of gender, with his golden kindness.

Some days he could not think of anything that was physically praiseworthy about me, so he would become ambiguous, saying "I like your haerrrgh . . ." or "I like your sohesss . . ." with great enthusiasm during the "I like your" part, so that the rest seemed inconsequential. On rare occasion, he would ask if I had any spare change. On the days I saw him, no matter how long I'd cried that day, my eyes found the energy to smile at him.

Bill theorizes that the Compliment Man doesn't need the money he infrequently asks for, but rather, the man just wants to go out and compliment people,

---

[39]I would be very interested in the full history of that bag of chips, from the time it was born, to the time it came into my hands and everywhere it went afterward.

and he throws panhandling in as an acceptable motivation, so people don't think he's a weirdo.

Who knows? I know very little about the Compliment Man. But I know for the hours that he spends out on the streets, mining his vocabulary for kind words to bestow upon strangers, he is the summit of civilization. He becomes the Library of Congress, the National Art Gallery, and the Kennedy Center personified.

The Compliment Man and the woman who did not want to suck cock for money embody the essence of DC for me—heroics and heartbreak, life and death, sublimity and sorrow.

I realize on the walk back to Jeff's house that my task on this long journey is ultimately the reconciliation of these two unshakable extremes. Just how far I've progressed is impossible to tell at this point.

26

The Dramamine tablet I share with Maggie knocks me out from our morning departure in DC until, on the cusp of sunset, I wake on the entrance of a dream. As we drive into Jamestown, Virginia, the James River flows in metallic orange; the sun appears to be melting into the water and surrounding wetlands, burning upon the surface in a fiery orange-pink distillation of daylight.

We search for a place to shed the walls of the car and then slosh upon spongy ground to the very edge of the James. There the world burns before us in a shimmering molten flow, and upon a thin finger of land that stretches into the river stands the motionless silhouette of a great blue heron. The lissome bird's sharp, still form has the substantiality of a black cardboard cut-out against the fiery turmoil of the sun's hasty departure. We linger in the darkening dusk, equally as insubstantial as the heron, until the darkness erases us altogether.

Belittled by the night, we make our way back to the car and drive to Newport News Park, where we plan to camp. Smack dab in the middle of Newport News, Virginia, it is reportedly the largest municipal park east of the Mississippi River, with thirty miles of hiking and biking trails, nearly two hundred campsites, a lake, a golf course, etc. Yellowstone it ain't, but it sure beats sleeping in the front seats of the car in an interstate parking lot.

Upon waking we drive to Jamestown, the first permanent English settlement in this land, where John Smith met Pocahontas and the American Indians made the mistake of helping the people who would eventually steal their land and bludgeon their culture.

At Jamestown, I find myself fascinated with history, in contrast to fifteen years ago when I traveled here from Indiana with my mom and brother during spring break. I remember rolling my eyes and crossing my arms on my bony teenage chest when my mom suggested a visit to the historical park. I think I had wanted to go to an amusement park or a mall and I did my best to make my mom pay for subjecting me to history on my vacation. It seems that almost overnight history has earned my respect. Perhaps it has something to do with having a history of my own to grapple with, but suddenly stories of the dead and our collective past seem relevant.

From Jamestown we drive south out of Virginia and into North Carolina to the Outer Banks where we settle in at the Cape Hatteras National Seashore campground. In the morning we head west to Roanoke Island to visit Fort Raleigh National Historic Site, which commemorates one of the very first attempts by the English to colonize the Americas. In 1578, Sir Humphrey Gilbert gained a charter from Queen Elizabeth "to inhabit and possess . . . all remote and heathen lands not in actual possession of any Christian prince." The charter marked a turning point because up until this time, English interest in the New World had focused on looting Spanish ships and slave trading. But England had come to recognize the financial rewards of colonizing North America and decided to give it a whirl. The endeavor got off to a bumpy start—Humphrey failed miserably to establish a colony and died trying. But not long afterward his half-brother Sir Walter Raleigh decided to continue his half-sibling's work. The Roanoke tribe of American Indians helped Raleigh's band of colonists find a good piece of land on what we now call Roanoke Island, but as winter blew in the settlers' general ineptitude at farming left them in a precarious position. They began to steal food from the tribe, which led to a precipitous deterioration of relations.

The two groups' dissonance might have been mended but the English took a final decisive step. Pretending to be interested in a peaceful discussion, the colony's governor Ralph Lane arranged a parley with Chief Wingina. When the chief approached the appointed meeting place, the English open fired on him. And once he was dead, the English beheaded him.

The move didn't help the starving colonists and soon they were so desperate for provisions that they boarded the first available passage to England. The colony was thus deserted in 1586.

Raleigh, however, was a real trooper. He soon sent another group of settlers, this time including women and children. When they arrived in 1587, the new colonists were surprised to find the Indians on Roanoke still angry about the beheading of their chief and generally unwilling to help the colonists settle in and survive. Within a few months, the governor of the desperate colony, John White, returned to England for supplies. White's trip commenced a week after the birth of his daughter, Virginia Dare, the first English child born in North America. He would never set eyes on her again. When he returned, after a delay of several years, he found his wife and daughter vanished, along with the rest of the colony. The only remnant of their presence were the letters "CRO" carved into a tree and the word "Croatoan," the name of a nearby island, carved into a post. Though White and Raleigh searched Croatoan and the rest of the region, the colonists were never found and to this day their fate remains a mystery.

The grounds of the Fort Raleigh National Historic Site offer little suggestion of the people who once tried to make a home there. Trees and shadow cover most of the site. Still, the mystery of those lost lives lingers in the Southern summer air, which hangs in heavy humid clumps that sluggishly part as I press my way through. The Park Service brochures say that the most likely explanation for the disappearance of the colony is that most of the settlers were killed in battles with the Roanoke tribe; those that survived joined the tribe and were assimilated.

But that doesn't explain the carvings in the wood. Croatoan.

Coward Among Us

From Fort Raleigh we return to Cape Hatteras, lounge for a while on the beach, and then drive to our campground as sundown is approaching. Upon arriving at our site, as we are climbing out of the car to get food a-cookin' Bill and I simultaneously dive back into the car and slam the doors shut.

"Aaaaaeeeeeehhh!" Bill lets out a high-pitched squeal and starts flapping and flailing his arms at an angry Air Force of mosquitoes that has entered the car. Together we work to dispatch them while mosquito legions swarm outside the car, bouncing off the windows, trying to discover a way in. I know they can't possibly . . . get in . . . right? The windows are closed, but still . . . I feel a sharp terror rising.

Faced with a murderous bloodletting, we reconsider our plan.

We could leave, drive to the nearest town, try to find a hotel. But it's late and there are no towns nearby and we're both tired. And we still have to pack up our tent so we will have to come back tomorrow. That's a dumb idea.

Could we just stay in the car? We could skip dinner. Bill brings up the bathroom factor. I consider suggesting some sort of creative means of dealing with this bodily function but I'm guessing Bill would not likely entertain any option I put on the table.

In the end we agree, at least one of us has to get out of the car.[40] And given this fact, we might as well sleep in the tent. So we begin brainstorming a multi-faceted plan to get from the car to the tent, alive.

"Okay, what do we need?" Bill says, holding his hand up so we can keep track with his fingers.

"Water," I say, and grab the bottle.

"Books," Bill says, and grabs our books.

"Journal, cards, flashlight," I say.

"Check, check, check," replies Bill.

"Dog," I say, then notice that this item is staring at me with a purposeful solemnity.

Right, she has to eat yet.

"How am I going to get her food? It's under all that stuff in the way-back."

"You're just going to have to climb back there and excavate," Bill says.

I crawl over the front and back seats and onto the pile of our belongings that fills the way-back. I then rifle around for Maggie's belongings and procure for her a bowl of chow. When Maggie has finished her dinner, signaling with her customary belch, we prepare ourselves mentally for the mission. Bill's plan is to pause briefly to pee near the car. I plan to head straight for the tent, having maintained my default stance that urinary requirements are negotiable and at the current juncture they are secondary to circulatory functions. We have both decided dental requirements are not worth mentioning.

We pause for a moment of silence . . . then we both agree, we're as ready as we'll ever be. Finally, on the count of *one-two-three!* we throw open the doors and dash out of the car toward the tent. Bill stops briefly to pee then dives into the tent and zips it up. As for me, several steps into the fray—the drone of thirsty fiends invading my psyche—I feel I am going to piss my pants. So, I change plans midway, realizing I was foolish to dream I could make it through the night without going to the bathroom.

Cursing Bill's handy penis, I run to the bathroom, waving my arms about to create a current against the mosquitoes. Just then, a sea breeze stirs and throws

---

[40]Bill . . . bladder the size of a peanut.

the puny little blood-sucking bastards into a tizzy.[41] Within this reprieve, I slow to marvel at the sky, open to me from all directions, the stars not yet dimmed by the rise of a near full moon, which is beginning to glow on the eastern horizon. I can hear the ocean pulsing beyond the dunes. The air swims about me in a swirl of gentle warmth, the perfect temperature, which makes me feel like I am floating in the ether, naked and fluid with the sky . . .

"Aaaiihhhh!" I hear the regrouped blood zombies swarming and I feel them jamming their evil snouts into my skin, vacuuming out every last ounce of blood, leaving nothing but filth behind to make my skin itch and swell. I pee fast, cursing my dimwitted brain for lolly-gagging in the . . . lalala . . . beauty . . . moment when I could have been back in the tent by now. Naked in the ether . . . please, dipshit! I run back to the tent and plunge in, closing the door with clumsy madness. The dozens of mosquitoes attached to my flesh enter along with me. I start smashing indiscriminately at myself, in the air, and against the flimsy walls of the tent, bellowing when the soft tent fabric foils my splat and a would-be-dead mosquito emerges alive from my splayed hand.

"Aahhhh!"

I continue my swatting frenzy until I become aware that I am the only one thrashing around the tent. For a moment I consider the possibility that Bill has grabbed the dog, darted to the car, and abandoned our plan and me. He is such a mosquito drama queen, melodramatic as a silent screen starlet, makes me look like Rock Hudson, but he wouldn't dare . . .

"What the . . . ?!!"

I notice a large lump of sleeping bag piled beside me, trembling oh-so-slightly.

Bill has long ago thrown himself inside his bag and mine and tucked the edges underneath his body. He's left me out here to die alone.

"Get out of there, you coward, and fight!" I demand.

He silently signals his refusal by tucking a loose edge tighter beneath his body, so that neither the mosquitoes nor I can reach him.

At this point I consider unzipping the tent and grabbing Maggie (who in this incident is uncharacteristically innocent of wrongdoing, and who Bill did not bother to include in his mosquito-bomb shelter), running to the car, and leaving the tent door open. The coward would have to come out eventually; it's

---

[41]Haha. Bested by the wind. Dummies.

too hot to stay under that bag all night. I dismiss the evil notion and continue my attack on the tent walls and ceiling. Bill pokes his head out when the greatest danger has subsided and begins to help me dispatch the remaining mosquitoes.

We fight them for about half an hour before they are all dead, bloodstains gruesomely polka-dotting the tent walls. Then we fight hallucinations and mosquitoes that are perched on the outside of the tent (but appear to be on the inside) for another hour.

In the morning, the mosquitoes have vanished, gone to rest in their tiny little coffins until night returns. Bill and I begin packing up the tent and notice that in addition to the char marks inflicted by its stint atop a New York campfire, our blue home now also sports blood smears by the dozens. At least we stole some of our blood back from the usurpers. We will leave the polka-dot crimson mosquito-carcass memorial as badge of honor[42] and a warning to future mosquitoes to approach at their own peril.

Rock, Paper, Scissors

Exhausted and anemic, we hightail it out of the barrier islands and drive west through North Carolina into the mountains. We arrive at a campground in North Carolina's Pisgah National Forest as a chilly darkness is approaching. After we have worked together to set up the tent we separate to get our nightly chores done quickly. Bill goes to fill our water bottles while I get a fire going and food prepared. When the food is about half-cooked, and Bill and I are huddled around the fire poised to eat a nice hot pan of rice-n-sauce, the WhisperLite stove blinks out.

"Goddamnit!" I say.

"Whisper-lite piece of shit!" Bill says

A continuous barrage of curses ensues, followed by a moment of tense silence. I look at Bill. He looks at me. Our steely eyes express the same indisputable fact: The other guy is going to have make the noble gesture and volunteer to leave the fire and walk forty feet to the car to retrieve the backup stove. Maggie, who has already had her dinner and is lounging comfortably by the fire with her head on her two front paws, is cloaking her anticipation over the opening

[42]Mostly mine.

hostilities in this latest battle. She shifts her eyes back and forth between me and Bill, like a spectator in a coliseum.

As our stomachs growl and the fire blazes, Bill and I begrudgingly jettison the expectation of an altruistic gesture from our travel mate and agree upon a legal route to settlement of the stalemate. As usual we look to blind justice, i.e., rock-paper-scissors, to determine who will have to fetch the stove.

Bill is starting to resemble a mouth-watering veggie hotdog as I prepare my strategy for the contest.

The first shake, we both go bold and strike with *rock*, leaving us in a tie.

The second time Bill *again* throws rock but I wrap it up with *paper*. I think he assumed that the event of a double *rock* usually leads a person to want to go with *scissors* in the second shake, with the expectation that the enemy will go with *paper*. I however, had sensed his treachery and decided to skip right to paper. I was right. I won.

"That's not paper!" Bill protests.

"Yes it is," I counter, calm and confident.

"*This* is paper, with your palm down!" Bill demonstrates the proper form for *paper,* using the jerky motions of a madman.

"If it's not paper, then what is it?" I ask with sharpening edge in my tone.

"It's not paper."

"Yeah, you just said that."

"It's not paper."

We stare at each other as our half-cooked dinner cools and the fire dims. I begin to mentally dress Bill with ketchup, mustard, and mouth . . . watering . . . relish . . .

"Best two out of three!" Bill dictates, and puts his hand up to ready himself, as if this is an indubitable answer to our dilemma.

I remain dubitable.

It's a universal fact, only the person who knows he lost says, "Best two out of three."

"No way! I won! Get your ass up and get the stove."

Inconceivably, Bill does not get his ass up.

"You didn't have the proper form! You easily could have switched to scissors at the last minute."

So! He's calling me a cheater!

"So! You're calling me a cheater!"

"I didn't say cheater. I just said . . ."

"Do you even remember the last time this 'form' question came up and Mike[43] was there and sided with me?"

"Mike always sides with you!" Bill howls as he turns from the fireside and storms to the car to get the stove.

I too leave the fire, but head for the tent, into my sleeping bag, into sleep and brooding dreams.

In the morning, after waking early to the sound of my aggravated stomach, I fetch granola from the car and sit down at the picnic table to calm my belly. Bill follows close behind and pours himself a bowl. We eat our granola in silence with down-turned eyes, but occasionally lift our heads to smile sheepishly at each other. For neither of us is it an admission of guilt or an apology,[44] but it is an unspoken acknowledgement of our mutual culpability in what will come to be called "Battle of Pisgah" or, in later days, "The War of the Rock, the Paper, and the Scissors."

[43]A friend of ours who always sides with me.

[44]When hell freezes over.

27

As unbelievable as it may seem, given the caliber of the competition, the dog is occasionally the most difficult person in the car.

In Asheville, North Carolina, we stop to resupply at a natural foods market. Maggie remains in the car while we shop, which is not usually a problem for short periods. However, on this day Maggie had company—odiferous, delicious company. Stashed in a paper bag in the back seat lay a small hunk of Amish Swiss I had purchased a few days prior. It was not exactly a small hunk but rather a glorified morsel, due to budget constraints. I had seen the treat in a small-town store. It had called to me from behind a glass door and I had heeded its call despite several insinuating eyeball rolls from parsimonious Peter. The cheese cost twelve dollars a pound, a whole day's budget, but I found an eighth of a pound cut. It was as if the universe had intended it for me. I was saving the treat until I could relax with it and really enjoy it. One cannot enjoy cheese properly in a moving vehicle, or in a vehicle at all for that matter. Or can they . . . ?

It did not occur to me that my methodology for consuming this precious cheese might clash with Maggie's general philosophy on cheese.[45]

Failing to account for this contrasting philosophy, I am actually surprised when I come out of the store to find Maggie in the front seat hovering over a single remaining tidbit of the cheese in dog-slobbery Saran wrap. I wonder if, when she first pulled it out of the paper bag, she thought, "Just one bite, they'll never notice." But she kept on saying, "Just one bite, just one bite, just one bite" until there was only one bite left and she thought, "They are bound to notice this," so she just sat in the front seat with the mess she had made waiting for her

---

[45]Maggie's Cheese Philosophy in three simple axioms: 1. Eat it! Fast! Before they catch me or change their minds. 2. Savor it later, after they can no longer take it away from me. 3. A cheese in the gullet is worth two in the general vicinity.

punishment, perhaps thinking to herself, "Those cheap-assed sons-of-bitches. Who buys an eighth of a pound of cheese!?"

Her punishment from me is a brief explosive "Maggie! Goddamnit. Maggie!" and a long dose of the silent treatment. She acts as though she feels guilty, but I'm pretty sure she considers the cheese, regardless of the paltry portions, to be well worth the punishment. It was, after all, twelve dollars a pound.

On down the road, Bill goes hiking in Great Smoky Mountain National Park, while I sit on a log with Maggie at my feet, enjoying some time alone. Maggie lays down with her two front paws clutching a stick that she methodically, and artfully, chews into little slobbery bits. Momentarily, this jars the still-raw memory of my defiled cheese and my eyes begin to narrow. I wonder if she is trying to recreate the scene for me, saying in effect, "Remember this? Huh? This log is pretty good, but that Amish Swiss was sooooo much better."

Then I think, even if she is playing evil psychological tricks on me, they are cancelled out by her ubercuteness. I can't stay mad at her.

Luminous Beings

Pine tree carcasses lay strewn about the forests of Big South Fork National Recreation Area in Tennessee, felled by a creature no bigger than a pinhead. There are few survivors. Alongside the healthy oak, sycamore, and maple, those pines that remain upright appear sick, naked, plagued by a beetle that bores into their flesh leaving pin-sized holes that perforate the dying and dead. The voracious little eater has brought the forest to its knees.

Spread of the beetle was hastened by hapless forestry practices that followed the commercial razing of these forests a century ago. We knew enough to dismantle the ecosystem but not enough to know how to put it back together again. Bill and I were warned when we got our backcountry permit, and by numerous signs since, to be wary, for the dead are falling all around. You can hear the creaking and groaning of those that will soon falter. The reality is disquieting. In addition to not wanting to be squashed by being in the wrong place at the wrong time, the forest feels somber. It's like watching a slow train wreck, knowing that many will die but having no power to prevent it. I have grown sensitive to this type of helplessness and it troubles me to walk within this ailing forest. The park service has no answers for the pine and the trees will probably continue to fall until there are none.

Still, it's good to be backpacking again. When you are living in the land of private property it is hard to feel comfortable unless you have some of that private property. Out here in the public forest I can wander and still feel at home, not worrying whether someone will question my motives for being here, or charge me some ridiculous price for a ratty-assed place to sleep.[46] My greatest concern stems from the ranger's warning not to leave valuables in our car, due to a recent string of burglaries in the park. Of course we have no choice but to leave our valuables in the car because we have no other place to put them. The only choice is to forego backpacking or take our chances. So, I stashed my computer in the way-back with the cameras, underneath a bunch of smelly and worthless stuff. Perhaps if the car is broken into, the thieves will not be inclined to dig through layers of dirty underwear and socks and a year's supply of rice-n-sauce packets and stale crackers, in order to find more profitable booty.

Out on the trail, I find it hard to conceive that anyone else, thieves or otherwise, even exists. Though the weather has been autumn perfect, sunny but not hot, there are very few people around. In fact, since yesterday we have seen no one. The fall colors here are not as striking as the older, moister Smoky Mountains, but the solitude is exquisite.

This landscape bears the textured mark of ages of wind and water falling, with numerous rock arches reaching improbably across great spans of terrain. The trails are permeated by the contemplative mood that envelops some special places in the South.

These forests are not old growth; few places anywhere on this continent now harbor the ancient forests that existed before European peoples washed across the landscape. American axes and eventually machines made the dispatching of a thousand-acre biological community simple, easy, routine.

But they are forests, thousands of acres, uncut by roads, far from the noise of human industry. To be sure, they are deeply wounded, but walking in these woods reminds me of a passage in the *Ecology of a Cracker Childhood*, where author Janisse Ray describes the feeling of standing in an old growth Southern pine forest. She says: "Here mortality's roving hands grapple with air. I can see my place as a human in a natural order more grand, whole and functional than I've ever witnessed and I am humbled, not frightened, by it."

---

[46]. . . in Burlington, while tossing her pantyhose over a clothesline.

Walking in the land of trees is a lesson in both humility and connection. For those who believe in an ultimate omnipotent creator it is a rare chance to experience the genius of the earth and every creature that came into being within it. For atheists and scientists, it is a chance to observe the perfect order of a system where nothing is wasted and everything, no matter how simple or complicated, has a niche. For me, it is an explanation, one I have needed all my life, but especially now. The forest is where I fit. It's a place of reconciliation—a reckoning for the prodigal daughter dislodged from paradise and plunged into the disconnected terror of a creature without a niche, without a home. I am Eve, only I didn't leave the Garden of Eden on a command from God after eating some fruit. I lost paradise when I stood by watching while Adam hewed it down, reducing perfection to board-feet, boxes, and toilet paper.

So much of the world humans have developed has reduced the earth, and us, to crude, disjointed matter—from curves, color, crisp clean air, and infinite texture, to strait lines, indistinguishable hard geometrics, monoculture, smoke and mirrors. We come to acquiesce in the idea that we are a part of this fabricated system, this meager creation of limited minds made of asphalt and oil, roads, buildings, utility poles, and plastic. But as Yoda said to Luke,[47] "Luminous beings are we, not this crude matter." We belong to the system of Earth, which came into being over billions of years from what was literally an explosion of light and energy. We are particles of Bang! So incomprehensibly wondrous was the making of the universe, our Earth, the massive biodiversity of the planet and finally human beings, that after ten thousand years of observation and study, we still don't come close to understanding the system or our place in it. The most cogent description I've heard came from Carl Sagan. He called us, like everything on this planet, "starstuff."

No amount of study will tell us how exactly the earth came about or in fact why, if that is even an appropriate question. But every breath and quirk of adaptation and color and habit of every species and bend of the land and act of water is a love song from our unknown origins. Unknown, but knowable, in the sense that the bond between a parent and child is indefinable and immeasurable and yet tangible.

---

[47]Nerd red alert!

Grand Teton National Park, Wyoming

Cape Canaveral National Seashore, Florida

Fort Stevens State Park, Oregon

Oregon coast

Devil's Tower National Monument, Wyoming

Point Reyes National Seashore, California

Yellowstone National Park, Wyoming

Yellowstone National Park, Wyoming

And no matter how far away Daniel seems to be now, we remain connected through this impossibly complex and beautiful system in nature that is both eternally inscrutable and immediately accessible. It is always waiting, deep in the forest and in the glittering spark of sunlight that bounces off the eye of a thrush before it flutters away and out of sight.

Crude Matter

While hiking out of the Twin Arches trailhead from our backpacking trip, Bill and I begin debating whether we took the easiest direction on the loop trail. Bill adamantly claims we took the best route for the hike because if we had gone the opposite direction we would have had to climb up the steep ladder that we instead descended to get to the trail.

"I think going down the ladder was harder than going up would have been," I say.

"You're just saying that to say the opposite of what I say," Bill replies.

"No, I just happen to think going down the ladder was harder."

"You would have said *up* was harder if I had said down."

"No, I would not have. Going down you have to go backwards with a backpack, which is obviously harder than going up. Plus we had to figure out how to get Maggie down, and getting her up would have been easier . . ."

Bill starts to run away from me. For a moment I just shake my head and watch him run, his backpack flopping up and down in a ridiculous manner. Then, compelled to assert my rightness on this point, I run after him and grab onto a strap on his backpack.

"You can't just run away," I declare. "I was saying . . ."

Bill jerks his body and yanks the strap from my hands, then runs ahead fast so I can't catch him.

Maggie follows Bill, who she believes to be the victor by virtue of him having outrun me.

But what she doesn't know is that what I lack in speed, I make up for in cunning. I know Bill is psychologically incapable of resisting a challenge,[48] so I yell after him: "I am not talking to you for the rest of the day!"

Bill skids to a screeching halt and rounds back toward me.

As he approaches he says, "Hey, do you know what time it is?"

Subtle. He knows I never wear a watch. I ignore him.

"How much further do we have to go?" he tries again.

Ignore. Fail.

After a few more unsuccessful attempts, he tries making me flinch by launching his head toward me until it is just inches from my face.

Inwardly I judge him a weak opponent, but I give no outward response.

Finally he grabs hold of my backpack straps and starts yanking me back and forth, nearly knocking me over. Maggie starts nipping at his heels. I refuse to talk or even look at him. I am the queen of silence, a fact he will soon learn.

I'm all set to keep my day-long silence when we approach the car and I see the back curtain is not pulled over our belongings in the way-back. (I know I pulled it closed when we left.) Furthermore, every last one of the belongings I pulled the curtain over are gone. The back is empty. I glance at the front of the car and notice the passenger-side front window looks strange, like it has something draped over it.

While I have been surmising the troubling situation, Bill has been thinking up cut-downs he believes will elicit a verbal response.

"Your mama is sooooo dumb . . ." Bill continues his quest as he opens the back hatch and starts putting in his backpack.

"Don't you notice anything strange?!" I ask him, almost as alarmed by his lack of perception as I am by the empty car.

"Ahhhh! You talked to me!" he exclaims triumphantly and pokes his finger victoriously in my face.

I swat it away, gesture wildly at the car and exclaim, "There's nothing there!"

---

[48]When Bill's older sisters wanted to get him to do something as a kid, rather than asking him outright, they'd bet him that he couldn't run to the fridge, grab a Coke, and bring it back to them in less than a minute. Or that he couldn't move the laundry from the washer to the dryer in less than two minutes. "Run! I'll time you," they'd say. Poor little rube.

Bill takes another look in the car, his eyes widen, and his mouth plummets open.

We stare at the car in silence for a few moments until I notice a ranger across the parking lot walking toward us. I approach him and start to tell him our stuff is gone but he stops me short.

"You've had a break-in," he says to our stupefied faces. "The thieves were interrupted and didn't get everything."

What did they not get? I scream silently in my head.

As if he had heard me, "I think the back was untouched. The ranger who took the call stored everything he found so it would be safe until your return. I'll let him know you're back."

When the other ranger comes a few minutes later I am relieved to find everything that had been in the back returned.

"A car drove into the parking lot just as the thieves threw a rock through your window," the ranger says. "The man in the car started honking his horn and the thieves, some local teenagers, grabbed a few things and ran."

The ranger then begins writing up a report for us, so we have to puzzle over what is missing.

"My mouth guard is gone," Bill says dejectedly.

Sure enough they pilfered Bill's mouth guard, a malodorous piece of plastic that protects his teeth from the loud and determined grinding he subjects them to while sleeping. He had to pay a dentist three hundred dollars to make the guard for him. The thieves were either smart-assed hooligans and took something they obviously could not use or sell just to spite us or they were incredibly stupid teeth grinders who didn't know people's teeth are as unique as their fingerprints and believed the device might save them some expensive dental work when they were older.

"They also got my sunglasses," Bill adds.

"And the checkbook," I say.

And then I notice the CD case is gone, including all of Daniel's special music—Johnny Cash, John Denver, Indigo Girls, Moxy Früvous . . . The first day we met, our mutual and decidedly uncool affection for John Denver was fleshed out into the open, like an unmentionable disease. Not really. We talked of perfect childhood moments dancing around the house to Denver's "Grandma's Feather Bed."

Bill notices my eyes welling up; he puts a hand on my shoulder.

"At least you still have the cases at home, and you can replace the discs," he offers.

"It's not the same," I say.

They were Daniel's.

The moment throws me into a somber mood, but I try to focus on how incredibly lucky we were that some kind soul drove into the isolated parking lot at exactly the right time and that we didn't lose everything—my computer and months' worth of journaling, all our cameras and film, rice-n-sauce . . .

We decide to head to Nashville to get the passenger side window replaced and clean up the glass, which is in shards and splinters all over the front and back seats.

I lay a towel down in the back so Maggie doesn't end up with glass in her pads and we head out of Big South Fork as rain begins to fall. I am still not talking, but Bill no longer feels a challenge to make me.

We arrive at a Nashville Saturn dealership just as they are about to close for the day. Lucky for us, the Saturn people can see what a rough time we've had and elect to stay late and help us. The man in charge of us becomes quickly enamored with Maggie, who sits grumpily in the car. He reaches his arm in to pet her and . . . wait for it . . . "*Rahrahrahrahrahrah!*"

She nearly bites his hand off, scaring the piss out of me, and him.

I scold her and apologize to him.

But he cuts me off saying, "Oh no! She's just protecting the vehicle. She's had a hard day. Maybe she even feels responsible for not guarding the place properly."

I smile gratefully at him, and then by way of an explanation he takes me to his office and shows me a wall of photos above his desk—hundreds of photos, all of his dogs.

Our Saturn angel then places an emergency order on our replacement window, which he says will arrive the following morning.

Fortunately for us, Bill has a good friend who lives in Nashville. After we leave the Saturn service center, Bill calls Hugh, who welcomes us to stay with him.

Hugh went to college with Bill and since then often happens to wind up living in the general vicinity of Bill regardless of where he goes. They both went to school at Notre Dame. When Bill moved to Tucson for graduate school, Hugh was living in Phoenix. And when Bill moved to Washington, DC, Hugh happened to live a block from where Bill found an apartment. Now, when Bill's car is broken into in rural Tennessee, it turns out Hugh is living a couple of hours away in Nashville.

Despite the fact that I have also ended up living near Bill for most of the past decade, I don't know Hugh well and have had few solo conversations with him. I base my perception of him on his connection to Bill and on one particular conversation we had the last time I saw him, in DC the previous November. Hugh, an attorney, had found some books to help me with the foundation Daniel's family and friends were setting up in his name. The day he brought the books to me we talked of tax law and bylaws and bureaucracy. We had not spoken of Daniel, or of his death, or of all that came before and after, though it was the first time I had seen Hugh since Daniel had died the previous March. I didn't really expect us to; we were not close.

But, then, just as he was leaving, Hugh turned back to me and said, "I'm sorry, for what you're facing."

People often say they are sorry, and certainly they are, but you can rarely see just how sorry they feel. They mourn for you, but not right at that moment, not visibly. I remember last November, I could see in Hugh's face and hear in his voice just how deeply sorry he was.

So, despite the frustration of the broken window, and the loss of Daniel's music, I am comforted by the respite at Hugh's house. He and Bill spend the evening catching up, we get a good night's sleep, and in the morning we return to Saturn and wait while they fix the window and clean the seats of splintered glass. We also become happily acquainted with a Saturn hospitality tradition of providing free donuts and coffee to folks waiting for their vehicles. Saturn may start to rethink this policy after they realize two vagabonds and a dog are showing up at their dealerships every day for the next year. That's their concern. We stock up on donuts, and hit the road again.

28

On a long southeasterly drive toward the Okefenokee Swamp, I observe the changing scenery and daydream while Bill drives and Maggie stands on the seat between us. Suddenly, I feel something fluttering on my head and begin thrashing my arms and yelping.

"*Aaaaahhh!*" I yell as I slap my shoulders and twist in my seat to look behind me.

What I see is Maggie's tail wagging against the back of my neck.

Bill howls with laughter.

"I think a spider stowed on board Mag's tail," I tell him. Then I look at Maggie, who is scared by all the yelling.

"You scared me, buddy," I say, petting her to calm us both down.

"Yeah, that spider I wag by my ass is terrifying," says Maggie, through Bill.

When the moment passes, Bill yawns and I am compelled to do the same.

"I wonder if that works on dogs," I say.

Bill and I start pretending to yawn to see if Maggie will follow. She doesn't. I read somewhere that means she is a sociopath.

We drive by a farmhouse with a cardboard sign out front that advertises in large block letters, "DOG BOXES."

"Need a box?" I ask Maggie. She gives no verbal reply, but her eyes say, "No, thanks, I'm good."

I take over as driver halfway to Okefenokee and Bill starts reading his book. As I drive, I comment on the sights and Bill makes no reply, just completely ignores me. So I start singing to myself that famous song by Stephen Foster about the Suwannee River.

I don't know all the words so I have to improvise. I sing progressively louder and louder, "Way down upon the Suwannee River, far, far away, I took a trip with just my liver and I fell in love one day." After that I lose the tune and go with an alternate tune for the lyrics, "I saw him standing there upon the bank so muddy and so bare, his scales so rough his teeth so sharp, his beady eyes went through my heart . . . Ohhhh . . . way down upon the Suwannee River, far, far away. I fell in love with an alligator, once on a summer's day."

Over and over I sing. Louder and louder.

Bill never even looks at me.

Later, after I have given up getting Bill's attention, I turn on the radio to listen to National Public Radio. For better or worse, we have given up our *no news* pledge. A story comes on about a company selling anthrax detectors like smoke detectors and Bill starts listening. Then he launches into a detailed commentary about the story on the radio.

"That's capitalism for you . . ."

That, of course, makes it hard for me to hear the reporter so I turn the radio way up.

He turns his head to glare at me but I refuse to look back. So he bends over to Maggie's ear and says, "I don't like her."

Maggie, who eschews involvement in all human conflict and has seen this wedge tactic of Bill's before, hops into the back seat and sticks her face out the window. The gale peels her eyelids back in a way that appears unpleasant to me but she has a huge grin on her face, so I refrain from micromanaging her wind-in-the-face moment.

When we pass a boiled peanut stand on the side of the road, I comment that we should stop and get some.

"I don't like boiled peanuts," Bill replies.

"You just said two days ago that you've never tried them."

"No, I said I hadn't tried *Cajun* peanuts."

"You did not."

"Did too."

"You're saying we came across a Cajun peanut stand in North Carolina?"

"So?"

"You are so full of . . . flexible reality," I say.

"*You* are so full of mis-listening," he retorts and sticks his head back in the book that has been sitting on his lap.

I really don't know what to say to that, so I go back to my singing for the remainder of the drive.

Dey Ate Us

Spanish moss drapes the Okefenokee Swamp in a dreamy shade of gauzy green. Spiders of every horrifying size and in shades of brilliant yellow, red, and green—like giant Skittles with legs—cling to webs that gleam in the dense swamp air. They are candy-coated taffy evolved into man-eating monster, an interesting biological niche, and if they weren't so nauseatingly terrifying, I could call them what they are—exquisite.

Alligators glide silently through the dark still waters that lounge upon the land. This nearly 500,000-acre peat-filled wetland is the largest inland swamp in the world and for nearly 7,000 years, wetland plants have lived and died here, leaving behind a spongy mat of decaying peat that forms the basin of the Okefenokee. In some places the accumulated plant matter reaches depths of fifteen feet.

The Suwannee River originates here and drains 90 percent of the swamp's watershed southwest to the Gulf of Mexico. What remains feeds the swamp ecosystem and provides habitat for gators, hundreds of bird species, and the Florida black bear—a bear subspecies threatened by habitat loss. This landscape itself has been threatened several times in the past when corporations have attempted to mine or drain the swamp for agriculture. Somehow, the Okefenokee has persevered and today most of it is protected as a national wildlife refuge.

As darkness falls, we head to the refuge visitor center to ask about nearby accommodations. When we arrive, we wait, and wait and wait while some people talk to the ranger for a long time, looooong time. As I judge their accents, they are from Germany or Austria maybe. Bill and I loiter around the visitor center and gift shop, memorizing exhibit information, picking up paraphernalia, looking at it, putting it down, waiting and waiting some more.

Just as the group is wrapping up their investigation of Okefenokee, as they are walking out the door, one of the men, sporting a waterfall of Crystal Gayle-long hair, turns back to the ranger.

"Ah der very meny mahsquitoes in da paak?" he asks.

The ranger begins, "No, not this time of year . . . but—" when the man cuts her off and says indignantly:

"No! No! Dey ate us already!"

Well, that ends the conversation with some finality. How can you trust a ranger who tells you there are "not many mosquitoes" when you, and your group, have already been ingested by them?

Nevertheless, when we finally manage to talk to the ranger, we put our trust in her because she is very helpful, even though she is trying to close and go home for the day.

"Do you have any ideas on where to stay around here?" Bill asks her.

"Well, there are a couple of campgrounds. There's one by the river, but, well, the locals come by the river near there . . . You know, it's fine, they're not really dangerous, and they usually stay away from the campground itself."

"Hmmm," I say, unsure how to interpret this statement and recalling how she downplayed the mosquito threat to the Germans. What does "not really dangerous" mean? There have only been a few *attempted* murders there this year? Or maybe loss of limb but not life?

"How about motels . . . are there any inexpensive ones?"

"There are a few moderately priced motels. You should be able to find one," she says. Then adds, "Stay clear of the Days Inn, though."

"Mmmm . . . okay. Thanks," we say, and head out so she can close up.

On the walk back to the car we puzzle over her last warning. Perhaps the locals at the Days Inn *are* dangerous and *don't* usually stay away from the motel itself.

What to do?

Bill and I consider our budget and subsequently choose to go to the one campground for which the ranger had no cryptic comments. But . . . it's closed. So we go to the campground by the river where the locals aren't really dangerous. When we arrive, the office is locked and dark but a scraggily teenager with a shaved head is loitering by the entrance.

Bill steps out of the car.

"Is the office closed for the night?" he asks the young man.

A response is slow in coming. The youth sucks his teeth a few times, looks Bill over and says, "The caretaker ain't 'round now."[49]

Why did he have to use the world "caretaker"? That's what people say in movies where camp counselors get cooked up in a stew. Doesn't he know that?

---

[49]I'm not making this up.

Bill is clearly unsure what to say next so he just waits.

From the car, Maggie and I watch them standing there silently.

Sigh.

Humidity.

Sleepy.

"You kin jest take a site n pay in the mornin'," the guy eventually says.

We meander the dark, unorganized campground, looking for a spot to pitch the tent. There are no sites marked, so we pull in on a patch of grass that appears vacant. Unreasonably but sufficiently spooked by the ranger's description of the campground, I sense a baleful, unwelcome heaviness in the air. We sit considering our options. In a few moments, our gangly young host walks by and Bill asks him if we should put the tent in a specific spot.

"HehHehHeh," the young'un chuckles to himself.[50] "It's no big deal, ya jest go where ya want," he says, then walks to a nearby camp where he picks up an axe and starts chopping wood and building a fire. It has to be 80 degrees and 98 percent humidity—what's up with the fire? I consider the possibility that the youth turned friendly in order to size us up, to determine if he was going to need more firewood, a bigger pot. The ranger had said the locals weren't really dangerous, but maybe this guy *wasn't* a local.

We pull out of the campground, speed past the Days Inn, and head for a rest stop.

---

[50]Subtext: Yankees! Wouldn't be worth a tinker's dam if they weren't so tasty.

29

There are few places in the country or the world more contrary to the spirit of this journey than southeast Florida. Not only is it a festering concrete blemish on the land, but its very existence has drained the Everglades and all of its wild inhabitants of their life force. We are here for one reason—Bill's aunt has a place for us to stay while we explore what's left of the Everglades. I've never been to the Glades and I don't want to miss it entirely.

We spend most of the day snared in a long series of traffic jams on a sea of pavement and are ready to gnaw off our own legs when the situation takes a tailspin.

Bill has a policy of waiting to get gas until he finds a price he deems reasonable. His justification, aside from being frugal, is that it is better for the environment if you only get gas when the tank is empty, thereby exposing toxic fumes to the air less often. Well, the gas light went on, he passed by several stations and then got on the highway—where we promptly ran out of gas.

With admirable acceptance of his culpability, Bill now climbs over the guardrail and scrambles down the steep freeway retaining wall in search of a gas station or phone. I stay in the muggy car, sucking in exhaust from the traffic, rain plopping in the window, semi trucks vibrating the entire car with the thundering vortex of wind that rages as they pass.

In no more than five minutes, a truck stops right in front of me on the freeway shoulder. The back of the truck reads "Broward County Road Ranger."

A woman steps out of the truck, approaches the car, and leans her head through the window on the passenger side.

"*RA!RA!RA!RA!*" Maggie tells the ranger to get her head the hell out of Maggie's home.

"Maggie!" I tell the twenty-pound dog with bared teeth and bad breath to get her ass in the back seat where it belongs. I feel bad yelling at her. She is just trying to do her job, but really. She scares the piss out of people.

"I'm really sorry," I tell the ranger, who has leapt back, well away from the window. I smile at her. She glowers back.

Once she regains her composure, she says, "What seems to be the problem?"

"Ran out of gas," I say sheepishly. Very convenient that Bill is not around to take the credit for this bit of foolishness. So I look like the ditzy broad with the psycho dog who forgot to fill her tank.[51]

"Could you try to start the engine so we can make sure it's an empty tank?" she asks me.

I try to start the car. Nothing.

"Okay, I can give you a few gallons. That will get you to a gas station."

"Thanks, can I give you some money for the gas?"

"No, it's a service of the county," she says, with the implied subtext: to keep the cars of dumbass drivers off the shoulders of the highway.

After my hero has put a few gallons of gas in the tank I look back to see Bill walking in the distance searching for a pay phone to call AAA. I start to get out of the car to run after him, but the road ranger commands me to go get gas first (subtext: and get my dumbass self and my car off the shoulder of the highway). I can hardly refuse her. I don't know if road rangers are issued guns, but she looks unbending on the matter. So I drive to get gas then double back to find Bill on 595 West. I try to drive slowly so I can spot him, but on the Miami freeway speed is compulsory. Fortunately, across eight lanes of traffic, I see a blur that resembles Bill walking on 595 East. I honk to him. Then I proceed to 95 North, then 95 South, and finally 595 East where I find him looking small and vulnerable as a mailbox in a tornado.

As I drive up I expect him to be happy to see me but when he opens the door he yells, "Where were you?!"

I start to explain but he interrupts, "I came back and you were gone, the car with no gas was gone, the dog was gone. I had concocted all sorts of *X-Files* and kidnapping scenarios in my mind."

After he calms down, Bill is able to listen to my explanation and finds it more than satisfactory. When I finish, he looks at me and says, "See what great stories we have when I run out of gas?"

---

[51]This has actually been the case on numerous occasions, so I look the part.

"Yeah, you should run out of gas more often. Three times a year is not enough. Hey! I've got an idea. Let's skip the Everglades and just drive around on this freeway and see how many times we can run out of gas in two weeks."

"I don't think the sarcasm is necessary. I'm just saying, look on the bright side."

He then looks out onto the sea of cars coming at us from all endlessly concrete directions. "We've gotta get to the West."

"How 'bout Key West?" I suggest.

"That'll do for now."

HoJos

Camping is not really an option in the Florida Keys, so upon our arrival in Key Largo, Bill must acquiesce to finding a budget hotel. We spend an age looking for a place to stay that will take pets, is not too far from a snorkeling outfitter, and that has rooms available for two nights. Finally, we settle upon Howard Johnsons.

When we get to our room we decide to order Chinese food but find that while there is in fact a phone in the room, said phone has no cord; it is just an old rotary dial sitting on a desk with no connection to the outside world. Lame. They could have at least put in one of those Mickey Mouse phones so we could ring Donald to bring us some chow.

After we have assessed the communications situation, Bill and I both refuse to go to the front desk to get a replacement phone cord.

Unflinchingly resolute in our determination not to leave the room and still gun-shy of the formerly infallible rock-paper-scissors solution, Bill ends up eating dehydrated mashed potatoes—made into a cold slop with tap water—and I go dinnerless.

I throw a dirty sock at him.

He throws the sock in Maggie's startled face.

I get mad at him for picking on her.

He gets mad at me for getting mad at him.

I ignore him.

We watch *Hello Dolly* on TV.

I had forgotten what *Hello Dolly* was about prior to seeing it again—it tells the tale of a woman getting over the death of her much-loved husband and entering the world again. The storyline makes me realize, I have been struggling more than usual the past few days. We have no greater stresses, really; aside from Miami's traffic and the omnipresent cloud cover. The real cause of my anxiety likely lies with my anticipation of Daniel's upcoming birthday and our anniversary.

In the Deep

If the word *eternal* can be applied anywhere, surely it is here, under the surface of the ocean where all earthly life began; where single-celled organisms flourished, died, decayed, and eventually transformed into more complex life forms. Thousands of millions of years ago, cyanobacteria began making food from water, carbon dioxide, and sunlight—with oxygen as a byproduct. These microscopic MacGyvers have been around in some form for 2.5 *billion* years. And for many hundreds of millions of years they quietly made their meals and discarded their oxygen—laying the atmospheric foundation for the explosion of biodiversity that followed. They helped make the air of this planet breathable for creatures like myself, the byproducts of their byproduct, who were then but a distant vision of a far, far-off future.

Life's beginning place exists on Earth, this is our Eden. And how enticing are the dark enigmatic leagues from which we all originated, where vision is surreal and memory, painless.

As I snorkel, Grecian Reef corals sway in brilliance beneath the gently rolling waves off the coast of Key Largo. I curse my needy lungs every time they force me to the surface and away from the world of parrotfish, filefish, shark, and coral. These natives seem mostly undisturbed by my presence, so I shadow them around and lose all track of time in the forests of feathery fans of lavender and mottled brain coral.

When the boat signals it is time to head back to land, I am far from ready but I acquiesce to my fate as we begin the boat ride back to Key Largo. I look around at the boatful of snorkelers that has accompanied Bill and me on this half-day tour, considering how this experience has affected them. The faces are content, some excited, all changed in some way from the ride out. But one man in particular captures my attention. He is in his fifties, very out of shape, belly distended, and as we motor from the reef, he turns his back to me and I am confronted by the scar that Daniel had—a lung surgery incision, upside down arch from shoulder blade to breast. Had things been different, I might have seen those scars as a life-saving sacrifice. But as it is, they represent butchery and failure, and also helplessness. I recall myself, with soft strokes of my fingers, dabbing vitamin E oil on Daniel's scar. He worried that it would remain a frighteningly pink disfigurement. I assured him that it would fade. I feared my touch or words would hurt him, so fragile he seemed. So I touched with all the softness I had inside me, maybe all I will ever have.

As we reach the dock and disembark the boat, I watch the scarred man walk slowly away, stopping momentarily to light a cigarette.

I feel suddenly very tired.

When we reach the hotel I lie down, with no intention of moving again for the remainder of the night. Bill and Maggie are comfortable with this strategy so we commence to festering. I begin picking foreign objects from my head; Bill follows suit. I find much sand and some of the tiny white balls of unidentifiable nature, which Bill calls "nernies." We stay up late mining for nernies and watching movies on TV—*Bad Boys*, *Teen Wolf*, and *Matilda*. Our evening is so remarkable we decide to write a song about our night in Key Largo, set to the tune of that 1980s song by Bertie Higgins.

We had it all, (we had it all),
picking nernies was a ball.
We can find it once again, I know,
just like we did in Key Largo.

Here's looking at you, kid,
watching Teen Wolf in the bed.
Staring at HoJo's late, late show,
passin' the time in Key Largo.

30

Six years ago today I met Daniel, in an Indian restaurant in South Bend, Indiana. Coincidentally, it was the owner of this same restaurant, a professor at the college I attended, that initially laid the groundwork for our acquaintance. This professor, Dr. Cyriac Pullapilly, led a semester abroad program for students of Saint Mary's and Notre Dame. On that trip that I became friends with a fellow student named Jon, who, after we returned to the United States, introduced me to Bill, one of his best friends from grade school. Because of my long friendship with Bill, I happened to be at Dr. Pullapilly's restaurant six years ago, where I met Daniel.

I reflect on life-altering chance as Bill and I move in silence from the Keys to Everglades National Park. When we arrive at the Flamingo Lodge we unload the car and settle Maggie into our hotel room. She will have to stay in the room for much of our visit, as she is not allowed on any trails in the Everglades. (Alligators have been known to eat dogs right off the leash.) With Maggie situated, we walk to Eco Pond, a nearby wetland pool constructed of treated sewer water.[52]

As Bill and I walk around the pond, we see several common moorhen, flocks of egret, ibis, heron, and a bald eagle flying overhead. It's a pretty good first experience of the Everglades, but eager to see more of the national park than the sewer pond, we walk to a nearby visitor center and ask a ranger for recommendations on trails and locations to find wildlife.

"Well, you can forget about seeing a Florida panther or a black bear, and you won't likely see any bald eagles. There are very few that travel here anymore," he says.

"Really? We saw one this morning at Eco Pond," Bill responds.

---

[52]Miamians use the Everglades' water, so the Everglades have to settle for effluent.

"Is that right? You're fortunate. In all my years here, I've never seen even one," the ranger replies. "But you'll definitely see alligator and many different species of birds. Oh, and lots of mosquitoes."[53]

From the visitor center we head to a nearby trail. At the trailhead, Bill elbows me and points to the sky. Another bald eagle flies above us, or likely the same one. We smile at each other quizzically then step onto a trail that crawls through a thick mangrove forest. The path seems unusually dark and as my eyes adjust I realize that the shadowy space around me is mobile and menacing. We are blanketed with ravenous mosquitoes before we've taken ten steps. Unprepared for such an onslaught, we turn about and run out of the forest.

On down the road we find a drier, breezier trail farther from the Florida Bay. As we set out, we run into some birders.

"Have you seen much out here?" one of them asks.

"Well, not much on this trail, but we've had two bald eagle sightings," Bill says.

"Really?!" replies one of them. "We'll have to keep our eyes open."

After a short chat they walk on down the trail. Within minutes a bald eagle swoops low, just above our heads, closer than I have ever seen one. Had I reached out with my hand, I could have almost touched it. We look in the direction the birders had walked, but they have their backs turned to us and clearly did not see the bird. Before I can call out to them, the eagle is gone.

We meander the trail for most of what remains of the day, but we return to Eco Pond for the last hour of sunlight and sit on a wooden bench on the boardwalk trail. All is quiet, except for some chattering from the moorhens. It's as good a place as any to be on Daniel's and my anniversary. For a while it is just Bill and me on the boardwalk, but at one point a man about our age approaches us.

"Are you birders?" he asks.

"Yes," I answer. "Sort of . . . but we are having trouble with this one." I point to a bird meandering the far shore of the pond. "Do you know what it is?"

He raises his binoculars.

"Where are you from?" he asks, while flipping through his bird identification book.

---

[53]Yes! Yes! Dey ate us already!

"Michigan," Bill replies.

Usually I let people believe we are both from Michigan, rather than open my reticent mouth. But for some reason I say, "Arizona."

"Where in Arizona?" he asks.

"Tucson."

"I grew up in the Verde Valley," he says.

"Really, I worked for a newspaper in the Verde Valley for a while," I say, surprised to hear someone mention this small region in northern Arizona.

"The *Verde Independent*?"

"Yes!" And we both laugh.

"It was my first job out of school. I lived in Cornville."

"That's where my parents live. Cornville is where I grew up!"

I stare at him in wonder, mouth agape. For a year, Daniel and I lived in Cornville, a town of about four thousand people, situated across the country from where I stand, and on the day of our anniversary, under a sky flush with bald eagles in flight, I meet somebody who grew up there.

The River of Grass

In the 1940s conservationist Marjorie Stoneman Douglas reported to the world that contrary to long-held perception, the Everglades was not swampland but rather a broad, slow-moving river that spanned a width of fifty miles and ran from its source at Lake Okeechobee to the Florida Bay. It was one of the most unique ecosystems in the world, home to an astounding diversity of plants and animals. Stoneman Douglas called it the River of Grass.

And even then it was in trouble. The flora and fauna of the Everglades ecosystem were adapted to the river's flows. As fish in the Mississippi would die if the river's waters were cut off upstream, so the plants and animals of the Everglades have died off in alarming numbers since its water flow began being severely restricted in the mid-1900s following human population explosions in south Florida. In the 1930s, a quarter of a million wading birds nested in colonies in the southern Everglades. Now there are eighteen thousand. The snail kite was reduced to fewer than four hundred breeding pairs due to water scarcity and contamination. The near-extinct Florida panther's numbers have at times been reduced to fewer than thirty individuals. Meanwhile the human population of

Miami-Dade County has ballooned from 260,000 in 1940, to more than 2.6 million today—and the demand for water has risen accordingly.

At times the river's flow has been completely shut off. Other times, it has flowed with pollutants from agriculture and other human activities. High levels of mercury, levels that would be toxic to humans, can be found in plants and animals throughout the region.

In 1947, on the heels of Stoneman Douglas's discovery, the federal government established Everglades National Park, the first national park created to save an endangered landscape. But as population and agriculture continued to grow exponentially in the second half of the last century, the Everglades continued to decline. The national park includes only one-fifth of the Everglades ecosystem—the fifth at the downstream end of the River of Grass. Because the source of the river does not lie in the park, the park service has little control over what becomes of it and much of the river's flow continues to be diverted to the Miami megalopolis and central Florida farmland.

Meanwhile the wild things of the Glades go on about their business as best they can. On a walk today, Bill and I stop at a watery depression on the side of a trail where a flock of white and snowy ibis, egrets, and a great blue heron have mounted an attack on a lethargic alligator. The gator's sluggishness and the birds' ire are likely connected, as the alligator appears to be suffering from a food coma—probably brought on by consuming a compatriot of the agitated fowl. The birds dive at the gator with beaks and feet and feathers in an uproar while the gator skulks sleepily, only occasionally thrashing his enormous jaws at the birds.

Eventually, Bill and I tear ourselves from the drama to find some breakfast. Afterward, I take a walk alone and end up back at Eco Pond. I am snapping some photos when suddenly I hear a loud *swish! swoosh!* in the water. I look down to see an alligator with its mouth clamped on a large, wide-winged, still-struggling bird. Judging from the bird's wing span and color, which I observe jutting out perpendicular to the line of the gator's mouth, the reptile's awkward feast is a great blue heron. A second gator then tries to nab the catch but the gator with heron's wings trailing from both sides of its mouth lashes its tail in stern warning and swims slowly away with its meal. It is a bittersweet moment, watching two creatures caught up in a battle such as this—what is death for the heron is life for the alligator, and when it is done, the world moves on. There was a time when we as humans fit seamlessly within this system of birth, death, and renewal. We took a sharp right turn at Albuquerque and in some ways we have gained, but in some deeper cavernous primordial place, we have lost pieces of ourselves and our pathway to peace within the world.

I find more and more that I am looking for those pieces, in the mountains of Baxter State Park, in the cranberry glades, in the Everglades . . .

On the Snake Bight Trail we approach in a high state of preparedness: long pants, long-sleeved fleece, head nets (hair nets we call them) and mittens in 80-degree weather. I am instantly sweating from every pore. Not more than fifty feet onto the trail we are both surrounded by a dark buzzing cloud, and even garbed with winter gear from head to toe, I am soon feeling the familiar mosquito sting all over my legs and arms. Inconceivable! We trudge onward.

On the narrow high ground between two channels, our 1.6-mile trail passes through prime gator territory. The muddy, sulfur-stinking channels are obscured from view by dense mangrove and mahogany, and various shrubbery. But there are paths here and there between the two waterways where gators have drug their heavy bellies and tails, leaving a slithery depression in the marshy ground. In a swarm of mosquitoes, my head darts right to left on the lookout for gators, then down looking for snakes. At one point, arrayed in the middle of the trail, lie the bone and feather remains of what was probably an egret or white ibis. Atop the feathery pile is a single bird foot, severed at a bloody ankle. It seems that a big cat—a bobcat or perhaps the Florida panther—has passed the trail before us. The gory pile lies as a totem of the wild and stops us in our tracks for a moment, until the mosquitoes whisper a simple entreaty: move or die!

At the end of our trail the Florida Bay sprawls out to the south. We follow a boardwalk across a stream lined with gators sunning themselves in the muck. On the near shoreline we see flocks of wading birds congregated at the spot where the stream enters the bay. Willowy roseate spoonbills glow bright as a sunrise against the gray palette of the day. Great blue heron and black-necked stilts loiter and feed on the fish and invertebrate life that inhabits the shallow bay shoreline. Bill stays on the boardwalk while I wander out in the muck toward the birds. Consciousness of time passing dissolves in wonder.

After a while, Bill yanks me from my trance with a squawky bird call, "*Caw! Cacaw!*" I look back to see an almost alarmed Bill jerking his finger toward the narrow stream that flows past the muddy bank on which I stand. Lumbering toward my turned back had been a rather sneaky and hungry-looking gator. I step slowly back a safe distance from the stream and afterward keep an eye on the creature. The gator, along with several that follow, lounges in the tidal pools where hundreds of birds fish and nap—an opportunistic spot for a hungry predator. A tense peace holds for now between bird and reptile but surely not for long.

The day is fading so Bill and I turn back. As we drive away from the Everglades—back toward the city that has nearly destroyed it—we lament our inability to see it as it was a thousand years ago, as it was intended to be.

31

Manatee Spring bubbles up from a cavernous subterranean source into a deep pool of skylight blue. Towering cypress encircle the pool, shading these waters as they flow about a hundred yards to the Lower Suwannee River, just before it enters the Gulf of Mexico. We meet here the waters of the Okefenokee one last time before they are consumed by their oceanic destiny.

Because this spring stays warm all year, relative to the Gulf in winter, West Indian manatees seek refuge here in winter months.

Hoping to encounter this endangered marine mammal, Bill and I take a sunset stroll upon a boardwalk that overlooks the pool and follows the spring to where it enters the Suwannee. We peer into the clear-to-the-bottom river looking for manatees, but instead we see a congregation of turtles traipsing about. They are floating, foraging the grassy bottom and paddling around, like odd little birds in a pale green sky. Here, fed by untainted waters direct from the sanctuary of inner earth, the Lower Suwannee is a river of glass.

We linger to watch the rise of a full, full moon—supposedly the fullest in decades. As the moonlight streams through cypress onto the Suwanee, owls *whoowhoo*, frogs grumble and gargle their croaks; fish leap and splash, and turtles soar in the luminous flow of the river set aglow by a moon so bright it mimics the dawn.

When the true dawn arrives, Bill and I rise and rent a canoe. At the mouth of the spring, just beneath the Suwannee's surface, enormous shadows appear—manatees hovering as dark puffy clouds in the silent underwater river-sky. They are nearly the size of our canoe, but they glide through the water with a mesmerizing grace that seems the birthright of even the bulkiest of sea creatures.

Hello, manatee.

We watch them grazing on the grassy bottom while fish and turtles commute in the spaces above and beneath them. Before long, most of the manatees disperse in search of greener pasture but one solitary swimmer, who has become intrigued with our boat, remains to glide around and beneath us. As it passes below, its back glances upon the bottom of the canoe, sending us into a gentle roll.

Mythological in essence and form, manatees are amorphous yet utterly distinct from this so often violent world. They seem weightless in the water, but are in fact, giants, capable of growing to ten feet long and weighing 1,200 pounds. They move through the water with subtle shifts of their tails, but much of their movement stems from a native ability to adjust their buoyancy in relation to the water. Because of this it seems as though they move simply through the power of thought rather than physiological effort.

People have dubbed manatees "sea cows," but their closest land relative is the elephant. In the water, the manatee is related to the West African and Amazonian manatee and the dugong. One branch of its immediate family has been terminally severed: the Steller's sea cow was hunted to extinction in the 1700s. So far the manatee has avoided that fate, but only just. They are listed as endangered under the federal Endangered Species Act. It would seem that their size and lack of natural predators would protect them from most any threat, but they are soft as anything of the flesh, and their curious nature contributes to their vulnerability. Not only do they not shy away from the unknown, they actually seek it out with the sweet inquisitiveness of a child.

I hang my head over the side of the boat and find myself staring directly into dark ingenuous eyes set against an expressionless face. They stare right back at me.

My heart takes one booming, bursting beat beneath my ribs.

I stretch my hand out toward the creature, but stop short of touching it. Further encouraging manatees to be trustful of humans and boats is unwise, as illustrated by the scars that slice along the length of this one's broad back. Slashings from boat propellers are so common that researchers identify individual manatees by their scar patterns. Scientists employ the creatures' human-inflicted wounds in the effort to protect them from human-caused extinction.

Boat traffic and habitat loss pose the greatest threats to the manatee. Recently the species has responded well to conservation efforts, when they are implemented. In areas where boats are prohibited and pollution controlled, manatees have rebounded. The problem remains that most of the manatee's habitat is not adequately protected. This year, of 325 known manatee deaths in Florida, only ninety-four were due to natural causes.

How long can any species survive such an onslaught? I wonder as I watch the gentle creature glide away.

Turtle Wrangling

Soft, luminous sand sets the Gulf Islands National Seashore aglow. A cool November wind blows in from the Gulf, but the sand is warm on my feet as we stroll the beach picking up cigarette butts. Bill and I have decided to seek some volunteer work in this national park today, to mark what would have been Daniel's thirtieth birthday.

A ranger suggested cleaning trash from the beach, so we walk slowly along the alabaster edge of the land, picking up plastic bottles, aluminum cans, plastic utensils, candy wrappers, potato chip bags and the omnipresent butts that many smokers seem to think don't count as litter.

As I drop butt after shriveled, ashy butt into my trash bag, my mind goes back to a Tucson, Arizona, sidewalk. Shortly after Daniel moved to Tucson, I was showing him around my neighborhood and we saw a woman ahead of us cast her butt to the ground and then walk on. When we reached the place where she dropped the cigarette, Daniel bent down with lips pursed, picked it up and tossed it in a trashcan that was only a few feet away. He looked in the direction of the woman, now halfway down the block, and yelled, "Trash can! Right here!" We walked on and he told me how one time he had seen a guy sitting in a parked car toss a cigarette butt out of his window.

"I picked it up and threw it—with smoke still trailing from the ash—into the car and onto the guy's lap," Daniel said.

"What did he do?" I asked, shocked by this action so uncharacteristic of the Daniel I knew.

"He stared at me, kind of shocked. I stared right back," Daniel said. "Then I said, 'There's a trash can right in front of you,' and walked away."

As I replay the memory, I hear myself scolding Daniel, saying, "You really shouldn't do things like that. That guy could have had a gun or something . . . blah . . . blah . . . blah."

One of the many things I wish I'd never said to him.

I emerge from the faraway theater of my mind when I hear Bill exclaim excitedly, "Turtle!" He has spotted a huge sea turtle twenty feet down the beach and just a few yards offshore. We set our bags of trash on the dry sand and run with abandon and great expectation into the frigid gulf. Icy, biting water up to our waists, Bill and I identify the turtle, the most common type of sea turtle—not a leatherback or green or hawksbill, but a stunning specimen of the feral automobile tire family. Bill and I look at each other with the disgusted disappointment of a kid who gets hand-me-down socks for Christmas. Then we run out of the water while we still have thawed flesh on which to run.

Upon exiting the bitter water, we sit down on the dry sand to warm ourselves and then notice our trash bags staring accusingly at us. We look at each other and back at the turtle impersonator (inturtle-ator), sigh, then splash back into the water. The galvanized turtle puts up a fight but we manage to lug it out of the water and up to the trash bin and gratefully return to our dry land trash quest. On down the beach Bill spots another turtle, which, as we expect, turns out to be an enormous tractor tire anchored in the bright sand beneath the crystalline gulf waters. Because it is nearly half buried in the sand, and the waves keep knocking us over and re-burying it, we have to heave for about half an hour to free the stubborn piece of junk.

As we are beginning to make progress, when we have finally dislodged the tire from the weighty sand and begun to haul it onto the beach, an old couple strolls up to us.

"You found yourself a bargain!" the old man says.

Why, you smartass old bastard, I think to myself. I imagine wrestling him to the ground, forcing him to listen as I recount how hard we worked to get that damn tire out of the ocean, and then tossing him into the frosty surf. However, despite my struggle—with the garbage we humans pile upon this earth, and the weightiness of a world without Daniel—I laugh with the smart-mouthed, endearing octogenarian and his bright, charming, white-haired companion. They walk on down the beach laughing at us and holding hands, and Bill and I scoff at their cuteness and return to picking up trash until we have filled our bags and tired our bodies and the morning has passed into late afternoon.

In the evening, when we sit down to dinner at our campsite picnic table, I lift my bottle of water to the sky and say, "Daniel, happy birthday, I miss you!" Then we follow the Ethiopian custom of throwing drink on the ground before a meal to welcome those who have died to the feast.

We eat quietly, each lost in our own thoughts.

I have pages of memories of Daniel scattered chaotically in my mind, his living and his dying, but not until that rare moment when it all shuffles into proper order, does it seem real and my soul goes to pieces.

Life seems all wrong in the context of his death. This current reality cannot be true: either I'm mistaken that he ever existed, or he's not dead now. I feel sometimes the urge to bang my head against a tree, like one might pound a pinball or a soda machine to make it work right.

I doubt it would prove effective, but the pain might make me forgetful of my confusion for a while.

32

Our time in the crowded East has ended and we make haste to the relatively wide-open West, starting with Texas. Bill, Maggie, and I pass a long day on an uneventful drive.

Bill is quiet. He has been feeling low the past few days ever since he read an email from his family about a chair that had belonged to his dad. The overstuffed maroon La-Z-Boy symbolizes a lifetime of TV sports, movies, and solitude—the choices his dad made that removed him from the picture of Bill's childhood. When his dad died, the chair should probably have been put in storage for Bill to have when this trip was over. But Bill shuns the inclination to cling to symbolic belongings, and belongings in general. So the chair was given to a friend of his sister, who later decided he did not want it. Now the chair has gone to a friend of Bill's brother-in-law, a person Bill has never met. The homeless chair stirs feelings of confusion and loss. Bill is stuck with the odd reality that death can clatter and clang its great finality and yet here is this piece of velour furniture wandering from place to place, an overstuffed maroon memory lumbering through Bill's consciousness.

There is nothing out here to distract one from such clunky recollections, and much to encourage them. Earlier I saw a jackrabbit dead on the side of a dry Texas road, and somewhere from the depths of memory echoed a phrase: "A jackalope is a rabbit what has antlers on its head."

It has been five years since Daniel said that. He had ridden a train for four days from Buffalo to Tucson. After I picked him up at the Tucson train station, we stopped at a café for lunch and Daniel regaled me with his train stories. The train it seems had a self-appointed Julie McCoy, an affable cruise director that kept the passengers entertained throughout the trip from Houston to Tucson with a series of jokes, geographic factoids, and contests. Daniel had won the train trivia contest and was given the grand prize of an Amtrak blanket, which he passed on to a family who did not have any warm clothes with them. While passing through west Texas, the train attendant's voice came crackling through the speaker system urging passengers to keep an eye out for the fabled jackalope. "A jackalope is a rabbit what has antlers on its head," the Texas drawl over the loudspeaker explained.

Daniel's laughter bounced off the tables and walls and ceilings of that small café, and into the recesses of my mind where it has been reverberating ever since, waiting for a long stretch of lonesome Texas highway to resurface.

The Big Bend

This morning I wake with a stiff, stabbing backache from last night's bed, a concrete slab along the Amistad Reservoir. But catching sight of the Chisos Mountains as we drive into Big Bend National Park quiets my crotchety vertebrae. Red rock formations, hills of pebbly white stones dappled with jade-colored pads of prickly pear cactus, and minerals glowing minty green upon sheer-faced mountains make my trifling human pains suddenly uninteresting. Javelina loiter at the side of the road, filling the air with a stench that befits the feisty, wild, piggish creatures. Tarantulas creep slowly across the road and we stop the car to let them pass in safety.[54]

I had never heard of Big Bend before starting this trip, but even at first sight I know I'll remember it as one of the most stunning landscapes I've seen. The Rio Grande makes a whimsical and grand change of direction in southwestern Texas, where it delineates the border between the United States and the Mexican states of Chihuahua and Coahuila. Here, within the big river's ribbon of riparian green, sits Big Bend National Park. Located in the northern Chihuahuan Desert, it is bordered by mountains on three sides. The political boundaries that cut the southern terminus of the park are forever marred by the bloody wars that created them. But another boundary exists here, one designated by limits imposed by nature rather than conquest. The Mexican long-nosed bat is one ambassador of an envoy of tropical plant and animal species who reach the extreme northernmost limit of their ranges in Big Bend. Similarly, many northern species travel only as far south as the Rio Grande. The land surrounding the big bend in the Rio Grande comprises a rare junction of nature's north

[54]And to keep a close eye on them lest they try to stow aboard on Maggie's tail.

and south. And, with its supreme isolation from the world of human endeavor (a hundred miles to the nearest town with a hospital), the meditative world of river, bird, and plant life predominates.

At the park visitor center we learn that Maggie will definitely have to stay in a kennel while we backpack. Dogs are not allowed in the backcountry, probably for several solid wilderness reasons, but the reason the ranger gives us relates to mountain lions. They have been known to kill pets. The ranger also cautions us about the javelina—a.k.a. collared peccary. I start to smile when the ranger broaches the ill-tempered pig subject, but she soon conveys seriousness of the issue. Apparently, javelinas run in gangs of six to twelve, and like the Crips and the Bloods or the Sharks and the Jets, they carry chips on their shoulders the size of a city block. Give them a reason and they and the rest of their posse will bring on the hurt. Actually, javelina will generally ignore people, but if one of their family is wounded or threatened, the whole group may attack. And though they are only about twenty-four inches in height and weigh less than sixty pounds, they are equipped with razor-sharp tusks—thus the name javelina, Spanish for "javelin" or "spear."

No doubt the hairy little beasts are tough, their primary food source is the painfully long-needled prickly pear cactus. So we take to heart the ranger's advice, to stow all food away, take Maggie to a kennel, and try to stay out of their way.

We find a "kennel" for Maggie, which is really a ranch where dogs have the run of the place. While we are touring the grounds, Maggie peels off on her own examination of the digs. It doesn't take long to ascertain that this kennel rocks, so Bill and I get ready to take off. I call out to Maggie so I can say goodbye. She doesn't answer. Or come running. So we look around the house and finally find her lounging on the couch in the owner's living room.

"Maggie! Get down." I scold her.

Maggie considers me, then looks at the proprietor.

"No, no, it's fine," the home/kennel owner says. "I want her to be at home here."

With that, Maggie begins licking the Texas dust off her paws, effectively dismissing us.[55]

---

[55]I wonder if she thinks the past five months spent on this road trip have been nothing more than a means of delivering her to the lifestyle she has always deserved. Won't she be disappointed when I show up again in a few days . . .

Bill and I set out exploring Big Bend. We had planned on crossing the Rio Grande into Mexico for dinner, carried by a small rowboat man—correction, small rowboat, not sure how big the man is—who charges a dollar for the trip. When we arrive at the bank of the river, however, the regular-sized man has already shut down his operations for the night. After a short discussion about illegal border crossings, water moccasins, and pollution, we roll up our pant legs, take off our shoes, and start to wade across the legendary river.

As the Rio Grande washes over my bare feet, I think of all the other people who have made this crossing, only in the opposite direction and with a peril that I cannot possibly understand. I have read of desperate people entering these waters when they rage with flood and being swept away or watching helplessly as the child they hold is wrenched from their arms. I think of desperation and drownings and of disappointment, finding out how inhospitable a new country can be.

Bill's mind and eyes are on his nemesis, the water snake. For this reason, I lead the way, feeling out the ground in front of us for solid, snake-free footing. After the dry summer season, the water, even at its highest point, comes just above our knees.

Midway through the crossing, two men, about our age, arrive at the bank on the American side. They are pondering whether to make the crossing as we are. When we have made it safely to the Mexican shore, one of the men calls across to us, "Has the boatman gone home?"

We nod that he has.

"How was the crossing?" they ask.

"Not bad at all." I show them where the river is shallowest and they follow in our footsteps. When they finish crossing, we all set out on a short walk to the small village of Santa Elena. On the way, we talk.

"Where are you from?" Bill asks the men.

"Washington, DC," one of them says.

"Really, so are we. Where do you live in the city?" Bill continues.

"At the corner of Nineteenth and Columbia Road. It's a building called the Shamut."

"I know the Shamut, I lived two blocks from there, at Nineteenth and Florida," Bill says. "We have some friends that live in the building next to yours."

We all shake our heads, thinking the cogent "small world" phrase that has been driven so deeply into cliché hell that I cannot here vocalize it.

We talk of work and other things and then as we walk into the same restaurant and sit down at tables next to each other, I approach a deeper subject.

"We've been gone for most of the last three months, but I was wondering if things have changed in DC since the September attacks."

"Things have changed," one of the men answers. "You have to watch what you say. People are so worked up over the attacks. At work I have to be really careful."

People are afraid, so afraid that mere words—the slightest hint of self-reflexive thought, sound that casts doubt about who is evil and who is good—turns eyes dark and mistrustful.

The conversation makes me glad to be far from home—both because I'd rather not witness the culture of fear that has cast a shadow on a city I love, and also because I'm in a restaurant where I can gorge myself on the *mas bueno guacamole en el mundo* before wading back across the Rio Grande in the autumn darkness.

Emory Peak

With food, water, and shelter on our backs, Bill and I hike seven miles, from the desert foothills to Emory Peak. I am bent and aching when I jettison my pack at our campsite and sit down on a rocky formation clinging to the steep edge of the mountainside. From this viewpoint the land drops off and a desert plain sprawls beyond the Chisos Mountains into a seemingly infinite distance muddied by the day's fine dusty haze. Somewhere in that haze is an invisible line denoting the boundary between Mexico and the United States, but it looks like an unbroken river valley from here.

I am munching some trail mix, which draws the attention of a fearless gray-breasted jay. The cerulean bird hops from the red-skinned manzanita tree beside me to the immense flat boulder on which I sit and back again, casting a steely eye and plotting a takeover of my bag of nuts and fruit. I ignore it, but secure my snack on the rocky ground between my legs.

After a while, Bill joins me on the rock with our dinner in hand. We dine on noodles as the light over the far away nebulous land shifts from golden to gray. From this altitude, it is hard to imagine there could ever have been anything other than tranquility as far as the eye can see. When the earth has fallen to shadow, we shuffle back to the tent and lie down.

I am primed for sleep and fall quickly to the task of dreaming, but within a few hours the clouds that had been idle and divided during the day unite with a force of rain and lightning and thunder that rattles the mountain.

Jolted awake, Bill and I both stare at the blue fabric of our tent ceiling, which is periodically set aglow with the sky, and we wait tremulously for the sound to follow. *Craaaack!* Eventually light and sound are near simultaneous, and the thunder that smacks down upon us ignites my body with electric adrenaline, the boom rumbles endlessly in my ears and I see Bill sitting upright, a strobe-lit silhouette against the sky. I am too scared to make my usual entreaty for panic, and I can see that Bill may not need any urging in this situation.

But all he says is, "That was close."

He lies back down and we wait through bolt after bolt of angry-loud light to see if we'll make it through the night.

Gradually, the electrical storm passes on, leaving us unscathed, but rain continues to pound through the night, leaving little peace for sleep.

Day two is not much better.

After two nights of rain and lightning, with baggy eyes and bent backs from little sleep and heavy packs, we descend again into the Chisos Basin. Clouds shift and allow the sun a brief opening to shine upon the sheer face of cliffs that frame the valley before us. We linger in the desert foothills where the tentative sun glitters on cactus moist and swollen with the arousing rain. It is a spectacular moment, one for gratitude from the arid land and all who live upon it.

Shortly though, my pack reminds me how anxious I am to be rid of it and return to the posh life of car camping. When we reach the car, we unburden ourselves of our packs and drive to our next home at the park campground in Rio Grande Village. After a shower and some lunch, Bill is ready to move again and I am feeling mealy-minded and convincible. So we steer the resentful Saturn down a holy hell of a dirt road on the western edge of the Sierra Del Caballo Muerto–Dead Horse Mountains. The dusty road is really more like a desert wash with delusions of grandeur. And, though the sign at the turnoff for the road says, "Recommended for high clearance vehicles only," Bill is too determined to be dissuaded. The Saturn rattles and shakes down the washboard road and large rocks periodically scrape along her underbelly, but she deposits us at the trailhead for Ernst Tinaja intact.

We are unsure as to the nature of the attraction we pursue as we begin the short hike to the tinaja, but the hike itself justifies the nerve-scraping drive. The trail cuts through a desert wash, bordered at first with slabs of polished rock and on down the trail by steep canyon walls of striated salmon-colored limestone. Beneath our feet lies a pebbly sand bleached alabaster by the intense Texas sun and the raging rush of storm waters. Here and there, wildflowers dot the secluded wash.

The Ernst Tinaja itself consists of a series of round deep pools cut into a rocky channel, constructed of flaky layers of eroded rock in unthinkable shades of spring—lavender, pink, and peach. The fine brittle nature of the shale and the pastel hues of the earth make the land appear to have been constructed from the discarded shells of a millennium of Easter eggs.

From the tinajas, we double back to our campsite and get to sleep early. Before dawn, we rise and head to a hot spring at the edge of the Rio Grande. When we arrive, sun appears on the horizon, dimly lighting shale cliffs and illuminating scattered pictographs and petroglyphs from ancient civilizations. A pool of steaming water at the edge of the fog-capped river is lit by a lavender glow—a reflection of the purple haze of clouds parted in the East by the blazing sunrise.

Rocky cliffs behind the hot spring pool, which lies between the cliffs and the river, radiate red-golden warmth. With no other people around, the morning's silence remains unbroken, except for the gurgling gait of the Rio Grande beneath its veil of mist. Bill and I ease ourselves into the water and sigh at the perfection of the moment. The air is scented by the recent desert rain—for that alone I would walk in a cactus field barefoot. I lie back and float effortlessly in the three-foot-deep pool, a perfumed breeze delighting the air, water rushing in my ears.

This moment could begin to heal almost any hurt this world can contrive.

After about fifteen solid, sweet minutes of solitude, up walks a man clad all in black leather with a shaved head. Bill flashes me a brief apprehensive glance, which I interpret to mean, "Uh-oh, skinhead?" But our concern is short-lived. We exchange greetings as the man enters the pool, then after a few quiet moments, Bill breaks the silence.

"Where're you coming from?"

"New York originally," the man says. "But I've been on the road for a few years."

"What motivated you to leave?" I ask him.

"Some events in my personal life," he says and does not elaborate.

I tell him the same is true for us.

"Do you still have homes somewhere?" he asks.

"No, we sold everything or gave it away," Bill says.

"That's fantastic!" He flashes a first warm smile. He clearly enjoys the fact that we have shed our possessions—though our journey in a car seems fairly posh compared to his journey around the country for nearly two years on an Enduro off-road motorcycle. He can only carry what fits into the small saddlebags of his bike. At times he sleeps outside with just a blanket. Other times he uses his knack for finding the seediest motels for dirt-cheap prices. He has followed warm weather for eight seasons, just because something compels him to get on his bike and move, and to keep moving, until another something suggests it's time to stop.

"I'll probably ride one more season, then go back home," he tells us.

I imagine him going back to New York, and wonder if he will recognize his hometown. I ask him for his insider (as a New Yorker)/outsider (as an expatriate) view of the terrorist attacks on New York a month ago.

He chuckles and looks to the sky. It is the reaction of a man looking back on his culture from someplace far away. As an observer of culture on many levels, he seems to possess an uncommon detachment and objectivity. He wonders whether people will find the capacity to think critically about the terrifying events and put them in the context of history. He sees the obliteration of the World Trade Center and destruction at the Pentagon as a powerful demonstration that the impossible is never quite out of the realm of possibility. In the theater of history and time, nature and human nature can always surprise.

"When things like this happen it makes me want to hang around," he says, "just to see what's going to happen next."

33

In the dark, early morning hours Maggie wakes me (and perhaps others in the campground at Guadalupe Mountains National Park) with a few short, but dog-serious barks. I sit bolt upright in my sleeping bag, muffle her noisome snout, and listen. I hear feet shuffling, a rustling at one corner of the outside of our tent; I smell a familiar stench, and then hear the snort. A javelina is just on the other side of our tent wall, surmising the contents of our home. This has pissed Maggie off. She was already furious with me for making her leave the Big Bend ranch/kennel, but this takes the cake. She shakes with pent-up bark and tries to break the grip of my hand. My breath goes shallow as I recall the Big Bend ranger's javelina warning. I try to use Jedi mind tricks to get the javelina to move along, but the stinky beast is either not feeble minded enough for me to overpower, or is too intrigued by the smells coming from our tent.[56]

Gradually, as minutes pass without a sharp tusk in my ass, I calm myself, recalling that javelina are generally not aggressive unless provoked. I probably spilled some dinner on my shirt, but I wasn't dining on prickly pear cactus, and I'm pretty sure rice-n-sauce will not be an incentive for the beast to charge. I have to stay awake until it leaves though because Maggie still has some things to say and my hand is the only thing preventing her from broadcasting her thoughts to the sleeping campground.[57] Finally, the troublemaker moves on and Maggie and I return to sleep.

When the sun rises a few hours later, we drive north to Carlsbad Caverns National Park in New Mexico. Bill and I sign up for a tour and once underground,

---

[56]Not having showered in a few days, we probably rival the stench of the wild pig. Perhaps it has mistaken us for family members and is hoping to free us from the captivity of a rival gang.

[57]Including Bill, who has not stirred in the slightest throughout the commotion.

it would seem we have left the planet. In Carlsbad, the magic of millennia has wrought the unreal.

Millions of years ago, water began infiltrating cracks in the earth's surface, dissolving limestone and eroding the belly of the earth into these fathomless caverns. Once the caverns were formed, about 500,000 years ago, the percolating water began to deposit calcite it had picked up on its downward journey. And where those deposits were made, stalagmites and stalactites were created in all manner of unimaginable shapes and patterns and colors. Depending on the flow of the calcite rich water, the deposits took the form of immense columns of jagged teeth, curtains of gauzy bone, ribbons of milky glass, or brittle cave lily pads floating in foreverdark pools.

It takes a special kind of creature to be able to survive in a place like this. For bats, it's a good place to rest out the daylight hours in peace. But for some cave creatures, every breath, every movement, every moment is lived in this utter darkness, in this secrecy so profound that even we pesky inquisitive humans have not yet found them. Creatures of this far-below world are still being discovered, unacquainted to human eyes, science, or any particle of light that has ever fallen to Earth.

Carlsbad's dark beauty is an indelible wonder and a lesson worth remembering—there is so very much of this world that we don't see, don't know, don't understand.

From the dark underground, we travel northward to Carlsbad's polar opposite, where the brilliance of sunlight reflected on gypsum particles is blinding and there is no place to hide. The process by which the region of White Sands National Monument was formed seems as unlikely as the end product, a sea of luminous white sand stretching toward the dark San Andres Mountain Range and an unbroken canvas of desert sky. It began 250 million years ago when gypsum settled at the bottom of a shallow sea that covered this region. The sea eventually dried and the land rose into domed mountains which later collapsed, forming the gypsum-rich Tularosa Basin. For many years, rain water collected and subsequently dried in the basin, leaving a crystalline form of gypsum. Those crystals broke down as the forces of nature played upon them, forming sand, which was then carried by the wind and deposited throughout the basin on the ever shifting 275 square miles of incandescent dunes. Situated at the northern edge of the Chihuahuan Desert, they form the world's largest gypsum dune field.

I return again to my childhood dream of being able to walk in the clouds, in the unblemished ether of the pointy bible-grandpa, where dirt, death, spiders, and sour washcloths do not exist. I imagine our hike in White Sands is the closest I will ever come. I don't know if my childhood imagination yearned for the softness of a great puff of cottony cloud or an escape from the chaos of life and death that I was then only beginning to understand. But in White Sands I clutch a tangible fistful of what I was yearning for. I experience myself against the pure white nothingness of cloud. It is so, so quiet, to ears and eyes. So restful to anguished places in deep cavernous spaces.

I see my feet sinking into a yielding illuminated earth, and aside from my own body, Bill, Maggie, and the distant mountains, all I envision is the bright rolling sand and the pale-gray clouded sky. In places, a hardy island of plant life—a sumac pedestal, a gnarled cottonwood tree—interrupts the negative space. Occasionally I spy a determined beetle plodding through ripples of sand. But living is hard in this dry gypsum land, and the life forms that exist are stealthy and unobtrusive.

What the eye sees here are calming patches of anchored shapes of dunes and mountains animated gracefully by light and shadow. Sometime late in the day, the clouds part and the rolling hills become awash in pale golden ivory—like moonlight captured in a gypsum glass. It is for a moment a meeting place of two worlds, where illuminated clouds merge with the fertile dirt of the dark burdened earth, where I walk on the very precipice of the known and unknown, light and dark, life and death—tranquility showers over me.

34

When we pull the fly off the tent this morning it is coated with frost. The moisture from our breath has frozen overnight. So have I. A constant shivering through the night has twisted the muscles of my back into a knot. Bent and disgruntled, we drive north to Salinas Pueblo Missions National Monument.

The story of the Pueblo Indians in the Salinas Valley of New Mexico is a painfully familiar one. Over many thousands of years the people inhabiting the Salinas Valley gradually built a thriving culture in some of the harshest desert land conceivable. Then, Europeans arrived in search of gold, and when that eluded them, in pursuit of religious and cultural domination. For the glory of god and king, Europeans stole food from the Indians and forced them into the backbreaking labor of building churches for European gods. What did the Indians get in return? The guarantee of an everlasting soul.[58]

Speaking of bad deals, our Saturn has begun to leak fluid from the engine into the front seat floor on the passenger side, so we are bound to find a Saturn dealership in nearby Albuquerque. On the bright side, they will have free donuts and hot coffee waiting for us.

When we arrive, I grab as many donuts as I can manage with two hands, stick a coffee under my arm, then head outside to wait. I sit down in the sun to warm up before what will surely be another freezing night of camping. As my blood sugar begins to spike, I observe my surroundings. Next door to the Saturn building towers a gray granite well-manicured memorial to consumerism, materialism, and excess—a self-storage building, sporting an enormous sign that reads: United We Stand. Adjacent to that, sits a small, decrepit, almost unnoticeable cemetery in the grassy square that buffers the self-storage building from the nearby highway. A warped, rusty, and broken-down, bowing-almost-to-the-dusty-ground

---

[58]This product is not guaranteed. No refunds, see select stores for details.

chain-link fence denotes the boundary between the once-revered world of the dead and the shiny, new, plastic world of the living.

Brittle brown grass surrounds small rusted metal crosses and dingy stone arcs marking final resting places of long-forgotten lives. Who were these people? Surely what lies beneath this ground is little but bones by now, but without exception, the sad memorials to their lives seem to be abandoned, unvisited, untethered from history, family, or friend.

A short distance from the cemetery, cars whiz past on a highway that takes no notice of the dead. Car dealerships and self-storage are the gods of this twenty-first century world—we have places to be and extra stuff that needs storing. The graves are invisible to most. Only the lucky few who sit munching free donuts waiting on the asphalt for an oil change or auto repair have time to adjust their eyes and notice the crumbling sanctuary beyond a fence plastered with wind-blown garbage. My only company as I consider these human remains shipwrecked in strip-mall suburbia are Nutter Butter wrappers, Super Big Gulp cups, and other disposable detritus, which stare blankly at the anachronistic wreck of a home for the dead.

Aircraft roar overhead while cars flash past belching a grimy haze of polluted destiny left to hang on the air long after they are gone. A gusty wind stirs garbage to dance upon the ground. Crushed cups, lids, and straws from Wendy's and Kentucky Fried Chicken shuffle listlessly about while plastic shopping bags float restlessly, as they all await their final resting place atop the bones of humanity.

If White Sands was the destination I longed for as a child, a place where confusion dissolves in liquid light, then this spot marks the antithesis. There is a choking sadness, a palpable isolating dust that walls the chaos of human hubris from the timeless order of nature; there is a searing embodied truth screaming out to everyone and no one about the hard-broken reality of the life we have fabricated from the silken star-stuff of the universe. I want to shut my eyes, cover my ears, but no matter, the vision is with me now.

Thankfully, like everyone else, before long the car is fixed and we move on down the road.

It's good to have something to be thankful for; today is after all Thanksgiving. Earlier in the day Bill and I bought some items for a feast: boxed mashed potatoes, frozen corn, frozen green bean casserole, and Hostess cherry pie.

Though I am still pretty stuffed from my Saturn donut binge, I suggest we stop somewhere and make our special meal.

"I don't think so," Bill responds, somewhat sadly. "I think I just want to go for a hike."

He doesn't add "alone" to his sentence, but it is inferred.

"Okay," I say. "I'll stay in the car with Maggie."

Bill has been feeling bad all day, but staying quiet about the cause. He drives us to Petroglyph National Monument and then heads out onto the rocky hillside. While he's gone I write in my journal, go for a short walk with Maggie, and take what seems like a lengthy nap. I am awake and starting to worry when Bill returns. He gets in the car quietly and we drive to a rest stop to camp for the night. I can gather he doesn't want to talk about what's the matter. Perhaps he is just feeling low, or maybe my ups and downs are finally getting to him. Could be he's just tired of being in this car with me. His silence is unusual, and worrisome for me, but I leave him to his thoughts.

$19.95 for Two, Pets Okay

At the rest stop I feed Maggie, then hollow out a place to sleep in the back seat, amid all of our crap piled halfway to the ceiling—including a bag filled with our uneaten Thanksgiving feast, which melted today and will probably refreeze tonight.

When daylight finally gets around to showing up, Bill and I wake with parched mouths in a tomb of frosted glass. We quickly open the doors and gulp some lung-stinging air and some ice water from our bottles. The temperature dropped to 12 degrees overnight.

Hastily, we start the engine, crank up the heat, and head down the road to El Malpais National Monument. El Malpais means "the badlands" in Spanish. This land turned bad somewhere between two and three thousand years ago when lava oozed from McCarty's Crater, killed everything in its path, and then hardened to form a shell of volcanic rock that covered much of the region. Where lava flowed the land remains an ebony river, or a scattering of porous reddish-brown volcanic rock. Where it didn't flow, life lived on.

A community of Puebloan people made their home on the banks of the hardened lava land from 950 to 1350. According to their mythology, the landscape's obsidian stream was a dried river of blood that flowed from a monster killed by twin heroes in ancient days. Whether blood or lava, little was spared when the devastating event occurred. But small islands and narrow ribbons of earth escaped the molten flow's destruction and continue to support remnant plant and animal populations from the time before the earth's scorching tide.

One animal in particular remains perturbed by the mess left by the volcano. Maggie has to wear dog booties while we are hiking here because the sharp obsidian earth will shred her soft foot pads. She is demonstrably insulted by the booties, and with every step shakes one back leg and then the other trying to get the boots off. It's really funny when she runs while doing this; she looks like a dingo-shaped bucking bronco.

In the late afternoon, we all sit on a sandstone bluff overlooking the Malpais and watch a magnificent sunset of smudged oil pastel pinks and roses, mauves and peaches, of fire streaks and golden rays.

When darkness overwhelms us, we set our minds to seeking shelter. Because of the persistent cold, we settle on the Franciscan Inn: $19.95 for two, pets okay.

This is by far the most rustic motel we've stayed in. The bathroom floor of green plastic tile is chipped away to reveal an older shade of green plastic tile. The tub consists of loose, mildew-caked tile (with paint splotches where someone tried to paint over the mildew), a white plastic shower curtain made of Saran wrap, and towels the size and thickness of Kleenex. The bathroom door has a hole where the knob should be. Old wooden chairs are padded with hand-cut squares of cardboard-thin carpet remnants that fray at the edges.

One fantastic feature here is that the "laundry mat" is right next door to our room, and the machines are so old and loud and the walls are so thin that we can hear when the laundry is finished, rather than having to leave the room to check.

In the early morning we drive farther west, to El Morro National Monument, where sheer bleached sandstone cliffs tower over pools in the high-desert floor, providing a shady haven that attracted people from various cultures over the past thousand years.

The area was once home to ancient Puebloan cultures and is called A'ts'ina, or "place of writings on the rock," by their modern day descendants. Puebloan ancestors of the Zuni people rested for many years at the oasis in what is now northwestern New Mexico. When they abandoned their pueblo in the 1300s, they left inscriptions and pictographs on the walls of the sandstone cliffs.

Hundreds of years later, Spanish conquistadors were drawn to the pools and sheltering cliffs of El Morro. Along with many others, the infamous Juan de Oñate, who in 1598 colonized the region of New Mexico, carved his *paso por aqui* in the stone guest register. Eventually, Indians revolted against Oñate and Spanish missionaries and effectively made Spain's long-term domination of the isolated El Morro area impossible. But after the Mexican-American War in 1848 the United States took control of the New Mexico territory and military expeditions violently uprooted the Indians.

Many of these players in the tragic theater of history left their mark on El Morro. But when an east/west train route was opened in 1881, the oasis at El Morro lost its attraction for travelers—who could suddenly speed past without ever noticing the stone art of Puebloan peoples or the carvings of conquistadors. Shortly thereafter, the federal government prohibited further inscription on the cliffs, which were set aside as a historical record of all who had once traveled here.

So Bill, Maggie, and Krista will not be leaving our mark on El Morro. Instead, we drive back through Albuquerque and south through Socorro to the Bosque del Apache National Wildlife Refuge. I set out on a walk around a pond enveloped in a cacophony of bird voices. An estimated forty thousand snow geese winter at this refuge, and they make their presence known. Watching a flock of snow geese take flight from a New Mexico plain is like seeing a crisp white sheet the size of a football field rippling and rising from a clothesline in a strong summer breeze. Only much louder. The geese all seem to have something to say, something urgent. And even if they are just flying a few hundred yards to take a dip in the open water, their choreographed flight suggests the same urgency as their voices.

Despite their clamorous presence, Bosque del Apache was not established for the snow geese but for a less populous member of the community, the greater sandhill crane. In 1939, there were on average seventeen endangered sandhill cranes that wintered in the region. After sixty years of habitat restoration and protection at Bosque and other locations, sandhill counts are now estimated to be seventeen thousand. Like the bald eagle, these cranes are a potent symbol of how a simple consciousness of our actions and some latitude for nature can accomplish so much. And one glance at these birds is all the impetus anyone ought to need: Sandhill cranes are like ballerinas stretched on a rack into gawky but perfectly graceful creatures.

For the sandhill, the Bosque is an essential stronghold because history was not kind to the cranes. Bosque del Apache, meaning "woods of the Apache," was so named by the Spanish because Apache Indians used to camp along the riverside forest. In their attempt to subdue the Apache and wrest control over the region, the Spanish established El Camino Real, "the royal road," from Mexico City to Santa Fe, which ran right through the middle of the present day reserve. The development and deforestation of the subsequent centuries wreaked havoc on the habitat of the sandhill crane and other wildlife of the region. Their numbers gradually dwindled until the National Wildlife Refuge System protected thirty thousand acres along nine miles of the Rio Grande, a critical source of water for wildlife in the dry New Mexico desert. Today Bosque is one of the premier places for bird watching in the Southwest, because birds are bound to congregate around this rare wetland habitat.

35

Rest stop camping is becoming a nasty habit as we attempt to avoid sleeping in a frost-covered tent. The car provides a negligible amount of added warmth but something about solid walls makes you feel like you're more protected from the elements.

Upon waking, Bill and I find that our bone-dry tongues have adhered to the roofs of our mouths overnight. When we have pried our cemented maws open, we rehydrate but our mouths have begrudged us the rationing because we barely speak until noon.

Bill breaks the silence.

"Want to have our Thanksgiving now?"

"There's a fairly good chance that the green bean casserole will make us sick; it's been thawed for a long time," I say.

"It won't make us sick. And then we'll have something to be thankful for," Bill says.

"Okay."

It is unequivocally the worst Thanksgiving dinner I've ever had, but we don't get sick, and we do give thanks, and the meal provides a welcome change of pace from Noodles & Sauce. Afterward we hike a few miles on the Catwalk National Recreation Trail, a series of suspended walkways over a canyon of pink lavender boulders and enormous golden-leaved sycamore trees in the Gila National Forest. The Catwalk view of the narrow Whitewater Canyon provides an impressive introduction to the Gila.

Though I lived in the next state over for many years, I have never before visited New Mexico's Gila, the country's largest national forest preserve outside of Alaska. Within the 3.3-million-acre national forest sits the largest wilderness in the Southwest and the first designated wilderness in the world, the Gila Wilderness. The idea of wilderness first took root when former forest service employee Aldo Leopold began professing it in the 1920s. Leopold had worked for almost two decades in the forest service, lots of time to observe the impact of government management of the land. Lands that were considered "protected" by the forest service were in fact being degraded by the government's lack of knowledge and restraint. Road building and other construction in forests was common, and done without thought to the implications for the land, wildlife, and water quality. So Leopold lobbied Congress to establish an area within the Gila forest as wilderness, and he is largely credited for the 1924 groundbreaking congressional authorization for the Gila Wilderness. Leopold went on to write one of the foundational texts of the modern conservation movement, *A Sand County Almanac*, published in 1949, a year after his death. His words and actions fueled a movement that spared millions of acres of land for generations of wildlife and plants and humans.

Without Leopold, and those like him, we would be lost. Taken as a whole, each generation of humanity has tended to believe that the land is a possession to dispense with as we please, without thought to the animals or plants who thrived there for millions of years or to future generations who might like—or perhaps *need*—to walk in an ancient forest or encounter the unmolested wild. Thoreau said, "In wildness is the preservation of the world." There is more to this statement than an argument for land preservation or wilderness policy. The need for wildness is written within our genes, in a language we are just beginning to understand. And in wilderness we will find the Rosetta Stone that can unravel this ancient language of our bones. In wilderness we save what is left of the natural world, and maybe someday, when we are ready, we can rebuild our broken relationship with our paradise lost.

For now, we have to focus on holding on to what we have left of nature. As Leopold said, "That land is a community is the basic concept of ecology, but that land is to be loved and respected is an extension of ethics."

Without an ethical relationship to nature, there can be no real peace. But ethics require sacrifice, a tough sell in a culture obsessed with convenience, comfort, and personal liberty.

A night spent in the Gila on the verge of winter is quite the opposite of comfortable. In preparation for what is certain to be a bitter cold night in the tent, I wear five layers of protection, including two sleeping bags. The foot-thick cocoon I have constructed provides little comfort and for hours I am jarred awake by cold.

In the morning, having slept little, I depart the tent to grab a water bottle from the car; it is frozen solid. I consider what that means for the blood in my veins, which passed the night under the same climate conditions.

Then, with icy slush slogging through our arteries, Bill and I skulk down the road from the Scorpion Campground to the Gila River, grumbling all the way. Maggie prances ahead of us blissfully, her dog breath turning to frosty mist in the morning air and her toasty spider wagging back and forth.

We sit and wait for the sun to break upon the canyon walls as our toes freeze into stinging nubs. After our morning photos, we thaw ourselves with oatmeal and hot chocolate. The sun begins to warm the landscape and us and we take a walk to the nearby Gila Cliff Dwellings National Monument.

Puebloan peoples built these dwellings about seven hundred years ago, nestled into enormous caves that overlook a beautiful side canyon near the Gila River. The structures have been ravaged by time and various human elements.[59] Still, the essence of the stone structures remains. I can imagine living a quiet, content life in those dwellings, when fires warmed the many rooms of the community built into a hillside and handwoven blankets padded the stone floors and benches.

Manson's Paradise

Not far from the Puebloans' cozy digs, there is a natural hot springs on a bank of the Gila River. When we arrive at the pool there are several people already soaking—one bearing a striking resemblance to Charles Manson—and several hikers on the trail behind us. The sign on the trailhead said, in no uncertain terms, "Clothing required at hot springs." Still, the people sitting in the springs appear not to be wearing any clothes. I think to myself, what if they really are wearing suits and I go in naked and the people behind me wear suits? Given the extent of Bill's and my general isolation, and cultural awkwardness, I figure it best to follow the written directions. But just to be sure, I ask Bill.

"You wearing a suit?"

"NnnyaaIthinkkso," he says.

---

[59]Ranchers housed their herds in the dwellings, treasure seekers pillaged, and morons came in and lit sticks of dynamite to scare off rattlesnakes.

That doesn't really clear anything up for me but I step behind a boulder and put my suit on, as does Bill, and we lower ourselves into the heavenly hot water with the definitely naked people. I grumble to myself that only squares wear suits in hot springs while Bill says hello to our companions.

"Hi, where are you all from?"

A young woman, about our age, with long brown hair speaks for herself and her boyfriend, a good-looking tall dude she's been cuddling with. "We work at the Grand Canyon but I'm from Tucson."

"Oh, what part?" I say.

"Central, pretty close to the university."

"Oh, my mom lives at First and Fort Lowell," I say.

"My mom lives two blocks from there. I went to Amphi High School."

"Really, my brother used to coach swimming there."

"Cool," she says, and then starts to stand up. "I have to jump in the river, it's too hot. Anyone else?"

Mmmm, hell no. This is the same river we had to cross to get here and it's not actually a river, it's snowmelt from the mountains.

I turn to the man-who-could-be-Manson, sitting to the right of Bill.

"Where are you from?" I ask him.

"Well, I live part of the year in Austin, working construction jobs and saving money. Then I take off and travel around, going wherever I can get to for as long as I can stay."

He turns to the guy who works at the Grand Canyon. "A couple of years back, I was rescued out of the Grand Canyon."

"Whoa, what happened?" we all say in one way or another.

"I'd been hiking in a remote side canyon for about a week and was heading back out when a flash flood came raging toward me. So I scrambled up the canyon wall and into a cave. It saved my life probably but then I was stuck. And I had almost no food left because I was on the last days of my trip."

"Shit, how'd you get out?" Bill asked.

"Well, the floods kept me holed up there until I ran out of food completely," he said. "When the water receded, I started the hike back to the rim, but I was still easily twenty miles out and didn't have the strength to make it. But I got lucky. When I didn't return to check out as planned, the park sent a rescue squad. By the time they found me and hauled me out, I'd been almost a week without food."

The rest of the people in the pool are now shaking their heads in amazement, likely thinking, *geez, this lucky son-of-a-somethin-or-other ought to be dead.*

I think that sounds about right, and I almost ask him right then, "So, did you come straight here from the rescue?"

This guy looks like the kind of person who recently escaped starvation—wiry, unshaven for years, and tough, like he's just escaped from a medieval dungeon and headed straight for the hot springs. My mind occasionally gives me signals not to trust this Manson on the run, escaped from prison with nobody the wiser. But he is just so damned interesting and friendly. Still, Manson was supposedly a charmer.

Long after the other two people leave, Bill and I stay talking to the man(son) from Austin. When the sun is considering setting we drag our pruney selves from the water and start the hike back, leaving our new friend to soak alone. About halfway back on the trail I hear splashes behind us and turn back to see the thin scruffy-bearded man clambering after us. Oh shit. Here comes Manson. My paranoid mind has been right all along. Bill and I stop to wait for him and when he strides up he holds out his hand to Bill.

"Is this yours?"

It's Bill's glove, which he had dropped in the stream without knowing it.

"Yeah. Thanks a lot," Bill says, and we walk the rest of the way back to the trailhead together. When we reach our car, Manson says, "If you liked that hot spring, you should check out the one on the Middle Fork trail. It's paradise."

The following morning we take his advice. The trail travels through canyons and over streams beneath a towering world of eroded stone cliffs and columns. Normally I would consider it one of the most stunning landscapes I've ever seen, but my only concern here is sitting my butt down in some scalding water.

Road fatigue and the frigid, restless nights wear on me. I have been doing so much better than in the east, I think, but a subtle darkness shadows me. In the past few days, the only time I can release it completely is immersed in a hot pool. Unfortunately, after hiking four miles on the Middle Fork trail, Bill and I start to fight over whether or not we should be allowed to stop along the trail and take photos. The argument can be traced to an unfortunate miscommunication from earlier in the day. Bill was under the impression that when we decided to hike to the hot springs, it was for the purpose of enjoying a trek through the outrageously beautiful canyons of the Gila Wilderness, taking photos, and then spending a short spell in the hot springs before hiking the seven miles back to the trailhead. I take responsibility for the misinformation that Bill was basing his perceptions upon. I should have told him that the sole purpose of the hike was to accomplish a single, highly time-sensitive task that was to sit my ass down in the steaming water and leave it there until it was good and prepared to face the world once more.

Bill does not know this, so when he stops once, then again to climb a rock face and snap some photos, I can hardly blame him. Yet, I do.[60]

I say something like, "Come oooonnnnn!"

Bill says something like, "What's your problem, hold on a minute. Jesus!"

And all becomes an angry downward spiral from there. Bill walks ahead, alone and fuming. I don't see him for a mile or so. In the meantime, I begin to worry that he has fallen or that Manson has found, brainwashed, and recruited him, or something. So I call out to him. No answer. I call again, and again. That he doesn't answer me gives me no real cause for alarm—he can be powerfully stubborn and silent when he wants to. But that Maggie does not come running back to me makes me very nervous (most dogs, if they hear their supposed "best friend's" panic-stricken scream, would come bounding back to help).[61]

I keep walking but wonder if I should turn back and try to find Bill. I imagine him stranded with a broken leg in the middle of a rapidly rising stream, too weak to call out to me. Fears that live in the deepest recesses of me begin to rattle their chilling cries. I know for certain that I am imagining things, but I also cannot shake the certainty that just when I least expect it, I can lose everything. I turn back the way we had come and start looking for signs of Bill, still calling into the lonely canyon.

"Bill! Biillll! *Bill!*"

It then occurs to me to look down for footprints. Sure enough, there are prints from Bill's boots and Maggie's disloyal little feet leading from the streambed in

---

[60]The reader may be wondering at this point, "Why is this person such an insufferable hag? Doesn't she know that any good story needs a hero and the hag is *never* the hero?" Well, smart reader, I am not the hero of this story, simply the magnificently flawed narrator (a fact that will become irrefutably clear in the next chapter). I will leave it to you to decide which of the other two carmates is the hero.

[61]I really ought to know her better by now.

front of me. My eyes narrow as I stomp down the trail. I imagine arriving at the hot springs and seeing him already soaking in the soothing steamy balm of mineral water, looking smug and rested. I growl at that vision and walk on.

When I finally find them, waiting for me about a mile farther down the trail, I charge up to Bill and yell, "I'm going back! I just need some water so I don't die of dehydration . . . Then I'm going to my mom's! You don't even care, you just leave!"

He refuses to give me the water. "*What* is wrong, Krista?"

"*Give me the water!*" I roar.

He gives me the water. I take a few swallows then throw the rest at the anti-Lassie who is sitting contentedly at Bill's feet.

"He doesn't even like dogs!" I roar at Maggie, then I turn and run back down the trail.

Bill follows me for about two miles then grabs my arm and spins me round.

"What is wrong?"

"I was calling to you! You didn't answer! I thought something had happened, I was afraid you were hurt, that I'd lost you . . . you were gone!"

"I'm sorry," he says and pulls me tightly inside his arms. "I didn't hear you. I just wanted to walk by myself because you were in such a bad mood."

"Well, you didn't have to scare me like that," I say, crying, but starting to calm down.

"That's why I said I'm sorry."

"Okay. Fine."

"Fine," Bill responds.

"What's Maggie's excuse?" I ask, sniffling.

"I can't speak for her," Bill answers, with a smile in his eyes.

She is trotting ahead of us, pretending to be oblivious to the whole scene.

Foregoing Manson's paradise, we walk back to the trailhead and back to our campground, where we build a fire and dry our socks and feet. My shoes and socks get too close to the fire and melt at the toes. This doesn't concern me, as I am preoccupied composing my mea culpa. Once I have warmed up, I apologize to Bill. And to Maggie.

"I was afraid. And you were acting so strange on Thanksgiving, and never even said what was bothering you. I thought maybe you were too tired . . . tired of me and my broken self. I can be alone, I'll be fine. I've gotten stronger since . . . everything. I'll be fine on my own now."

Bill grabs my hand and squeezes it, looking intently into my eyes. When he is sure my wall of fear has cracked a little and I am able to listen, he continues.

"It's okay, Krista," he says. "Everything is okay. I can't tell you what's been on my mind, not right now. But I will at some point." He pauses for a long moment then says, "I know this is not always going to be peaceful, that you and I can't live in a car together without things getting tough sometimes—we just have too much to work through. But I think we should make a pact that neither of us is going to threaten to leave again, that we're going to see this trip through to the end, no matter what it takes. I understand you're struggling and that's not going to stop and we'll keep fighting because this is hard, what we're doing and how we're doing it. But I'm not leaving, not you and not this trip. I think we both need to commit to this. At least for this year, no walking away."

He continues looking at me, waiting patiently for my reply.

I stare back at him for a long while, searching myself, wondering if I'm capable of what he is asking. Of letting go of all the terrors that pain has etched in the soft cavernous walls of memory, where voices echo in scream or whisper, *Run away . . . run away . . . hide . . .* As I look into his pale gray eyes, full of an earnestness that beams even in the dim and dying firelight, I feel strong, trusting, and able, for right now.

"No walking away, I promise."

Rock Bottom

We sit by the fire quietly for a while before I head to bed, hoping against hope that I have hit rock bottom. Once zipped into the tent, I shiver several hours away while my body temperature tries feebly to warm my sleeping bag. Right about the time I am feeling warm enough to fall asleep, my bladder expresses the desire to be released of its contents. I scoff at it and turn over on my side to ease the pain, then manage to fall into fits of sleep. Every fifteen minutes I turn to a new position in hopes of quelling my bladder and my aching back. A few hours before daybreak, I am so exhausted I fall finally into a deep, treacherous sleep. My mind slips immediately into dreams of bathrooms. It takes some time for my evil brain to overwhelm my will but just before daybreak, I find my dreaming self happily sitting on a toilet.

Ahhh . . . thank the good lord.

My eyes spring open, then roll skyward as the unpleasant realization of what I have done sinks in. And I lie in the darkness bemoaning my stubborn refusal to face the cold and feeling grateful that I am wearing four layers of clothing and that I have a clean change of clothes.

When the darkness abates, I put on clean clothes and wake Bill.

"I pissed myself," I say sheepishly, to his barely opened eyes.

"Huh," he says sleepily as a smile starts to spread across his face.

"I peed while I was asleep."

"Why don't . . . (*guffaw guffaw*) . . . why don't you just get out of the tent and go?" he says, laughing at me.

"Why don't you take your pants down and squat in the snow in the middle of the night?"

"Because I don't have to."

"Neither do I."

"The fact that you urinated yourself suggests otherwise."

I have no response at the ready for this irrefutable fact, so I just say, "It is really cold out there."

"And in here," Bill agrees. "Maybe we should leave a day early for your mom's house."

I like this plan. We are not really prepared to winter camp in the Gila, and we are only cutting short our stay by one day. Plus I am now wearing my last clean change of clothes and I am not confident about what will transgress over another freezing night in the tent.

36

Our visit at Mom's house—which will serve as a brief warm haven and home-base for a few weeks—begins with Granny giving Bill and me the skinny on recent events in her world. The issue foremost on Granny's mind today is the Gila woodpecker making a home in the saguaro cactus that sits a few feet from the house in Mom's front yard. I would show some excitement over the presence of the striking bird, except Granny's tone lets me know she's not happy with the squatter.

"Look at this screen! He sits out there pecking into that cactus and tossing his garbage against this screen. It's ruined!"

It is ruined. Some element in the cactus fiber tossed onto the screen by the insensitive woodpecker has disintegrated the mesh fabric.

"I go out there and cuss at him and what's he do?" Granny asks us, and then answers, "He sasses me, that's what. Just sasses me!"

I hear the male woodpecker chattering defiantly from atop the saguaro and I look at Granny with fists balled and pumping and cannot predict a victor. But then, something about the exasperated fatigue in Granny's voice and the soft cloudiness of her blue eyes makes me feel the screen-shredding bird holds the advantage.

From the front lawn and the cheeky woodpecker, Granny turns back toward the house and Bill and I follow. As she opens the front door, I hear her grumbling in front of me, "I hate that sassin' woodpecker."

From there we turn to the inevitable conversation concerning the battle between Mom and Granny about the manner of Christmas tree we will be decorating this year. The debate has been raging for at least three years. It started when Mom began using a huge ficus plant as a Christmas tree, thereby avoiding the felling of a living tree. Well, Granny and at least one of my two siblings have been endlessly chagrined by the substitution. According to Granny, the ficus is not strong enough to hold the ornaments and always gets droopy a few days after we decorate it.

Rather than being limited to the holiday season, the ficus plant dispute is waged throughout the year until the final determination is made a few weeks before Christmas; then sour grapes are grumbled through the holidays and eventually the cycle is begun anew.

This year the ficus tree, apparently troubled by its role at the center of the controversy, appears ready to bow out. Brown, crunchy leaves shower continuously around the base of the embattled plant.

"I think it's dead," Granny says.

"Strange, it was a mature tree and seemed to be so healthy," I say.

All Granny will say to that is, "I had nothing to do with it! I tried to save it."

I trust my granny, but with the ficus plant eliminated, she has gained monumental ground in the impending Christmas tree battle.

Even if she did poison the ficus, I won't fault her for it. Granny has always been a big part of my life, ever since she and my grandpa helped see us through the turmoil that followed my parents' divorce. But more recently, I've stumbled onto an even deeper connection to Granny.

Six months after Daniel died, I drove cross-country for an extended visit with my mom. The day I arrived, Mom was at work but my granny, who had just moved from Kansas to live with Mom, came out to meet me as I got out of the car. She put her arms around me and squeezed as hard as she could, and this cloud-haired and sometimes crotchety angel from another era became for me a bridge to some peace of mind that had been eluding me.

Whether it was going for two-hour-long shopping trips to purchase four or five items on my granny's grocery list; eating cinnamon toast (hers with diabetic sugar) at the kitchen table discussing the digestive prowess of prune juice; or creating the first and only installment of my granny's memoir, my perceived complexity of life and memory dissolved when I was a participant in her life. She passed the time making cookies and staring with patient acceptance into the face of death, as one waits in a doctor's office for a checkup. The love of her life had died fifteen years earlier. She kept Grandpa's photo next to her reclining chair, from which she watched *Wheel of Fortune* and critiqued Vanna White's fashion sense ("Look at that getup!"). She missed him every day, but she still lived and loved and appreciated every moment with a family who adored her.

For the first time in my life I was beginning to understand how much I had to learn from Granny. Her daily routine included the slow practice of scheduled necessity but allowed for the experience of any manner of serendipity—be it the celestial softness of a flower petal or the buzz of a hummingbird from the desert willow in the backyard. Granny took profound pleasure in simple things because the complex questions of life and love and death had already been answered a hundred thousand ways in her eighty-seven years.

The speed at which Granny moved used to unnerve me, when youth inflated my concept of self and destiny. But now I had no place to be and I looked forward to no earth-shaking excitement around some mythical future corner. I was only twenty-eight, but I had come to know that many surprises waited in various forms, from champagne to shadows, in the silent obscurity of the future. I was now in no hurry to greet them, which left me free to just glide along with Granny. In her world, so near to illness and death, life made sense to me. Maybe in the modern world there are only certain spaces where youth and old age can meet and connect. For Granny and me, it was the moment we both existed in a state of flux between life and death. I was brought to that space by following Daniel as far as I could, short of relinquishing my own physical existence, to the porch of that house with no windows that contains the absolute end or the final beginning, or whatever. I sat on that tranquil threshold with Granny, only she was prepared quite naturally to cross it, and I knew I would have to gradually return to the world of the living. But as long as we were in that space together my mind remained untroubled by the passage of time, the beckoning of fortune, or the predation of fate. I was able to sit with her on that serene stoup and see the world through older eyes.

I came to understand many important things during that month with Granny, but one of the most valuable lessons had been inching toward my consciousness for the preceding twenty-eight years. That is: A person can say things like, "You're going to hell for living together before marriage," or "Leaving that wet wash cloth on top of that dry towel is not just disgusting, it's immoral," and still love you so much that she writes your name on a slip of paper and carefully balances it on the glass of prune juice she pours for you each morning before you wake.

Keats

Daniel's mom Barbara, who is spending the holidays with family in Phoenix, has driven to Tucson to spend the day with us. When she arrives, Barbara and I head to a nearby coffee shop where we talk of family, mutual friends, and our travels. And, though I much desire to leave this sad eventuality in the less hurtful realm of theory, I make the decision to speak with Barbara about my plans for burying Daniel's ashes in the woods of the Northeast. Almost two years have passed since his death and I've made no mention of my plans for his ashes. And on the subject of the burial of her son, Barbara has never pressed me.

Getting to the subject takes more energy than I had expected. We talk of many things before my mouth will speak the words I've been meaning to say all morning. Once the first words have reached the air, they coax their followers behind them until sentences float in the space between us. I search her eyes for a sign, some relief from my need to know how she will feel about this. I promised Daniel I would take his ashes to a quiet place under a strong tree. I meant to do that, the quietest place with the strongest tree. But the place I've found is far from Buffalo and I need to know that this will not hurt Barbara more than she has already been hurt.

"I think it's a wonderful plan and I want whatever Daniel wanted," is Barbara's response. I feel the strain in her voice, though it is subdued by her great determination to accept the unacceptable. *A wonderful plan to bury her beautiful twenty-eight-year-old son's cremated remains.* The grieving grip what they can of a life that has slipped through their bewildered grasp. When nothing is left, a quiet place to think of what once was means more than one could ever have expected it would.

Later in the day, when Barbara has returned to Phoenix, sadness sidles up to me. With no nature to distract and a warm bed at the ready, sleep has been creeping back into my brain and occupying the regrettably voluminous space of undeniable desire. Beginning with my travels to India while in college—where I first digested a true sense of the injustice and iniquity of this age of first, second, and third world countries—sleep settled into my blood and fused itself to molecules of would-be motivation. I crave the smell of my pillow like an alcoholic does the tinkling of ice in a highball glass or a sex addict the touch of bare skin. I'd like to believe I'm a reformed sleeper. Before I met Daniel, twelve hours of closed eyes a day was not unusual, and for that twelve hours to lengthen into fourteen or sixteen was not unheard of. I think my record was seventeen.

Daniel urged me out of bed in the mornings, sometimes exasperatedly. He coaxed me from the couch at night, not always successfully. Since he died, I have struggled to remain awake, to honor the life that was torn from him. But I waver at times, times when finding reason to rise evades me, times when the face of reality withers into a hideousness I cannot countenance.

Sleep is my alcohol, my heroine, my intermittent death. I'm not the only one. John Keats wrote odes to sleep.

> *Then save me, or the passéd day will shine*
> *Upon my pillow, breeding many woes;*
> *Save me from curious conscience, that still hoards*
> *Its strength for darkness, burrowing like the mole;*
> *Turn the key deftly in the oiléd wards,*
> *And seal the hushéd casket of my soul.*

37

Agua Caliente County Park is a rare, spring-fed desert oasis adorned with lush ponds and noisy with birds—coots, mallards, ring-necked ducks, herons, thrashers, wrens, and kingfishers, to name a few. While walking the shaded grounds of the park this morning, I recall the first time Mom took Daniel and me to Agua Caliente, six years earlier. The Tucson summer heat had both of us refusing to go outside, and grating on Mom's nerves because we were omnipresent inside. To get us out of the house, Mom said she would take us to an oasis of wetlands nearby. In response, the eternal thirteen-year-old in me reminded her snottily, "Water around here dries up in the summer, remember?" Then, I bet her a million dollars that such a place did not exist in the 115-degree heat of the summer. In any case, we all got in the car and drove to Agua Caliente.

I had to ask Mom if I could owe her the million. As we walked around the oasis the scorching heat lifted from body and mind and Daniel and I talked about how we could get married there, on one of the bird-ruled islands in the quiet ponds.

As that time comes back to me this morning, I contemplate the jarring reality—for me to have lived another life, now gone except for in my memories; and then to be living this one, so permanently and fundamentally altered. I feel fortune for the memories and confusion for the incongruence. I inhabit now a universe forged not over thousands of millions of years, but in one instantaneous implosion, which though witnessed by my eyes, makes no sense. Lands that only yesterday were whole and connected, are now broken into distant islands. Seas have merged with incomprehensible oceans; the surface where my feet once stood firmly has become a swallowing liquid and I have yet to evolve the capacity to breathe in this sudden sea. So I continue to hold my breath, as I try to decipher which world could be real, the former whole or the present scattering of lands. Eventually I must accept that no matter how irreconcilable, both the now and the then, the moment and the memory, the land and sea are real—real products of time's unstoppable drift.

Hummingbird

Today I await another impending shift rumbling in the voracious belly of fate.

Yesterday morning Mom and I took Bill to the airport for him to catch a flight to visit his family for the Christmas holiday. It was a strange goodbye; we have spent nearly every moment together for the past five months. But a little break is likely a good thing. I know he needs some time to think, and perhaps he will be ready to talk with me when he gets back.

After leaving the airport, Mom and I stopped back home to see if Granny wanted to join us for brunch at a nearby diner.

"Granny, you up for some greazzzy eggs and hashbrowns?"

"No honey, I took some nitro and now I need to rest a while."

She has had nitroglycerin on hand for years due to a heart condition. I didn't think she took it often, but the offhand way she mentioned it put me at ease.

"We will make breakfast here then," I said.

"No, you guys go ahead and go out. I'm fine."

If time was merciful, our decision to heed Granny's assurances could be revisited. But life knows no such mercies.

We got in Mom's car and drove a few blocks to Don's (the "o" is a fried egg and the "n" is three strips of bacon), a little diner in a Tucson strip mall. After a short meal we returned to Mom's house to find that Granny was missing. We looked all over for her, growing increasingly alarmed as each moment passed and she was not found. Every corner I turned, I feared that she would be there, lying on the floor. She was not in the house or yard but her car was in the garage. Mom called the Medic-Alert to find out if they had come for Granny. They said no.

"Mom," I called out when she hung up the phone. "Granny's chair has been moved."

"The lamp is crooked too," she said. It was then that I noticed the empty medical vials on the table. We knew the ambulance had come and an emergency medical team had been in the house. Mom called 911. The operator said Granny had been taken to Tucson Heart Hospital.

We got back into Mom's car and quietly sped to the hospital. I had this expectation that we would find her in the waiting room there, ready to come back home. As old and sick with diabetes and heart disease and arthritis as she is, she has always seemed invincible to me.

Instead we waited for an hour and by the time we were allowed to see Granny, she was not breathing on her own.

Now, as I stand beside her bed in the emergency room, a thick ventilator tube snakes its way down her throat. Every time she wakes her eyes fill with panic as she begins to gag on the obtrusive tube. She tries to get her hand on the caustic snake, to yank it out. The nurse tells us to hold Granny's hands and try to assure her everything is okay, as the increased sedative works at putting her back to sleep.

As I watch her sleep, her face wrenching with the periodic sensation of the tube, I try to calm the panic in myself. I feel the pain and acid in my stomach that would simmer as I watched Daniel suffering the tubes and needles of modern medicine. I want to get her out of the hospital, for them to take that tube out, and for us to walk her out of those suffocating white walls and away from all those miraculous machines. But her doctor says, because the tube is already in place, we should wait and see if Granny has a chance to live through this. And if she lives, whether she will have any of the faculties of her former self.

Sitting in the hospital lounge, I recall a story Bill had told me of a recent experience he had with Granny. It seems he had walked out into the dining room to find her standing at the sliding glass door that leads to the back porch. She turned her head and saw him, then turned back to the outside where rain was falling softly on the grass she and Maggie had been dutifully tending for the past week.[62] And she said, "Glorious rain! I'd like to go take a walk in it!"

Bill thought of her arthritic hands, insulin shots, heart medicines, hearing aids, back pains, and fatigue. But it was like none of that existed while Granny's eyes danced in the rain.

We heed the doctor's advice and Granny stays in the hospital. Several days after her admission doctors remove the ventilator tube and Granny begins to breathe on her own. We spend the Christmas holidays in the hospital—hoping Granny's strength will return to her.

---

[62]Maggie's role was to run a loop around the yard to scatter the doves off the grass seed when Granny would command, "Get the birds!" Maggie was very good at her job and was rewarded with bacon from Granny's breakfast plate.

One evening, about a week after Granny's attack, Mom and I are sitting in the hospital waiting room talking, and Mom relays something Granny said about me earlier that day. "Krista is so good. She's had lots of practice." I know she meant that I feel comfortable being near her as she is afraid and hurting, because of my life with Daniel. Her words offer an evaluation of all I have been through, and in her eyes, I passed, and she approves. It's a judgment I never expected to hear from her. And at that moment, all of the things about me that Granny has throughout my life thought needed changing—from not wearing dresses, to being a slob, to "living in sin," to losing my faith in her religion—and all my disbelief that someone her age could understand me or teach me anything, fall to nothing.

My gratefulness for this time and resolution with Granny feels anachronistic in the culture I live in. Suddenly I am aware of one, very potent motivation for modern society's disenfranchisement and marginalization of old people. Coming to understand my love for and connection to Granny is an exercise in pain. She is eighty-seven. Even if she lives through this, she will die in a foreseeable future. I have come to accept pain as the emotional shadow of love; without shadow, light would have no dimension. But I have felt the pull of commercial culture—the desire to be the happy, young, beautiful people with the Coke or McDonald's burger, or heck, both! Then I'll be twice as happy, beautiful, and young. It's hard not to want to be those pretty commercial people with the painless soda pop lives, but the tendency toward instant gratification, avoidance of pain, and pursuit of personal comfort is incompatible with a valuing of elderly people. The reality is, if you love and respect an older person, you are welcoming pain and death and loss into your life.

Still, the desire to avoid pain is understandable. It is so draining and I feel so tired of it. So tired I nod off in the waiting room for I don't know how long. I wake to Mom shaking my arm.

"Krista, the doctor wants to talk to us." By us, she means the two of us and my brothers and sister-in-law, who have flown in over the past few days.

We go to Granny's room to find her sitting up. The ventilator has been out for several days but she is still unable to talk in anything but a whisper due to the abrasion of the tube on her throat. She is weak, but seems her old self more or less.

The doctor tells Granny she needs to get nutrition and hydration, probably through a tube or central line in her neck and then will need months in a care facility to get back to walking or going home.

Granny shakes her head slowly but resolutely.

Or, he says, we can take Granny home and help her be comfortable for the next few days.

"Do you want to get better?" my mom asks Granny.

Granny shakes her head no.

Mom's voice crackles the alternative, "Do you want to come home?"

Granny shakes her head again. "No."

"I don't understand. . ." Mom says.

"You have to let me go," she whispers.

"Of course we will," we all assure her. "But can we take you home?"

"I'm too tired . . . I'm too tired." She looks at us for a while with exhausted eyes. "You have all been so good to me. I don't want to be a burden."

We protest, but she won't believe us.

"I love you all. Goodbye," she says and closes her eyes. We each look from her to each other. Granny doesn't move or speak and we are unsure what it means, unsure what we should do. We wait and watch for movement on her chest. The room is utterly silent. Then suddenly, she opens her eyes and says, "My butt hurts."

With that opening, we urge her to consider coming home.

"You could be in your own bed and watch Maggie chase the birds in the backyard," Mom says.

"Maggie, Maggie . . ." she repeats softly, and falls to sleep.

As she sleeps we make plans for her to return to Mom's house.

Strange that such news can make me happy, but it does. I knew she did not want to die in the hospital, but I did not know if she would allow herself to come home. A lifetime of taking care of her family makes submitting to the care of others a foreign concept.

A few hours later an ambulance deposits Granny in her bed at home, which we have moved closer to the window near her hummingbird feeder.

I sit on the floor beside her bed, listening to Granny's oxygen tank humming and sighing. I feel I've stepped back in time two years. The scene is set the same, with all the familiar props: Ativan, morphine, alternating pressure pad. Only the caustic queasiness in my heart is not there. Granny is ready to die and I am helping her. Daniel was not and I was desperately, desperately helpless.

Granny reaches a hand out from her hospice bed. I take it and she says, "It's . . . cold . . . on the floor." And a few minutes later, "I'm afraid you'll catch cold."

Though Granny's eyes seem to be focused on some faraway beacon, her attention remains on her family and is still captured by the beauty of this world. A hummingbird visits the feeder outside her window and she reaches her hand out toward it.

"Hummingbird," she says.

It is her last word.

All my family is in the room when Granny breathes her last; my aunt and uncle have come and even Bill has returned in time to say goodbye. When she is gone I lie my head down and weep, still holding Granny's hand, still resting a palm on her soft white curls.

38

Sirius shines down on Earth with unwavering loyalty. But for seventy days of every year it slips behind the aurora of our sun, making the Dog Star all but invisible.

Sirius's return, when the star first becomes visible on the eastern horizon before the glare of the rising of the sun, is known as the "heliacal rising" of Sirius. In ancient Egypt, this celestial event occurred just before the yearly flooding of the Nile, which wrought death, disease, and violent disruption but also new life in waters laden with rich river silt, the foundation of all life in the Fertile Crescent.

Sirius's arrival, with its portent of pain and plenty, became the cornerstone of the Egyptian calendar. And the Dog Star became a demigod. Every year, Isis, Osiris, and their son Horus, were believed to embark as a trinity on a seventy-day odyssey, following the path of Sirius through the underworld, until they all returned in a scorching season to usher in the raging floods of renewal, in the dog days of summer.

39

The days pass into weeks and Maggie continues to guard Granny's lawn. She runs a tight, tireless circuit in the small yard to scatter the birds whenever they collect on Granny's grass. I occupy myself with a more sedentary task, supervising Maggie's work from the glider in Granny's rose garden. Though I slept for nearly eleven hours last night, I lack the strength to make much more of this day.

I feel no motivation to move and in fact am inclined to lie down right here on the glider and go back to sleep. The dryer vent is humming in vibration through the wall; the sun shining warm on my hair is lulling my eyes closed. The only problem is the tireless birds, discussing their work and plans just to shame me.

"Twitter, twitter, tweet tweet, song, song, sing, sing; look at that lazy ass over on the swing. We'll gather our seeds, we'll clean our wings, while she snores and dreams and farts and swings."

That is what they are saying about me.

What I say back to them is: *You with your light feathers and hollow bones and peanut brains, try having a frontal lobe weighing you down!*

Birds don't use drugs. Birds don't have religion. Birds don't oversleep or overeat or oversing or binge and purge. They also don't have dark consciousness casting a pall over everything they do. Lucky little fuckers.

Oh well, I'm sleepy . . .

Just as I am nigh on a dream, Bill appears. He kneels down in front of the swing, puts his hand on my arm, and says softly, "It's time to go."

I sigh and gaze up at him silently for a while. I know he is right—we need to move onward. Bill has been very patient with me as I process losing Granny and forestall our already belated departure from Tucson. So I nod and make no protest.

40

In the morning, we pack all of our junk back in the car, set Maggie in the back seat, and choke out a hard goodbye to Mom before pointing the Saturn north toward Utah.

A few hours into the drive, Arizona's Lake Powell appears, capped by clouds hanging in a taffeta mist that wreaths the reservoir's sandstone spires. The lake beguiles, enchanted by the brooding drama of a winter storm. But the spell is broken by the image of a neighboring power plant ceaselessly belching billows of filth to mingle with the hoary clouds that blanket the sky. The power plant's intrusive presence reveals a truth about the scene that Powell's tranquil exterior belies—that drowned at the bottom of the lake is an ecosystem of unsurpassed beauty, a treasure trove of archeological sites, and the haunting memory of now-extinct fish and plants, all fatalities of humankind's manipulation of the natural world.

The construction of Glen Canyon Dam, completed in 1963, dumped five million cubic yards of concrete—enough to build a highway from Phoenix to Chicago—atop the Colorado River. The dam's blockage of the Colorado drowned the landscape from Page, Arizona, to nearly two hundred miles upstream in Utah. All for the insatiable need for electricity and the control of water resources to feed human populations that far exceed the capacity of this fragile desert ecosystem.

The dreamy reflections of red rock on the caged waters of the Colorado can almost make one forget who and what once breathed in the halls of Glen Canyon. But I see the grimy haze above the power plant and hear echoes from the past rumbling through the unseen canyon. A single word reverberates: failure. David Brower, executive director of the Sierra Club in the 1950s and founder of several of the world's most influential environmental organizations, considered Glen Canyon Dam to be his greatest failure. Brower and the Sierra Club fought a hard battle to save Dinosaur National Monument in Utah from the damming of the Green River and when they won it was considered one of the environmental movement's greatest victories. But the price was compromise—the price was Glen Canyon. And Brower did not realize until it was too late that the irreversible loss of the canyon, the lives of countless wild species all killed in a single violent moment, should never have been negotiable.

It wasn't the first lamentable compromise for the conservation movement and it wouldn't be the last, but Brower mourned the sacrifice of Glen Canyon all his life. He also used the experience to galvanize the environmental movement for other battles, including a Department of the Interior plan to build a series of dams that would flood parts of the Grand Canyon. During the process, an Interior Department official stated that the reservoirs created by dams would enable people to see the walls of the Grand Canyon better from boats. In response to this, the Sierra Club bought full page ads in the *New York Times* that read: "Should we also flood the Sistine Chapel, so tourists can get nearer the ceiling?" After that, opposition overwhelmed the department and the projects were scrapped.

And Lake Powell remains a powerful symbol of the sharp line between failure and compromise.

Old Man in the Meadow

As darkness approaches, we hastily enter Canyonlands National Park. Much too hastily, for in Canyonlands we arrive at a troublesome, recurring question. That is: How many times can two people run out of gas in one year? Counting the three times before we started this trip, the answer would be five.

We knew we were going to be short on gas as we turned onto Highway 211 toward the park. Not only did we fail to refuel, but Bill drove the tank down to near-empty (until the gas light came on) on a dirt road pursuing "the needles." He had seen a photo of it and was determined to get there. I was not, so Maggie and I waited for the sunset by a pool of water while Bill drove around and sealed our fate. He was so focused on his destination that he didn't even notice the gas gauge going down, and down further, until he picked me up and we started to drive out of the park.

"How long has that been on?" I ask Bill, seeing the gaslight.

"Um, not sure exactly," he replies, sheepishly, but not sheepishly enough given the situation.

"What are we going to do? There's no gas station for eighty miles," I say.

"Yeah, I think we need to turn around and go to the visitor center and call AAA."

When we get to the visitor center Bill gets out and uses the pay phone to call for help. He returns and we sit in the car quietly for about ten minutes.

I say, "So, what is this, the fifth time we've run out of gas?"

"This doesn't count because we didn't actually run *out* of gas."

I look at him skeptically.

"We still have gas in the tank," he explains.

There's a part of me that wonders if he really believes there is a distinction here, but I'm sure that silence is a more peaceful path to follow for the interminable wait that lies ahead of us. So I suck my lips tightly into my face to prevent further discourse.

AAA arrives an hour and a half later and gives us enough gas to get to the nearest town. From there we drive back to Canyonlands and find a place to park for the remainder of the night.

When the sun has rounded the world and again approaches the swath of Utah on which we find ourselves, Bill and I wake in the sleepy station wagon and head to Mesa Arch. The arch sits on the edge of a sheer cliff with a couple thousand feet of nothingness on the other side. The precariousness of this perch has me feeling the earth could fall away from under my feet at any moment. In response to this sensation, part of me bellows, "What a way to go!" while another part of me wants to cower to the ground and whimper. Neither part wins out so I stand rather still on the cold plateau staring through a slit in a mounded eye of rock until the sun appears through the opening in a blast of blinding color.

After sunrise and a few short hours of exploration, I press Bill to get on the road to Meadow, Utah, where I have heard there is a hot spring waiting to envelop my ass. We argue about this for a while, because going to the hot spring means postponing or foregoing a trip to Capital Reef National Park and Bill is not keen on this idea. Eventually though, Bill gives in.[63]

Just south of Meadow, a four-mile stretch of dirt road ends in a cow pasture in a valley ringed by mountains. We arrive at the muddy lot with a mess

[63]He wisely recalls my stint as a snarling cur in the Gila hot springs episode.

of broken down barbed wire fence around it and happily find only one other vehicle in the parking area. Bill waves to the person in the white minivan as I park the car.

I put my shoes on in the driver's seat while Bill gets out of the car and pulls some towels out of the roof storage. I hear the white minivan's door open, then close, and hear an older, disembodied male voice address Bill.

"You going to the hot springs?" he inquires of Bill.

"Yes," Bill responds. I believe I hear an odd squeak in his voice. Then, as I bend down to tie my laces, I catch sight of the man attached to the voice. At first I just see a pair of bare legs, but gradually I take it all in: I see legs and more legs and far past any conceivable spot where pants ought to have been, I see a bare little wrinkly-old-man penis.

"I put a log out there so you can walk across the water that puddles in the field. But you have to jump to it," the voice that belongs to the penis says in a slow western drawl.

"O . . . kay, thanks," comes Bill's response as he walks around to my side of the car.

"You ready?" he asks me, sounding overly casual.

I step out of the car, close it up, then, out of politeness and/or curiosity, feel compelled to turn and greet the person on the other side of the car. I gaze upon a man who could be ninety, and then again, he could be 117. What I know is that he is old. If wrinkles worked like tree rings, he could be dated back to the Pre-Cambrian period. *All* of him has clearly spent a lot of time in the sun as he wears an alligator-hide tan right down to his foreskin.

"How're you," he says, in a gruff old voice.

"Good thanks. Great day," I respond, noting the cigarette that droops from the corner of his mouth like a withered, non-functional appendage, and flops about as he speaks. The cigarette seems to have no purpose hanging there; he doesn't take one puff that I see. It's as if the cigarette has merged with his face and the only way to remove it would be a surgical procedure he can't be bothered with. So it just hangs on for the ride. Wheeee!

"Ye-ah," he agrees. "Good day for a soak." The cigarette bobs and dangles, bobs and dangles.

"Welp! See you later," I say, waving to the naked old man in the parking lot, as Bill and I walk off to the barbed wire fence that borders the meadow.

Thoughtfully, someone has hung a dingy old pink carpet remnant on the fence for safety's sake and we both grab onto it and climb over and step into a broad field of long golden grasses protected by a ring of snow-capped blue peaks, the winter sky above them a cloudless royal velvet.

The "trail" to the hot springs spans about a hundred yards and consists of a soupy gray clay and patches of grass that cows have trampled, blending in their pies here and there. We slog through the cow slop, crossing several icy streams, which are painful to wade, but the pool we find at the end of the line is well worth it, as it appears to have been dug up in Hawaii and replanted in this high valley of Utah. Unlike the other hot springs we have been to, it does not lie near a river but consists rather of a clear deep pool, fed by an unseen spring. The walls and bottom of the pool, which look to be very deep, are moss-covered volcanic rock, except in patches where white sand reflects the sunlight and sky in aqua blue.

Bill and I take off our clothes and ease in, the nudity policy having been well illustrated in the parking lot. I enter the water with a degree of pleasure and indulgence that would make a Puritan weep. This is *it*. If there is a spot on the earth that screams, "There is a GOD, and that GOD is GOOD!" this is it. I cannot feel my bones aching or my muscles spasm or really feel my body at all aside from a warm sensation that fills my brain. I have melted into the paradisiacal landscape that surrounds us. Except for the mildly creepy vibe coming from the naked parking lot attendant, this place suggests perfection is not an empty concept.

I grab on to a rope that spans the width of the pool and lounge. When I glance over at Bill, I bust out laughing at the distortions light and water have made of his body. His head is normal but it appears his shoulders and upper arms are no more than an inch thick. His waist and chest are wide enough but only appear to be about ten inches long. His hips look like they've been run over by a steamroller. He points and laughs at me as well, hopefully having something to do with the water illusion. We are busy laughing at each other when Bill notices our friend walking through the field towards us, clothed in nothing more than tennis shoes, tube socks, and the Naugahyde he was born in. The brief flawless moment has passed.

He lowers his knotty self into the pool, shifting his gaze slowly from Bill to me and back again, and puffs on his lip appendage.

Lacking another approach to his arrival, we strike up a conversation.

"Have you been here before?" Bill asks.

"Oh, I been here thirty times or more," the old man says. "It's privately owned, you know."

We didn't.

He continues after a brief silence. "Once I was asked to leave. The owner mentioned something about the liability risk of the pool."

I doubt that was the reason.

"But I didn't leave."

I don't doubt that.

Our acquaintance lives in Idaho, we learn, but he has been to this hot springs enough to know the recent history of it, including who owns it and which girl drowned in one of its pools, which guy dove down and came up with an ear gushing blood, and the depth of the pool (thirty-seven feet according to a few guys who were diving there a while back).

"Schools 'round here bring girls and boys out to the pool on field trips," he tells us. And, though he doesn't think to mention it, I'm sure he's greeted them naked in the parking lot.

"One day I was here, four gals came out, soaked in the pool a while, then they got out and lay right down in the mud and cowshit."

He muses thoughtfully on this mental image for a few moments, then takes a slight draw on his cigarette, which is little more than a butt at this point. "They rubbed it all over their whole bodies, everywhere, even their boobs and their snatch!"

More pause for mental images. We're all onboard that train now.

"Then they all jumped in the water to wash it off."

He looks at Bill and chuckles."It stank!"

Bill's face contorts indecisively, uncertain whether he should wear the expected hearty-har-har smirk or a more natural did-he-just-say-what-I-think-he-said grimace.

The resulting facial confusion goes unnoticed by the old man, who is now climbing out of the pool. He squats immodestly at the edge while he replaces and lights his appendage, then he takes one long pull on the freshie and flicks the ash in the pool.

We need to leave anyway, but that helps us make up our minds as to when; so we climb out of the pool and prepare to walk back to the car.

"Nice chatting with you," Bill says by way of goodbye.

"What, you're leaving?"

We nod. He grabs his tube socks and quickly pulls them up to his knees. We dry off and start putting our clothes on.

Incredulous, he says, "You're not going to put your clothes on are you?"

"Ye-ah . . . I'm kind of cold," I say.[64]

Bill, for some inexplicable reason, stops putting his clothes back on and walks naked with our guide, whose bare ass and spindly old legs stride about ten feet ahead of us all the way back to the parking lot.

[64]Plus my snatch is feeling a little overexposed.

41

Somewhere west of Las Vegas, we stop at an interstate rest stop for the night. I fall quickly into sleep and dream about Granny, only in the dream she is still alive, alive and dying. She is anxiously trying to get her Christmas cards out before she dies and asks me to help her gather the stamps and envelopes and do the mailing. I do as she requests, as quickly as I can, but at one point I stop and lean against a table and begin to cry, angry tears flowing furiously from pent up sadness and exhaustion.

I have read that almost all imagery in dreams comes from scenes in our waking lives but is jumbled by the subconscious. Generally I cannot match dream visions with their origins in life, but for this particular dream I immediately pinpoint the exact date and time of its genesis: March 24, 2000, at 1:30 p.m.

42

The Big Bang Theory in a very simplistic nutshell, can be described thus: In the beginning there was nothing, nothing at all. No space, no matter, no gravity, no time. There was nothing. And then a dimensionless trove of creative energy exploded.

Sure. It sounds almost as implausible as a grandpa in the sky pointing things into existence. But, as is necessary for scientific theory, there is actual physical proof of the Big Bang—so much proof that some scientists spend their entire careers interpreting this evidence and charting out, in fractions of seconds, what happened in the moments that followed the explosion.

Okay, "explosion" is a pathetic and misleading term for this event, because what happened in the milliseconds and seconds and minutes following the Bang is something incomprehensibly enormous.

Within a minute: space, gravity, and other forces are created. From nothing, *nothing*, the universe grows to a million billion miles across; the elements helium and hydrogen are created.

Within another two minutes, 98 percent of all the existing matter in the universe is created. During this minuscule spec of time, raw materials and physical laws were set in motion that would, over the next fourteen billion years, evolve into the world we know today. And that exact moment of explosive violence—when the singularity of nothing but creative potential pulsed into a universe so complex that after thousands of years of human study we still cannot comprehend it—that moment is known as T=0. Time equals zero. The beginning point.

One final wrinkle . . . some cosmologists believe it is possible that T=0 is not necessarily one singular point in time but the latest in a series of universal beginnings that stretch back far beyond fourteen billion years, to infinity.

43

The universe ended March 24, 2000. All energy, matter, mass, the laws of nature and time itself were compressed into a black hole, quietly and without comment or pause from the billions of beings who mill about on this tireless spinning sphere. Many had predicted the millennial Armageddon, but curiously enough, when it happened, only a handful of people even noticed.

In that final moment, I sat on the edge of a hospice bed in a small room, in a small condo in northwest Washington, DC. At 2:21 p.m., the earth heaved and the sky shook and the beloved hand I held in mine turned to a cool, smooth, precious stone.

Daniel was twenty-eight years old. The universe, fourteen billion. But young and old died that day, and I was set adrift.

March 24, 1:30 p.m.

Because I was twenty-eight years old, I think I can be forgiven for not understanding what was happening shortly after noon on March 24. But I was also admittedly prone to denial. By early March, Daniel was barely eating. I cooked every food I could think of to entice him, but he had no interest. And he no longer wanted to come to the park with me as he had throughout the previous year, even when his mom and I had to carry him down the stairs in a wheelchair. I still asked, about food, about going outside, I continued looking for hopeful signs that he still had interest in this world. But he sometimes grew agitated with me. He tired of my resistance to a reality that he expended all his waning energy trying to accept. So I stopped asking.

But there was still a part of me that believed he would live, a part of me that could not believe otherwise, no matter what.

In the days leading up to March 24, Daniel had been having episodes where he would fight for breath momentarily, his face tightening. I would give him a dose of morphine and the fight would subside. But that afternoon, for twenty minutes Daniel had been fighting for air and clutching at his chest as sweat poured down his face in torrents. Barbara, who had been with us for several weeks, had gone to the store for some medical supplies, so I was alone with Daniel and my confusion.

I had given him a dose of morphine but it didn't seem to have any effect and I feared that any more would be fatal. He had never become so agitated, so distressed and panicked. I tried to calm him any way that I could, mostly by wiping the sweat from his forehead before it could reach his eyes wide with fear. I continued to pull cloth after cloth from a pile I kept by his bed, and one after another they became soaked and cold and useless. I only had one left. And the sweat continued to pour.

Up until that point, throughout his year of treatment, I had believed my presence by his side helped in some small way. I had to believe. But at that moment, in our bedroom that had become transformed by medical machinery that hummed with a satisfied purposefulness, all at once my uselessness in the face of his suffering struck me violently across the face. I reeled from the blow and doubled over, leaned my head against his bed, and sobbed.

My breakdown only lasted a few minutes, maybe less; he needed me and I choked my despair down enough that it could not unravel me completely. But my mind holds that moment as a singular experience in my adult life. It was a moment that harkened back to an earlier time, before I could walk or talk or take any initiative for my own well being. It was as if right then I recognized finally that Daniel was dying and I became an infant sitting alone and naked in the middle of a cold floor, hungry and scared, and unable to do anything about it but cry. He was leaving and all I could do was scream in the hope that someone would come and pick me up off the floor.

Crying is the first noise we make—the only form of communication we are most certainly born with. And it means only this: make it stop. Make the pain stop. Make the confusion stop. Somebody please, please make it stop.

That day with Daniel, nobody came, and it didn't stop.

After a half hour of panicked gasps for breath, Daniel's breathing slowed. I sat on the bed with him holding his hand, leaning in close to his ear and whispering words I hoped would calm him. How much I loved him, how lucky I felt to have spent the past four years with him. For a moment I looked into his face and his eyes recognized me as they had not seemed to in more than a day. I told him I was going to the kitchen to get more morphine, but he tightened his grip slightly on my hand and for some reason I knew not to let go. He breathed one or two more breaths, and then no more.

He was gone. And in an instant the matter of my life became compressed into an infinitely dark and distant singularity.

44

It is possible that T=0 is not a single moment in all of time, but a point in the cycle of time. I have heard[65] the pattern of the universe described as cycles of expansion and contraction, as a great pair of lungs that expand for billions of years and then contract for billions of years. And at the moment just before the explosion of matter and space and time, just before inhalation and expansion, time equals zero.

But it could also be said that T=0 lies at the end of exhalation, at the point where the energy and matter of the universe is most completely contracted into a dimensionless speck of utter nothingness holding the energy and creative potential of an entire universe.

In reality, they are the same moment and T=0 is both ending, and beginning.

---

[65]À la Bill Bryson.

45

After Daniel died, daily life consisted mainly of getting out of bed; getting to work; sorting through Daniel's clothes; stumbling through the eviscerating bureaucracy of death certification and estate settlement; driving with a friend to the funeral services office and standing with arms outstretched as a man in a dark suit handed me a small black container of significant weight and announced without human emotion: "The cremated remains of Daniel DiTondo."

This was no longer my world. I lived life as an observer, an apparition from a now non-existent universe. The things I did, it didn't seem to be me doing them. With one notable exception. My link to Bill tethered me to what had become a foreign place and at times our friendship helped me see that there could at some point in the future be a beginning.

46

The Joshua tree is a taciturn species. Except in times of windy upheaval, it says little, and never more than a whisper. Oak and willow, aspen and cottonwood rustle, sway, dance, and shimmer, they converse, give counsel, suggest. Joshua trees meditate, detached from all accompaniment, even the weather.

I look for a word, some solace from this dusty land, and either the trees are unwilling to utter, or I—with anger and resentment fomenting a fog in my mind—am unable to hear.

I had against all logic hoped this day would not come. But unavoidably I am faced with sunrise on a day I wish had never happened. It is as if, somehow, if March 24 did not come today, then all March 24s would cease to have any reality. And if there is no March 24, then I never felt the warmth of Daniel's hand drain in one unforgivable instant, I never watched the pink of his fingernails fade to blue, never felt the breath drain in slow pain from my own lungs as I realized what his hands were telling me.

Two years ago today I held Daniel's hand as he let go his hold on mine. Today I walk alone in the Mojave Desert of Joshua Tree National Park, hoping to find some peace and some piece of Daniel's spirit to help me make sense of the day and all that has passed in the two years since he left. Instead I find emptiness in myself and a landscape of indifference. I find words that want to be poetry, to gracefully encapsulate grief and render it a soft, harmless memory, but instead they fall angrily to the page in shards of sentences.

The time lost is a restless weight
Of bridled mirth and paths unturned
The pacing pith of soul's torment
That haunts the hours in search of one
A moment from a life unlived

A squandered light
A pulse undone.

I feel distant from my feelings and Daniel seems far away. I beg for a thunderstorm, for a fury of sobs, a release of rage; but I feel still air cementing a murky film over stagnant waters in my motionless mind. Why today?

Many times I cannot quiet my thoughts or still my torment. But now, at this moment, I cannot focus on Daniel. I can focus only on the chill of the wind and shadowy clouds that chased me into the tent. So I lay here, the stale tent air crowding in upon me. My only recourse is sleep and the chance that I might travel in dreams beyond this catatonia.

Merciful sleep does not come to me. I lay agitated and awake.

This morning had been a pleasant day of sunny calm, from the time Bill dropped me off at the trailhead, through my four-mile hike, until about an hour ago when the wind picked up with ferocity. Before that I had been out on a rock reading and observing a jackrabbit as it padded all around on the ground below me searching for scarce green growth to nibble. In my imagination the rabbit hopped upon my perch and sat with me until my loneliness subsided. In reality, the size of the rock on which I sat shielded me from the rabbit's notice, and when it had determined no food was to be found in the vicinity, it continued on its way, leaving me to shiver in the grim chill of the mounting wind, looking to the impassive Joshua tree for companionship.

During the night, a pitiless wind whips the tent unceasingly, bearing in on all sides with a suffocating pressure and ripping the stakes from the sandy ground. By morning, the only thing holding the bruising and bellicose tent to the earth is my insomniatic presence within it. I try to sleep between gusts, but every blast whips the nylon against my head and rattles the poles that hold it vaguely open. I give up. I step out of the tent, wrestle against the wind while I pack up, and hit the trail.

I hike a few miles from the restless camp to meet Bill and Maggie on a dirt road that crosses the trail. On the way, to escape my amorphous depression, I start talking to Daniel out loud.

"I miss you, sweets."

I hear no answer, just the sandy shuffling of my boots on the desert floor. It's okay. I'm talking for the sound of my own voice upon the air, an impotent but somehow satisfying rebellion against the silent void that enveloped us two years ago.

"I wish you were on this trip, painting all of the incredible sights we have come across."

Then I hear a rustling in a nearby bush and turn my head to see a creature bounding away from me, a desert mammal with spinnaker-sized ears. Was it a bobcat, or a coyote? A jackalope? I strain my eyes to locate it but it has melted into the desert landscape.

47

A warm rush of comfort washes over me when I find Bill and Maggie waiting at the trailhead. Uncharacteristically, Maggie has noticed my absence over the past day, and perhaps has even missed me. She stands on her hind legs and waves her arms at me. Bill stands regular but holds his arms out too.

"How was your day yesterday?" he asks as he envelops me with a hug.

"Hard to say," I answer. "Just hard."

"I have a great place to show you, it's incredible," he says. "Ready?"

"Sure."

We eat some lunch and set out on a walk among the odd plant life and lively rock formations that bubble from the desert floor in the park's Wilderness of Rocks.

And here the negative web that clung about me yesterday begins to lift and dissolve. I find that I can see better than I have for a very long time, maybe ever, and that I am walking in the perfect place to open my eyes wide. At first glance, giant sandstone skulls and heaps of melting butter-brickle ice cream solidified into stone seem the only inhabitants of this land. But life moves quietly here, as if it means to go unnoticed by the oppressive stare of the unblinking Mojave sun. Shrinking from a force beyond its reckoning, life waits, pasted low upon the desert floor, in the meager shadow cast by desert plants and under rocks, and in deep shadowy holes in the sandy ground; it waits for night and for the rare gift of a reviving rain, for respite from the omnipresent shriveling sun, for a moment to straighten tall, open arms, and breathe in the gentle time. Life is luxury when rain falls like liquid diamonds in the desert. Life's luxury, the livable-life, sets its own timetable and requires unending patience. Desert plants and animals, grown up here in this unlikely Eden, must learn to wait. And unlike humans, they bear the wait without complaint.

Take for example the creosote bush, known to wait a year or even two for a single drop of moisture. The plant, one of the most drought-tolerant in North

America, will shed its leaves when the sky gets stingy and moisture abandons. It will drop all the green that clothe and sustain, stand naked without comment or question. And if the rain still does not come, the plant will relinquish its branches, limb by lifeless limb, until to the eye it exists as only a bone-brittle shadow of death. The creosote stands bare, and barely there on the dust of the desert, bowing deeply towards death as slowly, impassively, clouds begin to form somewhere west of Eden. Salvation moves along on its own unhurried schedule, but eventually, the rain will fall and sacrifice will have saved the creosote, whose sweet scent floats on a rain-quenched desert like a cherry blossom petal on a pond. I have often inhaled this sigh of the desert, which speaks of survival, of unspeakable hardship, of lightning-crazed, stingy skies emptying long-hoarded rain; of birth, death, of birth again, of icy hands and pleading eyes, and a love that waits in crevasses and below our gaze on silent padded feet, beyond the bounds of comprehension for all but the briefest, most sublime moments in time.

When the desert rain descends, leaves alight on nascent limbs, preparing for the next long desirous drought. And for the creosote's perseverance in this hardhearted world, it receives life eternal. Almost. The bush has the ability to reproduce an exact genetic replica of itself, which grows from its base adding on to previous generations of the organism. The life of a creosote clone colony can span thousands of years. In fact, the world's oldest living thing is a creosote called King Clone living in Victorville, California. He's believed to be more than eleven thousand years old, older than human history, older than almost all of the many devices we have created to fabricate tenderness in this life that can so often withhold it. Conditioned air, humidifiers, dehumidifiers, lifted faces, pre-nuptial agreements, heated toilet seats, umbrellas. We as a species demand comfort. Alone among the earth's creatures, we do not adapt to the Earth's seasons of spare and plenty, heat and cold. We instead bend the Earth to our desire for comfort, because we are not satisfied with survival that requires sacrifice and only occasionally offers perfection in return. This uncompromising characteristic has allowed humans to thrive and multiply and dominate like no other species the earth has ever seen. It is also what keeps us so eternally discontented. We will stalk comfort to our mass grave while contentment and a battered earth observe, nearby, within easy reach, our paradise, not lost, but abandoned.

On the other hand, maybe we will learn. Progress takes time, but it does happen. Human beings were around for many thousands of years before we conceived the idea of written language and in the past ten thousand years, we have come so far. I see the potential for progress in myself. I have known luxury but until I knew drought, I had no ability to name it. I have, like the creosote, felt the distempered sun slice through my skin like a serrated scourge. I have wept for rain and shed my clothes and limbs when it did not come to cool me. And unlike the creosote, I have screamed at the injustice of this malicious measure that life poured upon me. I will very likely scream again and again, as some inescapable sense of entitlement provokes me.

But, as the resonance of my railing fades, I find the drought has honed my mind's ability to hear music dancing in memory. I see lavishness in laughter, opulence in what I once considered ordinary. The expectation of a lifetime winnows to a window, a moment. A glance of showering kindness. The embrace of understanding. A wag of a tail at the end of a hard trail.

It's enough. Enough to coax limbs alive, to cradle new leaves and create wonderment and wherewithal for what the future may bring.

I can at last see the creosote for all it is, admire its stoic persistence, and inhale its rain-induced sigh of relief. This simple plant, sage of the desert, ageless observer of ages, veteran of despair and plenty, conveys a cosmic message: comfort is not my due, and if I see things quite clearly, I, a foolish and fragile conglomeration of cells, am in no position to make demands.

But I can find some ease in the spare shade of the creosote.

48

At the apex of the Kelso Dunes, a vast expanse of desert stretches out to all horizons before rising into jagged peaks. On the far western horizon a round pink moon begins its descent beyond the mountains. But as one moon sets, another quite smaller moon rises unexpectedly. At the zenith, Bill and Maggie and I meet four college-age students who have slept in the parking lot and hiked the dune before dawn. As we set up our camera to take a photo of the rising sun, one of the youngsters approaches.

"You don't mind if we take off our clothes do you?"

"No," Bill says.

"Not if you don't," I add stupidly.

Maggie just silently snickers.

Really, this is a strange question to ask of perfect strangers, most especially because it is ass-clenching cold up here. I wear my fleece and windbreaker and I'm still shaking. I continue puzzling over the question until I notice one of the college students, the only woman, start to run butt naked down the dune and nose dive into the mountain of refrigerated sand. Following right behind her behind are her three male companions yelling with the abandon peculiar to college-aged naked sandsurfers at a 45-degree angle to the earth on a 45-degree Fahrenheit morning in Mojave National Preserve. We watch them belly flop into the sand and skid awkwardly down the incline, then tumble fifteen feet in a cloud of kicked-up Kelso before they regain their stance and run for another plunge into the dune.

"That can't feel good," Bill observes. And then, a neat-freak shiver running down his spine, he adds, "How *will* they get the sand out of their hair, and all their . . . crevices . . . and . . . crannies!"

"That'll take some time, I reckon," I say, feeling old and cranky compared to the bare-butted whippersnappers sliding down the dune below.

From the Kelso Dunes, we drive to an area of Mojave where lava once flowed and burned all that lived into a shiny black crust of nothingness. Since that time, plant and animal life have returned to the cinder cones area, but the landscape still bears the mark of that blistering river of fire. Lava tubes, left behind when the magma subsided and cooled, quickly capture our attention. The tubes are passageways through the obsidian earth, resulting from the cooling process of molten rock. They were formed over time, as the river of magma's surface cooled and hardened, while a tube of lava continued to flow beneath the hardened surface. Eventually the source of the underground molten-rock flow diminished and disappeared, leaving a tunnel of air where the lava had traveled.

Bill, Maggie, and I climb through a small hole in the earth where the ceiling of a lava tube collapsed. Though rubble nearly fills the opening, we scramble over chunks of hardened lava and into the dark tube where we are enveloped in the earth's subcutaneous silence. We shuffle along the passage, barely aided by a dim flashlight. The ground seems smooth and unobstructed but I still expect to trip over a boulder or fall into a bottomless pit. Ahead, another opening in the earth pours light into the tunnel from twenty to thirty feet above our heads, showering a diffuse spotlight upon the tunnel floor. While we stand in that circle of light, the clouds clear for a moment and the sun shines in warm contrast to the cool tunnel air.

Bill stoops to the ground and scoops some dust into his hand. He looks at me to make sure I'm watching, and then he tosses the dust into the beam. Magic. A million dust particles fall like a shower of golden stars.

Later that evening, on a dirt road near some cinder cones that long ago spouted fire upon this land, I lie in my warm sleeping bag in the folded-flat back end of the car. Bill sits perpendicular to me, also snuggled into his sleeping bag, reading chapter three of *The Fellowship of the Ring* aloud to me. The soft orange glow of the flashlight shines on Bill's face and extends in a circle of golden-orange light on the ceiling. I see the pages of the book reflected on the window behind him and Maggie dozing peacefully at my feet and I feel a deep contentment.

In the Valley of Death

Following a lavender moonset at dawn, we drive out of Mojave and north to Death Valley National Park, which is already in the throes of an anguishing, profanity-provoking March heatwave. What little decorum I can ever muster has withered in the 100-degree heat. This place is fucking hot.

The hottest place in North America, Death Valley has average summer temperatures that range from 110 to 114 degrees, the record high having reached 134. Average monthly rainfalls are measured in fractions of an inch and add up to only an inch or two per year. As with all harsh environments, the animals and plants that call this region home have developed adaptations other than whining in order to survive the blistering, buggering heat. To cope with the less-than-ungenerous provisions, plants develop roots that plunge into the earth as deep as ten times the height of a human being, or that spread in vast circles just beneath the ground.

In certain areas of the park, the land is utterly inhospitable to plants. At Badwater Point, salt flats deny the existence of life even as they exalt in their exquisite unwillingness to abide fruitfulness. At their lowest point, which also happens to be the lowest point in the United States, the elevation of the salt flats drops to 282 feet below sea level. An ancient saltwater sea once covered this land and when it gradually dried up, the salt lingered. Over the years, the interplay between hard but brief rains and the layer of surface salt has sculpted a patterned plain that boggles the mind.

As humans, we tend to glorify life and demonize its opposite. We use lovely words like "lush" and "fertile" and "verdant" to describe those areas where life dominates and ugly words like "sterile" and "desolate" and "bleak" to describe areas where life is subdued. The elevation of life above not-life was born at the foundation of language and lives in our anthropocentric perception. But at the salt flats, the splendor of the desolate is as self-evident as it is mesmerizing. A valley of white, surreally invariable flatness, wears an intricate textured pattern that spiders out in all directions. In reality the lines of this latticework are seams of salt that have accumulated at the edges of small, shallow, sporadic rain-puddles but they appear as brittle, alabaster veins woven upon a dry, pallid, endlessly flat face; the death mask of Death Valley.

And throughout the day and evening, the deathly wonder continues. Who could have known upon hearing the name—which conjures visions of massacres and mass starvations—what beauty in barren land resides. Who knew that the matter of the earth, unrelated, indifferent, and at times inhospitable to the world of breathing, bleeding creatures such as myself, could bare so much magnificence? I wonder if the revelation is one my mind can bear. That the static could be so dynamic—what does it mean about the stasis of dynamism?

Pestered by these weighty thoughts and the heat that closes in on the tent from all sides, I lay awake through much of the night, my mind swimming with the searing beauty of Death Valley. I also noodle over a nagging perturbation: what's with the name? I had always imagined "Death Valley" derived from some monumental event involving death, like an epic and tragic battle in which the good guys were slaughtered, or a mass starvation/dehydration of a noble people passing through the land in search of a better life or in flight from an evil foe. I figured sixty to one hundred at least must have perished here for the land to earn such a foreboding name. In reality, during the Gold Rush in the mid-1800s, a group wandered into the valley on their way west, and, though assuredly the passage was painful, most of the settlers survived. But the group named it Death Valley and the name stuck. Drama queens.

As sunrise approaches, I rouse a well-rested Bill and we drive to Zabriskie Point, where golden spikes of melting earth draw hordes of wide-eyed, panting photographers. After the sun has risen fully, and sweat again begins to surge, we ferret out some showers, which resuscitate our hygiene and spirits for a brief, comfortable while. A very brief while. Death Valley is one of those rare places where blue sky becomes oppressive. You plead for clouds to shade you from the sun, whose intensity is almost audible. But the only shadow here is a rain-shadow cast by the Panamint Mountain Range to the west, which blocks clouds and weather systems. And a rain-shadow is anything but cool.

Yea though I sit in the valley of the rain-shadow of death, I fear not. I possess a sustenance that will see me through this ordeal, provided by that all-powerful, leaf-clad bo-hunk, the Green Giant. For lunch, I spoon up my cold canned corn right out of the Green Giant tin and into my parched piehole. Refreshing! The only way I could have had a better Green Giant experience is if the can had been frozen and I had poured it into my pants.

49

In Sequoia National Park, the world's largest living thing resides. He is grander in scale than the blue whale and his name is General Sherman. This giant sequoia measures 275 feet tall with a base circumference of nearly 103 feet. If I had sixteen of me laid out horizontally, and each me clasped hands around the ankles of the next me, we could just barely wrap myself around the base of General Sherman. And if I could go back forty generations of my family, only then could I find someone who was alive when General Sherman sprouted, three thousand or so years ago.

Standing beneath this tree, I feel a crushing sense of awe, not just because of my puny stature, but also for my paltry understanding of the deep history of Earth, its creatures, the universe, and my tiny place in it. I also feel lucky. If it hadn't been for some very plucky conservationists, General Sherman might now be the frame of a house covered in vinyl siding in a smoggy Los Angeles suburb. Most of his sequoia kin are now little more than that, a reality that broke the hearts of people like John Muir, who witnessed it. When Muir was confronted with the clear-cutting of the giant sequoia he suggested with sad irony, "As well, sell the rain clouds and the snow and the rivers to be cut up and carried away, if that were possible." And if it were, we would.

As stewards of the land, we are a bumbling bunch. There are many with poor intentions toward the land, driven by greed. And there are the rest of us, with either no conscious intentions past our own lives or with the best of intentions, thwarted by insufficient knowledge of the complexities of nature.

Take fire for instance. Intuitively we understand fire to be synonymous with destruction. Because fire is death for us we have interpreted it to be so for trees, and so once we endeavored to save the sequoia, we began squelching fire. What we didn't know then was that sequoia trees need fire for their germination process. Even as it may kill some young and vulnerable trees, fire provides for the life of a whole new generation in the forest. What appears as destruction, a force that must be stopped, is actually the placenta of creation. Muir observed this dynamic in 1869 during his first summer in the Sierra Nevada:

Hot deserts bounded by snow-laden mountains—cinders and ashes scattered on glacier-polished pavements—frost and fire working together in the making of beauty . . . Reading the grand mountain manuscripts displayed through every vicissitude of heat and cold, calm and storm, upheaving volcanoes and down-grinding glaciers, we see that everything in Nature called destruction must be creation—a change from beauty to beauty.

This intense transition from *beauty to beauty* is the essence of the T=0 principle. The moment of ultimate violent upheaval can be the very self-same moment of the rebirth of creation; the fire that blackens the earth to brittle barren dust, may be the spark that ignites abundance in the growing season. We see this throughout nature, from the pine barrens of the Southeast to the grasslands of the Great Plains to the giant sequoia.

As for the sequoia, we now study where we went wrong and attempt to reverse our failures, but at the same time auto and industrial pollution travels from Los Angeles and obscures the sky above the Sierras in a brown-orange film that poisons the trees. The answer for the sequoia, as it is for all of nature burdened by human consumption, lies in thoughtfulness and restraint. But self-restraint is a hard sell. Like Spam it sits on the shelf until times of desperation. And with nature and the health of the earth, timelines are delayed and the moment of desperation occluded by belated consequences. We have already lost so much of what wild perfection there once was. Must we lose it all, starve ourselves entirely of our natural context, before we just go ahead and eat the damn Spam?

Who knows, if we try it, we may even like it.

On this journey, I find myself becoming increasingly agitated by the loss of nature in every corner of this country. I set out on the road to find magic in quiet places to cushion the hard edges of grief, and I have, beyond my wildest hopes. But I am also becoming acquainted with an entirely new source of grief as I come to understand the devastation we have wrought on the natural world. A loss that has been ongoing for more than a century has suddenly become personal for me. And at the ancient foot of General Sherman, I begin to understand why. Most people at some point in their lives look for a point of solace, a place where they can direct their questions, fears, desperation. I found that voice in the song of birds, the sound of leaves chattering in the wind, the heartbreaking vulnerability of a creosote bush standing baked and naked under the simmering desert sun. What does that voice say? I am not alone. I am a part of this symphony of life—a note in the infinite song of the natural world. I am really no more important than any other note. I am as important and crucial as any other note. I decide how my note will sound. And I am open-eyed, spellbound witness to the infinite other notes that exist in a time and space I am fortunate to be part of, whether I am a walking, living creature or a decaying collection of organic material or a scattering of minerals in the soil. I am a molecule in the eternal breath of the lungs of the universe, at the same time I am a universe all my own.

It is this second reality that has become problematic as our culture has embraced the very anti-ecological idea that the individual can be severed from, and is more important than, the system as a whole. As soon as we deny our essential connection to nature, we cease to have any motivation to preserve and protect it.

Finding the Future

In Yosemite National Park's Mariposa Grove of giant sequoias, pink fog feathers the sky above a sheltering grand canyon of trees. The great calm of the sky and the hush of the trees inspires tranquility in me. So while Bill goes for a hike, I sit in the car with Maggie and my journal.

My moment of peaceful introspection does not linger long. As I am writing, I hear some people walk behind the car and start talking about my current bumper sticker, "Be a patriot, conserve gas." I recently started a raggedy-assed bumper sticker campaign with homemade, hand-drawn signs pasted into the back window with scotch tape. It's pathetic, really.[66] But I feel so helpless as world events and fearful minds turn the sentiment of the country toward war in the Middle East, where access to oil is always a motivating factor. The easy short-term ego (and economic) boost of rallying the military machine has once

[66]Really pathetic.

again won out against long-term solutions of energy conservation, diplomacy, and global cooperation. So I am making bumper stickers as my measly protest.

At first I think the onlookers might be admiring my work. Then I hear sarcasm.

A young boy asks, "What does that mean?"

His dad replies, "That means they just drove their car from Michigan."

I get a little hot, but I stay quiet while they mill around a bit back there, mocking me. After they leave, I look to see what type of car they had driven, which is an SUV the size of an aircraft carrier. This gives me a mischievous idea. I pull out my sketch book and black marker and as fast as I can, while also monitoring the trail head nervously to see if they are coming back, I make a new bumper sticker: "SUVs Suck G-ass".[67] As I scribble my new slogan, my heart rate spikes and I snicker with nervous excitement, like some sort of humanoid creature that lives in a cave and has conversations with itself. "Yess, yess . . . this will show them, won't it, precious?"

When I finish, I run to the back, open the hatch, rip off the old bumper sticker, wipe the steam away from sleeping in the car last night, pull the soggy tape from the old bumper sticker, and slap it on the new one. The tape doesn't stick very well any more, but I press it down maniacally, willing it to hold just long enough for the man to see it. As I work fiendishly, I look back over my shoulder every second to see if my detractor is nigh. When I am reasonably satisfied my statement will stay put, I carefully shut the trunk, gather Maggie, and take a walk around the parking lot, keeping one eye glued to the trailhead where the man and his son disappeared.

As I am imagining the double-take the man will make if he glances at the back of our car again, I start laughing out loud. Maggie looks up at me, a trace of concern in her eyes.

What? I'm fine. What's the big deal?

The big deal is, I am not alone. I'm not sure how long she's been there, but during a sigh between chortling episodes, I notice a park ranger sitting in an SUV behind our car. She gets out of the truck and approaches our vehicle. I fear she wants to get a closer look at my bumper sticker and I cringe while she

---

[67]Bill came up with the idea a few days ago. At the time, I told him it was too confrontational.

inspects. I hadn't meant to offend her car, because rangers need high clearance vehicles to do their work. And I am sincerely hoping I don't get a chance to explain that distinction when she returns to her vehicle and drives over to where I am casually picking up Maggie's poo.

She rolls down her window as she approaches and says something I cannot hear. Certain I am in some sort of trouble, I open my eyes wide and suck on my bottom lip, hoping to look contrite, or dull-witted. When I do not respond she repeats herself.

"I just wanted to thank you for walking your dog with a leash," she says.

"Oh, okay," I respond.

"Remember dogs aren't allowed on trails," she continues.

"Yes, I remember."

"Did you spend the night in the parking lot?"

"No." Then I stammer that we had gotten there around sunrise. I sound very guilty of something.

"Where did you stay?" she asks.

I am really nervous then. We arrived in the park campground well after dark and couldn't find an empty campsite, so we hid in a dark corner of the full campground and slept in the front seats, without paying. Busted. I can't remember the name of the campground, so I stammer again: "Just up the road . . . the close one . . ."

"Do you mean a campground?"

"Yes."

She doesn't believe me. But after asking me about the other car in the parking lot, she leaves. I utter a sigh of relief as she drives away, then I saunter over toward our car and lurk behind a nearby tree. After about ten minutes I hear footsteps and then a pause near our car. I hold my breath, choke back some giggles, and wait to hear a response—a "What's that mean, Daddy?" and then a quick ushering of a young boy away from the car. But instead I hear a car door open and then a minute later, "Krista?"

I peek my head around the trunk of the tree to see Bill. What the?!

He sees me, and with a mixture of concern and amusement says, "What's going on?"

I quiver with excitement as I tell him what I've been up to.

"So . . . you're hiding behind a tree waiting for them to come off the trail?"

"Mmmmhmmm. Want to hide with me?"

"Okay."

As we crouch behind our tree, we chortle about crouching behind a tree. Then we start coming up with new ideas for the bumper sticker campaign. One is a modification of the anti-smoking campaign: "SUVs: a dirty, stinking, smelly, puking, filthy, rotten habit." Another uses the anti-drug slogan pushed by Nancy Regan: "SUVs: Just say NO." But I think the overall winner is: "Care about your country? Conserve."

When we finish tapping our brains for slogans, our friends still have not arrived and Bill begins to get restless. He lacks the patience for surveillance work.

"Want to go for a walk and see the trees?" he asks.

"Yeah," I say reluctantly. "But I don't want to miss them."

"I'd guess they could be a while." Bill coaxes me from behind the tree.

We walk into the grove of sequoia and my subterfuge is soon swallowed by the grandeur of the trees. My experience of these trees mimics my reaction to the Grand Canyon. The giants are unfathomable, containing the colossal stillness of a mountain, and yet they live and grow and breathe.

After we have been strolling for about twenty minutes and I have nearly forgotten my campaign, we see the man and his son approaching on the trail.

"Hi, how are you?" Bill says cordially.

"Hello," the man says back.

"Hello," the boy says.

I smile at them both as they pass and say my own "hello." I start to chuckle once they have moved further on. I am laughing mostly at myself but still I don't want them to hear for fear they will misinterpret my laugh as they did my bumper sticker.

Then I begin to doubt myself.

"Do you think I am a hypocrite?" I ask Bill.

"Yes." Bill says. "But not for the reason that man was suggesting."

"Thanks . . . We could have taken an SUV on this trip, but we didn't. We could drive forty thousand miles in the same time as an SUV drives twenty thousand, and still use less gas . . . right?"

"Right. But more importantly, we don't have a home or even sleep indoors most of the time," Bill says. "So we don't use energy for heat or air conditioning or lights or refrigeration. All those things use more energy than driving."

"Yeah," I say.

But I still feel uneasy. The point is not to put people on the defensive about what they are doing, but to forward the cause of conservation as the best, and probably the only, long-term solution we have for the energy, ecological, and political crises we face, well that and birth control. I didn't expect "Be a patriot, conserve" to raise the hackles of anyone. Though I'm pretty sure "SUVs suck G-ass" will. I doubt I can leave the antagonistic bumper sticker on the car.

As we are driving deeper into Yosemite, my anxiety over the morning fades and I recognize that something is happening to me, something important. Since losing Daniel I have been incapable of imagining a future in front of me and have had little desire to be a part of the present. Bill and Maggie have been a lifeline in time, but my overwhelming need has been to dissolve into the past. And now, after an intense moment in the Mariposa Grove parking lot that inspired a reversion to adolescence, I find I am once again connected to what happens to this world—if this morning's antics are any indication, I am perhaps passionately connected.

When I first catch sight of Yosemite Valley the thought comes closer into focus. From high above the valley floor, I realize, I remember this scene, though I have never before set eyes upon it. It is no déjà vu, but a tangible memory. At first I can't place the recollection, but then it crystalizes. Art. I am looking upon the archetype of paradise as seen through the minds of generations of romantic landscape painters and dealers in audacious velvet tapestries. I have seen the vision so many times but had never known that I was seeing Yosemite. In my memory, all of those paintings and photographs have the soft-focus of a dream, as if such a place could not exist aside from a mythology of a non-existent paradise.

Domes of gray granite shelter the valley above sheer cliffs streaked with ribbons of water falling toward a lush, fog-softened emerald valley. Though I can't see any at the moment, it seems to be a landscape where rainbows could be expected to appear at any time, whether or not it is raining. The sight brings grateful tears to my eyes.

In the morning, when I wake in Yosemite Valley, Bill hands me hot cocoa and a homemade birthday card for my thirty-first birthday. We eat breakfast in the now-quiet campground, then we set off into the morning mist. From there and throughout the day a dense caravan of beauty marches before my eyes. Of the sights I see on my birthday: deer walking tentatively toward me through a gauzy veil of fog hovering over the valley floor; the tallest waterfall in North America, water plunging against rock and leaping in spirit forms into the air; a robin tugging and stretching a worm from the soil and then gulping it down; a pair of ravens mating below the skeleton of a towering leafless tree; and mountainsides aflame with orange-gold poppies, redbud trees, and purple lupine. I smell wildflowers in bloom, rescue a ball from the Merced River for a crying little boy, and eat the greasiest pizza ever to oil my hands.

50

The morning after my thirty-first birthday sits in stark, stubborn contrast to the day before. I lay in a cynic's coma on a hotel bed staring at the ornate faux-copper border on the ceiling. To my right, I can hear Bill drawing a bath through the cardboard motel wall. To my left, I hear the Merced River raging. From beneath the bed, I hear Maggie rustling around.[68] A dark funk fills my brain, an audible unhappiness that translates into the scratching static of a poorly tuned radio, set at maximum volume. It is not exactly my surroundings that depress me. Though most places of purchased comfort have something of a plastic feel to them—with fake logs in a gas fireplace and walls of paper. On the other side of either wall lies something (i.e. the river and Bill) that comforts me deeply rather than cheaply. And under me is a troll I consider my best friend.

Still, as I lay here I think, *I'm thirty-one,* which is really quite young. But I feel so tired and old. Weight from the years I have lived thus far presses upon me like a lead blanket and I feel my body sinking further into the mattress on which I lie. Feeling the mattress slowly envelop me, I consider my life ahead. There could be thirty-one more years for me, or more. What if they are even half as difficult as the past three? My spirit shrinks to exhaustion at the thought of bearing all that could come.

The years from twenty-eight to thirty-one . . . those are the ones that trigger the fatigue and heaviness, that bring the tears. Not that there were not difficult years before that. My life as I can remember has never been without a subtle but deeply embedded anxiety—much of which grew from the uncertainty of watching a family come gruesomely unglued, mess oozing at the seams where there used to be connection and security. But I have lived with that for so many years,

---

[68]She often finds herself an under-bed cave to hole up in when we stay in motels.

and I was too young to have much of my conscious self invested in this broken system of relationships.

Not so with Daniel.

For this reality I pity myself as I stare with overly-wide eyes at the uninteresting pattern of the wallpaper (a swirly floral mess of purple and mauve and gray), and at the emergency sprinkler embedded in the textured white ceiling above me. Mired in this blank preoccupation, I await with tiresome trepidation the next moment in my next thirty-one years, or the balance of that for which I still breathe . . .

. . . .

. . . .

"Bbbbbggggbhutttt!"

A thundering dog-belch echoes from under the bed.

Then suddenly Bill bounds loudly out of the bathroom and onto on the bed and begins bouncing above me, twisting his fist toward my face, saying, "Want a noooooogie?" Then he flops down on the bed beside me and asks hopefully, "Want a ditch witch?" Then he hauls me up from the bed, flips me over his shoulder with great effort, turns me upside down and inquires, "Want a pile driver?"

With that, my thirty-first year is well in hand.

PPF

We leave Yosemite View Lodge and drive for about five hours through rolling hills of California green to Pinnacles National Monument. There we set out on the High Peaks trail, which winds up the side of a hill speckled with wildflowers.

We are passing near some brush when a loud rustling startles us. Thinking it to be a fitful squirrel, we continue hiking but suddenly from the bush comes *"GGGGGGTTT!"* and then *"FFF!!FFFFTT!!"*

I jump, then consider running my ass as far from that angry growling snort as I can, but I stop my scared-witless self by remembering that running is usually the worst self-preservation strategy when large wildlife are involved. Bill and I freeze for a moment, then we pace a wide, cautious arc until we are well beyond the brush containing the creature we startled, and who has more than effectively reciprocated.

We spend the next ten minutes standing stone still, debating whether or not the creature is stalking us and what to do about it.

"Let's get out of here," I say.

"No way, we have to find out what it is," Bill insists.

"Yes, I'm afraid we will find out what it is, very soon and painfully. It's too close, it's too large, let's go."

Judging by the size and character of the noises continually emanating from the brush we figure the elusive creature has to be either a small swine with a big voice or big bear with a regular voice. Or possibly a liger. I don't know of any wild pig species around here, so a bear seems the likely owner of the angry voice.

"We'll be fine . . . We'll climb up on that rock," Bill suggests.

"Fine," I say, knowing that this idea has no merit as a self-preservation strategy but not wanting to debate any further until we are at least on higher ground. So, we end up climbing some rocks to get a better view of the mountainside. There we strain our eyes to see some movement and wait for our beast to reveal itself.

After a few tense moments, Bill spies in the thick brush the shape of an enormous (three hundred pounds or more) black pig, and foraging around its feet are three tiny piglets. What looks like a hairy barnyard sow stands grazing on a national monument mountainside. The pigs take a path up the hill that parallels the High Peaks trail, so as we continue our hike we seem to be following them, or them us. We make sure to keep our distance as we discuss what could possibly have put them there, the feral pigs of Pinnacles.

It turns out the pigs derive from some combination of transported European wild boar and feral pigs brought by Spanish missionaries. They have made a nuisance of themselves in Pinnacles, and are believed to number between 800,000 and 900,000 individuals in the state of California. Like any species with a proficient breeding capacity that finds itself in an ecosystem without predators (California long ago exterminated all the grizzly bear and wolves), the population of feral pigs has gone out of control. In Pinnacles, the overpopulation of pigs has wreaked havoc upon the native plant and animal species, rooting up to fifteen acres of ground per day per pig, destroying vegetation and habitat for a variety of struggling species. For this reason, the National Park Service at Pinnacles has devised a Pig Management Plan (PMP), central to which is the Pig Proof Fence (PPF). The pigs who set up camp in Pinnacles—up to nine hundred of them in a rainy year—are going to be killed and the PPF is devised to prevent future squatters from setting up shop.

Pacific

On a trembling lip of land in Los Padres National Forest, North America meets the Pacific Ocean. We have struck the frenetic watery frontier of the utter West. Here at Los Padres the ocean rises in raucous assault against the land and in response California cliffs climb in defiant stony resistance. The motion, the drama, the determined noise of the anything-but-Pacific crashes upon the coast ceaselessly, each wave seeming to push higher and harder to break the will of terra firma and win this war of earth's elements. Of course the ocean prevails ultimately in wearing away its rocky obstruction, but with a gradual, nearly imperceptible, chipping that suggests no ultimate victor.

And under the nose of this bold posturing at the line of ultimate battle, lives a quiet world of creatures that subsist on the edge of two worlds. Starfish cling to the land even as waves pummel the rock. Crabs shuffle about determinedly. Anemones anemonize.

And there's us. Bill climbs a towering jagged stone arch planted in the sand, just as the enveloping ocean tide transforms it into an island. As the sun sinks toward the horizon, a band of residual light marks its descent in an undulating path of silver. And from the beach I watch a silhouette of Bill, his hands on his hips and his eyes cast out to sea, perched upon the precipice of a boisterous glittering Armageddon.

Our campsite at Los Padres sits on a bare edge of the ocean, loud with the voice of the Pacific, which sings itself into our dreams through the night. In the late morning we pack up and head north.

A leisurely drive brings us to San Francisco as sunset approaches, and we navigate to Lands End, overlooking the San Francisco Bay, searching for the Sutro Baths. What the Sutro Baths are, we do not know, but they are included as a red dot on our atlas, and because the dot is red and the title contains the word "bath," and we have nothing else to do, we are drawn to it.

Unable to locate the baths, Bill stops an older man to ask if he knows where the historic spot is hiding. Not only does this stranger know where our red dot is, he knows *what* it is.

Apparently the baths were built in 1894 by a wealthy former mayor of San Francisco named Adolph Sutro. With seven pools—one as large as a football field—a theater, three restaurants, a gym, and a museum, the facility was billed as the largest indoor swimming complex in the world. Sutro, a populist, designed the baths to be open to the public. The pools could accommodate more than a thousand swimmers and the entrance fee—which included a locker, towel, suit, and soap—was a quarter. Probably because the facility was so vast and well used, and the fee was so low, the Sutro Baths fell into financial trouble in the 1930s and closed in the 1950s. Then, in 1966, on the eve of its demolition to make room for an apartment complex, the bath facility burned to the ground.

"I was there watching when they burned," our Sutro historian tells us wistfully.

He pauses for a moment, waylaid by the memory, then asks, "Where are you from?"

"Michigan," Bill replies.

"My parents grew up in Michigan," the man says.

"Oh yeah? Where did you grow up?" Bill asks.

The man tells us he is originally from Buffalo, Daniel's hometown, and that he attended SUNY Buffalo, where Daniel went to college.

Bill talks a while about our trip and then asks the man what he does for a living.

"I'm a living poet!" he responds as if he is announcing for the circus.[69]

"Would you like to hear one of my poems?" he asks.

"Absolutely," says Bill.

"Suuure," says I. But I must admit, I am a bit wary when he pulls out a tattered notebook with a scrawl of smudged pencil that appears to be some sort of Morse code language. I smell alcohol on his breath and am worried about what might come out of his mouth. Given my phobia of being impolite, I know I'll listen to the whole thing, regardless of how long and/or offensive it might be.[70]

But, given his green light, our living poet begins to read to us with great feeling about ocean tides, a love poem. It is really quite good and the way he reads

---

[69]I don't know what a "living" poet is and I can tell by Bill's knowing nod and "Really?" that he has no idea either.

[70]"Ode to Snatch," an epic poem.

it is wonderful. He seems to love the sound of his words as they leave his lips, and, as if the words take physical form upon reaching the air, he follows their trajectory into space with grief-stricken eyes—each word like a lover on a ship disappearing beyond a distant horizon.

When he finishes speaking, we wait a few seconds to make sure he is through, then I say, "That was great." And Bill says, "Yeah, that was great, thanks for reading to us."

He smiles a big liquor-smelling smile and says, "Look for me, Jim Wilson, living poet! I'll win the Pulitzer someday."

"Okay, we will, Jim Wilson," I say.

As we start to walk away, Jim Wilson says to Bill, "Hey! What's wrong with her?" nodding his head toward me.

"N-n-nothing," Bill says confusedly.

"That's what I'm talking about!" Wilson yells and laughs as he climbs into his beat up old car and drives away.

We walk on through the wooded park, never finding even a trace of the Sutro Baths.

As daylight dims, we return to the car and I realize that Bill has grown especially quiet. I again consider asking him about this unhappy undercurrent that has been intermittently pulling at him for many weeks. Instead, when we reach the car, I turn on some music for the drive to a San Francisco suburb where we will visit our friend and Bill's former girlfriend, Katie.

In Pleasanton, Bill and Katie and I sit around her dining room table and talk of what has been happening in our lives. Bill and Katie lived together for three years, first in Tucson, with Daniel, and then in DC just the two of them. Since then, Katie has married and had a son, with another child on the way.

After we have had some dinner and caught up over casual things, I begin telling Katie about some plans for next fall, about the board meeting for Daniel's foundation and about burying Daniel's ashes. Suddenly my face tightens and I find myself holding back tears, unsuccessfully. When I look up at Bill I see that he also is crying. And so is Katie. I can talk about those plans sometimes without feeling the reality of them. But at that moment, with Katie, at a dining room table where we have never shared a meal, all the meals and moments of the life we four had shared come flowing back. The incompatibility of the past with the present moment wraps full around my chest and cinches violently. This, I realize, is the first time the three of us have been together since Daniel died.

Rather than allow my tears to escalate into all-out weeping, I ask Katie to show me where I will sleep.

She leads me to her son's room where I put down my suitcase.

"Do you want to take a shower?" she asks.

"No," I reply. "I'm going to write in my journal."

I am looking into her eyes, searching for something more to say, when suddenly she reaches out and puts her arms around me.

I don't know whether she could ever know how much this gesture meant to me. She had left while Daniel was sick, her life had taken a turn, and sometimes I had wondered if she ever looked back, if she ever thought of Daniel or Bill or me. In the force of her hug, I found the answer.

51

The waves at Point Reyes National Seashore crashed high and hard against the land today while the wind whipped the sand in a stinging merciless slap. At times the tempest died to a whirring whistle, but only to prepare for another shaking blow.

This erratic squall bears uncanny resemblance to my psychic condition over the past twenty-four hours, ever since we left Katie's house. The trouble seemed to arise when Bill took my bag to the car while I was in the shower and I had no clean clothes when I prepared to dress. I donned my dirty clothes and went downstairs where everyone was eating breakfast.

"Did you take my bag to the car?" I asked Bill.

He nodded.

"I still needed it," I said.

In response, Bill tossed the keys on the table in front of me and continued eating.

My brain hissed and bared its teeth. Nobody seemed to notice. I ate breakfast, went to the car to access my bag, then returned to prepare myself for the trip. When I was ready, we said goodbye to Katie, climbed in the car, and drove away.

All in all, not too bad a morning, a little bumpy, but not too bad. But as soon as we rounded the corner out of Katie's sight, we started to argue.

"Thanks for the help back there," I said in a snarky tone.

"I thought I was doing you a favor taking your bag to the car."

"You could have asked me first if I was ready. And you would have done me a bigger favor by going to get it when I said I still needed it."

"I don't see what the big deal is."

This was not the most sensitive response and certainly was not the response I was looking for, but it got me thinking. Did I know what the big deal was? I didn't. At least not until a few moments later when my mind returned to Katie's the night before, during dinner. The table, *that* was the big deal. Upon realizing this, almost immediately I started to cry and I didn't stop for a full day.

I had two images in my mind that could not sit next to each other without great upheaval ensuing. It was as if these memories were a wildebeest and a lion and any juxtaposition of the two could result only in pain and bloodshed. In one image, Katie, Bill, Daniel, and I sat around a table in Tucson, Arizona, sharing a homemade pizza. The other image was the night before. And every time I thought of that dinner table in Pleasanton, California, and I saw only Bill and Katie and me sitting around it, the emotional pressure surging through my veins and sinuses and eyes made my skull feel as though it would crack. The wildebeest will eventually fall prey to the lion even as the past will invariably be devoured by the present. That is the way of this life. But when someone whose very existence is woven into the fragile sinewy fibers of your own heart becomes trapped in the past, the severing feels like a tweezer clamping the tissue of your heart and ripping it apart, fiber by tender fiber, leaving nothing but a bloody excruciating mess of a still-beating heart.

This carnage, the predation of my substance and existence, encapsulated by the scene at Katie's house, turned over and over again in my mind, on what seemed to be an eternal loop. Over and over, and over and over I watched the rapacious predator rip the heart from my chest and swallow it whole with the past it had subsumed.

I stared out the window, lost in this hostile wilderness for hours while Bill drove. I would not, could not, explain to him what was happening, could not speak at all, and the tears would not abate.

He tried to get me to go for a hike at Muir Woods and I shook my head in refusal, then he took me to Point Reyes, where I opened the window long enough to feel the hard slap of the wind but refused to leave the car. Finally, mid-afternoon, he got us a campsite and set up the tent and I went inside and lay down with my sleeping bag. He brought my pad and pillow and slid them under me where I now lie.

My crying subsides for a moment but then my memory shifts to two or three minutes of time etched in the molten core of my mind. Daniel's face, incomprehensibly frozen. His too-thin, long legs, unacceptably still.

I remember those many days he would not eat. I think of the blood-thinning shots I did not give him, either because he did not want them, because I did not want to wake him after a night of fitful, restless sleep broken by the coughing and choking that shook his body, or because I was so worn from fear and sleeplessness. Even when he slept, I could not.

But he wouldn't eat. How could the shots have mattered? He would not eat. Food had made him vomit so many times, he no longer trusted his stomach. His fatigue of pain and discomfort had overcome his hunger for living.

We went to an alternative medicine doctor after all of Western medicine had failed Daniel. The alternative doctor asked me what I wanted for him. I wanted to say a cure, to scream at her: what the fuck do you think I want? I want him to live!

But what I said was, "I want him to not be nauseous so he can eat." How could he live if he did not eat? But what did Daniel hear that day? Did he hear that I was so desperate, I would take an appetite as a step toward a cure or did he hear that I had given up? So far from the truth.

As we drove away from the office that day Daniel said softly, "She didn't have a cure for me."

"No," was all I could say. Why not, "No, but maybe if you can get your appetite back, and your strength, we can find a cure that your body can handle." Why not something more? Anything more.

As I lie here, on the floor of the quiet forest, I wonder, how long, and how many thousands of times do I have to repeat it: "I did my best for him. Maybe I failed in many ways, but I did my best."

I did my best for him . . . my best for him.

Will I ever accept it? Well, not yet. I cry in a silent, breathless, but violent wail. I feel Bill's arms encircling, steadying me like an anchor in a turbulent sea. I can see myself at this moment, as I saw Daniel just as he was dying, and as he lay motionless in the dissolving of all that is. Instead of death, I become a distillation of this pain that has the power to stop my breath. My lungs feel the need to convulse for lack of air but the inside-out vacuum of a scream holds me, burning like an acid, erasing my being in paralysis and suffocation.

I fall into sleep finally, dreaming I am waiting for Daniel's funeral.

A long wait, too much preparation and wondering. Where is everyone, where is Bill? At a party for some other simultaneous occasion (life, I suppose). My mom comes, suggesting I wear some of her clothes.

I sleep for hours, giving my subconscious a chance to quell the violent feelings my conscious mind cannot subdue. When I wake, Bill is still at my side. Where would I be without him to hold onto me at these moments in an embrace that contains me, keeps me from spilling entirely outside of myself and being absorbed into the atmosphere? I wonder if he vicariously experiences some of the fear I hold from the time of losing Daniel, those last hours especially. Those moments pace like cloudy apparitions, scattered and restless in my mind. Disparate and violent weather systems, they are destined for collision when conditions are right. Bill is often present when the winds begin to rise and the skies darken, casting an eerie light on a restless, brooding sea. It must be frightening for him to see it in me. To hold me while my limbs shake and rattle. But he never falters, he just holds tightly and presses a gentle hand to my head until all has blown over and quiet has returned.

I look up at him, his face worried.

"I'm going to sit here until you tell me what is wrong."

I sit silently for a few more minutes then say, "I've been thinking of Daniel not being at Katie's. I can't stop crying. I'm afraid, really afraid I'll never be able to stop," I manage to tell him.

Bill just looks at me for a long, long time, sadness, love, and grief pooling and spilling over from his eyes.

Then he lays down next to me and snugs his arm tightly around my shoulders. We sleep the rest of the daylight hours. In the evening, we wake and eat some banana bread. Bill reads aloud from the *Lord of the Rings* to me, then we return to sleep.

In the morning I wake to the chatter of the hasty stream on whose bank we slept. I step out of the tent into a sheltering dome of adolescent redwoods and look gratefully around at the landscape in which I had spent a full day but which I had not noticed until that moment. In the calm of the morning, squatting along the streamside, I consider the preceding day. Momentarily Bill joins me.

Feeling infinitely calmer with every passing moment, I ask Bill what it is that has been on his mind for the past weeks.

"You've seen me at my absolute lowest. You know you can tell me anything," I say.

"I'm not sure this is the best time," he responds.

"What is? If not here beneath the redwoods, then where?"

"Maybe nowhere. Maybe it's just something I should keep to myself."

"Please don't. Don't we know by now that chances to say all we want to say don't last forever?"

He thinks on this a moment, then says, "Okay. I have been struggling with something for a while now. You know, I love you . . ."

". . . I know, I love you too . . ."

"No, just . . . let me finish. Everything that has happened over the past three years . . . losing Daniel, my dad, my aunt, my grandma, all of that has been so hard. But one of the hardest things for me has been seeing you suffer so much, all while Daniel was sick, when he died, and now for two full years after. Every moment you are in pain is torture for me. I know there has been some goodness for you, and for us together, but every time I see the pain and regret of the past pulling you down, it's like, it's not just pulling you down, but pulling you away from me."

He stops for a moment, looking into the cheery stream at our feet.

I sit quietly and wait for him to continue.

"I love you and I want us to have a future that isn't tied entirely to the pain of the past. It's selfish, and in a way I hate myself for it. But I know Daniel wanted you to be happy. I can wait as long as I need to wait. You can go away by yourself, for as long as you want. Years if need be. And I'll be here waiting. But I can't help but struggle wondering if there will ever be a time for you and me to just be okay. To love each other and accept, no, *embrace* a future life together."

When he finishes, we sit quietly, my mind turning his words over and over. I no longer know what it means to be okay, but I understand what he is asking me. I have in one way or another always loved him and I hold an intangible but unshakable certainty that the bonds we have forged through friendship, intense anguish, adventure, and beauty, are forever. But "forever" assumes a connection to the future, which demands an acceptance of the realities of present and past; a peaceful reckoning with the lion and its predatory appetites that, on the heels of my emotional wreckage over the past twenty-four hours, I am not confident I can muster. After a moment I take his hand and hold it tightly. For now, I have no response, but thank him for telling me.

We gather Maggie and drive to Point Reyes. Needing some time to think, I walk with Maggie one direction along the beach, Bill walks the other. I'm ambling along the edge of the land conversing with my self, when from the corner of my eye I see something rise from the shimmering surface of the ocean. I turn fully toward the vision and water suddenly erupts from a blowhole just above the surface of the water.

Searching for confirmation, I look around for others who speak my human tongue. Bill is a mile or more down the beach. I'm alone. I turn my attention back to the water and the whale appears again, and then again, each time bringing an involuntary smile to my face.

Mesmerized, I follow it down the shore. To the left is my companion whale, whose pace seems perfectly in sync with mine. To my right the sand displays a watery reflection of the ochre cliffs painted gold by the yawning mouth of the morning sun. When my eyes have settled long upon the water, the glare subsides and I realize I am traveling not with a partner, but with a band. The one whale is really two, a cow and calf, who swim in procession and seem to move as one, making shallow graceful dives, weaving upon the water like a single shining needle through a flowing silver cloth. Adding to our number comes a small round head bobbing in the waves between me and the whales, and gazing curiously at me from large dark circle eyes set in a soft dark glossy head. When I spy it spying on me, the seal dives beneath the white foam of the waves and disappears. But as I turn back toward the sand in front of me, my trusty eye-corner notices the head pop up and follow along. For a mile or more I march with the troupe until I see in the near distance a colony of elephant seals resting on the sand. I am still seventy-five yards or more away from them, but do not want to disturb, so I turn about, set my eyes on the ocean for one last look. Upon seeing a burst of spray, I begin my walk back with newfound clarity, back toward Bill.

In the afternoon we hike a dune trail against a dictatorial wind that forces the flowered ground into a frenzied dance of bowing and quivering. At the beach, sand assaults our skin but we linger, captivated by the sight of a wide band of frothing sea foam, sometimes flopping, sometimes skittering to the pace of the insistent wind.

Before long our struggle against the wind has exhausted us and we head back to the car. Maggie decides this is a good time to take a shit, while we are still a good distance from a trashcan. So she dumps her load in the sandy trail and I scoop it up in a plastic bag and continue walking. Within thirty seconds, I come to realize that the cruelty of the wind goes beyond its brute force. It has shrewdly adjusted direction just perfectly, so that the stench from Maggie's steaming turds charges with the accuracy of a nostril-seeking missile, right into the fragile nerves of my scent organ. No matter which way I turn, if I duck down or jump up, hold the bag behind me or in front of me, I may as well be storing Maggie's excrement upon my upper lip. I decide the only way to beat the wind, or at least shorten its dominion over me, is to run back to the car.

Bill thinks I am being stupid so he holds his leisurely pace. After about five minutes of chasing Maggie down the trail I am breathing hard and am pleased to see Maggie slow her pace. I slow too and look around the surrounding plant covered dunes to see what has captured Maggie's attention. As I turn to the left, I see a blondish form moving in the brush thirty feet from where I stand. I wait for it to come into full view and find myself gazing upon a mountain lion, who is in turn, gazing placidly down upon me. And she is gorgeous: powerful, gorgeous, and fierce.

The fact that I was able to come so close to the lion without either of us being aware of the proximity surprises me. It's easy to understand how I had overlooked the quiet animal as I bolted erratically through sand and against wind with a flailing bag of dogshit in my hand. But the cat should have smelled me or heard me. Then I realize, though I had been making a lot of noise, all was rendered silent by the whipping of the wind through brush and the gaps between the hills. And, of course, the wind had seen to it that all the putrescence of my parcel was being channeled directly into my nose, so there was none left for the mountain lion to detect. So, I assume as I gape at the casual grace of the cat, that is how I was able to come so close to the only big cat I have ever seen in the wild. The loud-mouth, ill-tempered, mean-spirited wind has unwittingly masked my arrival, allowing me to see up-close one of the grandest of wild creatures, and one of the greatest of the world's predators.

My inner predators are quieted by this encounter; my mind consumed with the question, why does it linger? It's possible that she is considering whether I am an appropriate or easy meal. She saw Maggie first—not much of a meal, but easy prey. Maybe I am just something to be observed and understood, placed into the cerebral context of the wild lion alongside wind, water, and wildebeest. Whatever her reasons, I feel for a moment . . . calm, acceptant, blessed.

When Bill catches up, the cat turns its back on us and begins to casually saunter up the hill, looking back in our direction occasionally, as if still uncertain whether it wants to depart.

52

Orion is known by many names in many cultures and languages. He has appeared in the great myths of great civilizations; in the *Odyssey* and *Iliad* and the Rigveda. He has been called Baiame and Mriga and Nimrod. In several stories he dies from the bite of a scorpion; others have him chasing the Pleiades into the sky. Due to his connection to the agrarian calendar, ancient Egyptians associated Orion with their god Osiris, god of rebirth and afterlife. Orion bridged the worlds of the living and the dead, so that no matter the separation, Orion could mend it.

Regardless of what he is called, or the divergent myths of how he came to live in the sky, Orion is understood across the globe and through time as a locator constellation because it is one of relatively few constellations that can be seen from anywhere in the world. With the guidance of the warm sun by day, and the cool glittering enduring presence of Orion by night, no matter where you are in space and time, you can never be truly lost.

53

Except for a man in a skiff with his dog at the helm, Bill and I see not another soul all day in California's Whiskeytown National Recreation Area. Bill sets up the tent facing Whiskeytown Lake, so the door of the tent frames the low mountains that lie on the other side of a narrow stretch of the lake. When the sun is at a late-afternoon angle, it hits the blue tent just right, illuminating the nylon like the cloudless sky of our own private world.

I have been reading a book about a woman who hiked the Appalachian Trail and when asked where she was from by fellow hikers, she always said, "Right here." I never know what to say when people ask me that question. But as I climb into the tent, my eyes are welcomed home by the sight of our sleeping bags laid out and fluffy and the fading glow of the sun lighting the blue nylon of the tent, leaf shadows from an overhead tree dappling the blue. I am struck with an incredible appreciation for the look and feel of the place where I rest and close my eyes. I could be sitting in front of a fire in a country farmhouse where I have lived all my life. I lay down in the sleeping bag-soft blue-lit universe and listen to the lake lapping lazily upon its shores. Bill ushers in Maggie, then climbs in after her, gets settled and starts reading from *The Two Towers*. I put my hand on his arm; he stops reading and looks at me.

"I understand what you were saying to me," I say.

He looks into my eyes deeply, but says nothing.

"I don't know how long it will take, but I know now, I won't stay lost forever. I will be okay . . . we will be okay."

He smiles at me, then stares quietly for a moment back into the pages of the book, and continues reading.

54

In the morning we rise before dawn in hopes of being the first visitors in Redwood National Park's Tall Trees Grove where the first, third, and sixth tallest trees in the world reside.

A locked gate serves to reduce traffic in the fragile grove, so when we arrive at the dirt road that leads to the preserve, I get out of the car and open the combination lock. I then drive the car through, put it in park, and hop out again to close the gate behind us. Just as I am clamping the lock down on the gate, I hear Bill from the passenger seat of the car, saying softly and strangely, "Ummmm, Krista?"

I look back to find out what he wants, and I see a huge black form ten feet on the other side of the car from where I stand. A bear! Shit, an enormous bear! I run back to the car (toward the bear!) while thoughtfully, but fruitlessly reminding myself, *Never run from (or at) a bear. Don't run. Don't run, stupid! Don't ruuuuunnnnn!*

As I fling open the driver's side door, the bear, now directly in front of the car, not six feet away, turns his oversized head slowly toward me, considers me for one quiet moment, then looks back towards the woods and resumes traveling. He has surmised that nothing in my vicinity warrants any of his attention and he continues ambling casually across the road, practically brushing our bumper with his gargantuan wobbling rump.

When I slip into the car Bill yells, "What are you doing!!?"

"I got back as fast as I could," I reply breathlessly. "I ran, in fact. Even though I knew, I shouldn't. Stupid, stupid . . . don't run at a bear . . ."

". . . No! You're supposed to get the camera out of the back!"

This doesn't register. I gently close my door as the bear moseys into the woods. Good god! That was the biggest bear I have ever seen, and certainly the closest. Maybe the closest I will ever see. Hopefully. It would have to be sitting on top of me to be any closer. Bill and I are wonderstruck and we gab and giggle about it for the next ten minutes, repeating over and over, "Did you see the size of that!"

Finally, when we have calmed down, I say, "So I thought you were concerned for my safety when you called out to me."

"No! I wanted you to get the camera."

He is right, I blew it.

But my failure is quickly forgotten in the deep emerald shelter of the redwood forest where trillium and bunchberry plants adorn and perfume the feet of aged giants. We spend the morning meandering the grove and breathing in the sweet air of the ancient trees before returning to the car and heading northward.

55

While driving toward the Columbia River Gorge, I begin to sing, compulsively. For some reason I have the song "America" from *West Side Story* in my head. "I like to be in America. Okay by me in America. Everything's free in America, for a small fee in America!"

"Dadadada in America, dadadada in America . . . dadadahnnnmerica dadadadadadamerica!"

I try putting in a CD and singing along with James Taylor or Tracy Chapman, but as soon as the disc finishes, the indomitable showtune returns. "Dadadada in America, dadadada in America."

I eventually accept my powerlessness to purge it from my thoughts and decide instead to attempt to use it to my advantage. Bill's brain is putty in the hands of a catchy tune. He hears music intravenously and regurgitates it like a colicky newborn. A few bars of any good melody and he'll be singing along without even knowing it.[71]

So I figure maybe I can use the subliminal prowess of "America" to sway Bill toward breaking our current budget of ten dollars a day. If I just set some words to the tune, I'll wager Bill will be powerless to refuse the suggestion. I try the tactic first with breakfast.

"I like to eat breakfast in America, go out for breakfast in America, pancakes for me in America, syrup on top in A-me-rica!"

Before long Bill is humming along so I say, "Hey, let's go to a diner for breakfast."

"Sure," he says.

It works! After some pancakes for me we hit the road again and I continue humming. Every once in a while, Bill realizes he is humming along and he bangs

---

[71]Last week, he had that '80s Rick Astley hit, "Never gonna give you up, never gonna let you down, never gonna run around and desert you," stuck in his brain for days.

the dashboard and yells "DAAAH!" Toward the end of the day, when we are getting near the state park where we plan to camp for the night, I suggest we give ourselves a treat and rent a cottage for the night.

"That'll be like seventy dollars. No way."

In response to this resistance I start softly humming, "hmmm hmmm hmmm America."

A few minutes later, Bill starts unconsciously singing the song. "I like to be in America. Okay by me in America . . ."

Then, in a fit of frustration he yells, "I need another song!"

I respond, "How about, 'Cottages, cottages, cottages . . . Cottages, cottages, cottages . . . Cottages, cottages, cottages . . . Cottage for me in America!'"

Bill appears unamused as he steers the station wagon into Viento State Park in Oregon, where we will camp for the night. Because the park is situated on the narrow swath of land between Interstate 84 and the Columbia River, the unwelcome noise of the highway and the pleasant roaring and rushing of the river combine to create a symphony of white noise. Hoping to tip the balance in favor of the river, we set up our tent as far from the highway as we can. The sun has long ago set and pitching the tent is challenging, but we feel pretty clever for the relatively quiet spot we have found without the benefit of daylight.

Once our sleeping bags are arrayed, we climb in, and I begin reading aloud to Bill. Within thirty seconds, the deafening *"WOOOOOOH! WOOOOH!"* of a train whistle drowns out my voice while scaring the living feces out of us. We have apparently set up the tent about thirty yards from a train track that had been hiding behind some trees.

The ground shakes for several minutes as the train thunders past.

"Agghhhh!" I grunt in protest.

Bill just sighs and offers optimistically, "Maybe it only has one run a night."

I shrug my shoulders, and raise his sigh with a significantly larger and more dramatic sigh. I am less than optimistic but have no intention of moving the tent in the dark.

I hum the refrain for "cottages, cottages, cottages" despondently, then return to reading aloud.

After a few pages Bill puts his hand on my arm and says tensely, "Stop. It's okay . . . but don't look up."

At first I am confused, but then I realize it must be a spider, and from the look on Bill's face it isn't "okay." It is a big, hairy, befanged spider—the kind that generations of my family have feared by day and dreamt of in horrific detail by night. I plunge my head into my sleeping bag while Bill tries to get the spider in his hand from the ceiling. But by some sickly fortune, it falls on my back. He swats me repeatedly trying to grab it.

"Aaaaahhhhh!! It's on me!" I squeal.

"No, I got it," Bill says unconvincingly.

He puts his hand outside the tent and shakes it, a gesture I interpret as theatrics intended to convince me of the spider's departure.

"Did you see it fall?" I ask him.

"Ummm, I think so."

Nice try.

"Are you sure?" I question.

"No."

We look all around the tent, and in my bag and in my hair with the flashlight. We find many things, but not the spider. I pick up the book to continue reading, but hesitate.

"Did you have to drop it on *me*?" I have to ask Bill.

"I didn't mean to! It's not that easy catching spiders, and I don't actually like it."

"Sorry, thanks for trying," I say.

I begin reading again, but every few pages I stop and ask Bill to look in my hair because it feels like something is crawling.

Eventually I calm down, finish the chapter, and we go to sleep, but just as we are entering dreamland, "*WOOOOH! WOOOOOH!*" We startle awake to sitting positions, and look at each other with a mild though palpable dread through the loud darkness. Before lying back down, I turn on the flashlight and give my sleeping bag another scan for the spider.

Thus, the pattern for the night has been set. We sleep, startle awake to the whistle, I search my sleeping bag for the spider, and then fall back asleep. Startle awake!, search for spider, fall asleep. Awake!, spider, sleep.

Exhaustedly, we rise after sunrise and take a drive along a steep mountainside that overlooks the Columbia River from the north. Wildflowers are blooming, alighting the landscape with yellow, purple, white, and pale pink heads thrashing in the powerful wind that channels through the Columbia River Gorge. Beyond the bright frenetic fields and the charging river stands the solitary jagged pinnacle of Mount Hood, observing the unending haste of the world around with stoic insouciance. As representative members of the hastiest species of Hood's surrounding world, Bill and I move on before long and make our way to Multnomah Falls.

Feeling tired from last night's unrest and wanting to avoid movement of any kind, I stay in the car while Bill and Maggie go hiking around the falls. I can see the famed waterfall somewhat from where I sit and the time alone gives me a chance to write, and rest my eyes. I am doing the latter when I hear a car pulling up beside me. I jolt upright to see a faded old brown van jerk to an abrupt halt a few feet from my repose. From the van, a short, rotund man with a golfer's cap and goatee emerges and says in the deepest voice ever to emit from a white man, "Ohhhh myyyyyy."

I know he's not talking about my raggedy-assed bumper sticker, because I have long ago removed it. So I turn to see what has provoked such a guttural uttering.

Oh right, Multnomah—it is after all the second-highest year-round waterfall in the United States, plunging more than six hundred feet from its source on Larch Mountain.

Following the man tumbles out a plump, geeky teenage girl, who also immediately looks up at the falls. She yells, "Wow!" Behind her lumbers another girl, and when her feet hit the ground and her eyes meet the falls, she catches her breath and gasps as though she's been punched in the gut, "Hhhhhuuuuhhhhh!"

I expect that to be the last of the drama queens (though the thought disappoints me), but then a blemish-faced boy of about thirteen, and with the same familial girth, pops his head out of the door and jumps down to the pavement. Of the falls, he exclaims, "Oh my gosh!"

And he isn't the last. Gawky teenagers just keep piling out of this van and coming up with new exclamations of wonder over the sight of the falls. I turn around in my seat towards Multnomah, expecting it to be blushing over all the unabashed admiration radiating from the parking lot. The falls seem gloriously underwhelmed. Which is good, because I don't want to burst its bubble. Multnomah is indeed breathtaking, but its splendor has for me been eclipsed by the strange phenomenon of these happy, un-sarcastic, non-ironic teenagers. What strange new breed of human adolescent am I observing?

When Bill returns from the falls, I tell him about the strange and wonderful van full of mutant teenagers. Still curious, as I start the car and pull away, I look at the van's license plate, which reads "Alberta." Bill and I look at each other, and nod.

Canadians.

The Price of Privilege

As we arrive at our trailhead in Olympic National Park's Hoh Rainforest, we are greeted by a mountain lion slinking through the forest's lush greenery. There's that word, lush. The rainforest gave birth to those words lauded by the living—lush, verdant, fertile. Here, life abounds and astounds, it's a matter of volume, of decibels of green in each of a thousand shades.

Sidled up against the western flank of the Olympic Mountains, this region is bathed in an abundance of moisture that collects over the coast. Where Death Valley sits under a rainshadow, the Hoh is situated under a rain-funnel. The forest receives between twelve and fourteen feet (feet!) of precipitation per year, that's up to 167 inches as compared to Death Valley's mere inch or two. The Olympic Mountains also protect the rainforest from climate extremes, blocking weather patterns that cause freezing cold and scorching heat.

Even in nature there exists the inequity of being born on the right side of the proverbial tracks. The western side of these coastal mountains means comfort and plenty, the eastern side can mean drought, scarcity, and struggle.

As Bill and I walk around the forest we see the beneficiaries of west-side plentitude. Everywhere green, upon green, upon green. Sitka spruce is the dominant tree species in the rainforest, but I am hard pressed to observe where the Sitka ends and its myriad plant-life accessories—draped over and around and beneath it—begin. Even the wooden pit toilet housing has become part of the ecosystem, with a wall to wall exterior carpeting of emerald mosses and a second skin of spongy, shaggy jade sprouting from the rooftop.

When I tire on the hike, I make myself plod on, thinking it best to keep moving. If I sit down to rest, even for a moment, restless plants caught up in the hasty pace of rainforest life might find my body as good a spot as any to set up shop.

You have to be quick here.

Even privilege has its price. On the sweet side of the mountain, everything is thriving and therefore competition for space and sunlight is fierce. The dense growth that accumulates in the canopy of the rainforest can be so thick that a shower of snow may settle upon the canopy but never make it to the forest ground. A taste of snow is no big loss for the bottom dwellers, but that same blockage can drastically reduce the sunlight that shines through to the surface. Plants that live on the rainforest floor have to either be crafty about competing for the sunlight that does filter through or make do with what they are able to capture. The *Oregon oxalis*, for example, has three leaves that it can adjust to ensure that the optimum amount of sunlight strikes their surface. In a matter of minutes, the leaves will fold down or tilt up, depending on the direction and intensity of the sun.

Other plants, faced with the ferocious competition for light and space, give up the rat race and adjust themselves to a life without light. The Indian pipe evolved into an albino plant because of the scarcity of sunlight on the forest floor—it no longer manufactures chlorophyll and instead feeds on sugars from fungi beneath the soil.

Always there is struggle. Desert dwellers have light and plenty of space, but little rain. Here it is the opposite. Whether it be against the elements of our environment and the misfortune we face, or against competition and natural selection—none are without adversity.

Sinister St. Francis

We turn our backs, sadly, on the Pacific Ocean and head east, edging our way along the northern coast of the Olympic Peninsula. Having ferreted out a nearby hot springs, we hike a few miles through wet woods, on a trail sprinkled with flowering skunk cabbage in Olympic National Park. At the end of the trail we find a series of shallow, stinky hot pools isolated in the forest. While soaking we meet a young man from Germany who is touring the United States. As we are discussing the different places we've visited during our travels, we stumble upon a common location—the hot springs in Meadows, Utah. The German kid says he hitched a ride near Meadows from a man who was on his way to the hot springs.

I want to ask the kid, "Was he about a hundred years old and naked except for tube socks and sneakers?"

Unlikely. Still, I imagine the young traveler on that Utah highway, flagging down a ride from a white minivan. I picture the German kid pulling open the passenger door and stepping back as cigarette smoke billows from the car, and when the smoke lifts, the kid's eyes grow wide as a scrawny butt-naked old man addresses him saying, "Hop on in, kid, where you headed?" (Bill later admits to the very same vision.)

While we are sitting in the hot springs talking with the German kid, a man suddenly appears and leans himself against a tree a few yards from the edge of the pool. He seems to just materialize—like he isn't there and we three are alone in the pool and then he *is* there. His face carries an odd smirk, like he has a secret we would probably benefit from knowing, but he isn't about to tell.

"Where are you all from?" he asks us.

As we respond he takes some crumbs out of his pocket and holds them out in his palm. In a few minutes, some gray jays fly up and stand on his forearm pecking at the food in his hand. He stands there, staring at us in the pool as the birds beak his hand.

"How long are you going to stick around here?" he asks Bill and me.

"We don't know," Bill answers evasively.

"Are you going to camp up here tonight?" he probes.

"Probably not," Bill says.

"Hmmm, that's too bad," the talking bird feeder says slowly.

Darkness is approaching,[72] and the presence of the sinister St. Francis encourages Bill and me to exit the pool and begin our trek back to the car. We both periodically look over our shoulders, expecting the creepy inquisitor to pop out of the woods at every turn. After we have made it back safely, I begin to worry about the German kid. He said he found Americans very friendly but I know of at least one, and possibly two, that may give the rest of us a bad name.

---

[72]Not really, but metaphorically and eventually.

56

On San Juan Island, I wake early to the bubble-wrapped jet-plane *vroooom* of a hummingbird inspecting the tent mesh for sustenance. I lie watching the frenetic busy-body, its drumming-humming encouraging me not to go back to sleep.

When Bill wakes we take a leisurely stroll along the San Juan coast while listening to the barking of sea lions echoing off the water from a nearby island. From there we travel to San Juan National Historical Park. The park marks the site of one of the most inane military events in United States history[73], where the life, or rather death, of a pig nearly precipitated a war between the United States and England.

By the early 1800s, both nations had pronounced themselves the rightful owners of the Northwest region of the current United States and British Columbia.[74] Eventually the two countries decided they would agree to split the land among themselves—the Brits would take Vancouver Island and everything above the Forty-Ninth Parallel, and the United States would take everything south. But the treaty that decided this partition of land did not elucidate the fate of the San Juan Islands, located between Vancouver Island and the United States mainland. So once again, both countries claimed sovereignty over the islands.

The two countries tolerated each other's conflicting claims and coexisted tensely for about thirteen years until, in June 1859, the insatiable swinish hunger for land came to a head over the death of a pig. A British pig wandered into an American garden and began rooting around, as pigs are wont to do.[75] An American farmer killed the pig at which point the Brits puffed their chests out and

---

[73]Stiff competition.

[74]This despite the fact that Native Americans had been living in the region for thousands of years before Europeans had imagined the place existed.

[75]They knew it was a British pig because of the polite way it belched after mowing down the asparagus, which it described as "jolly good!"

threatened to arrest the farmer. Both sides of the conflict then began amassing military might on opposite ends of San Juan Island, until—on the brink of war over a tiny pig on a tiny island—reason somehow prevailed. It took eleven years of military occupation of San Juan and the intervention of a neutral party (Germany), but eventually England peaceably left San Juan in the hands of the United States government.[76]

As we walk around the grounds of the park a great silence presides over the old empty barracks, redoubts and officers' quarters. Beneath our feet, rabbits tunnel, and in the trees overhead bald eagles scream their warning to all who will listen. We crane our necks to follow the cry and on the uppermost branches stands an eagle presiding over a nest, inside which there sits a gawk-awkward fuzzy little head, peeking with great effort because of a weak, floppy neck, over the rim of a gigantic mess of twigs and debris. The parent eagle notices us giggling at its crazy-looking little offspring and directs its piercing stare and scream precisely upon our heads. The address requires little interpretation, it is clearly time for us to vacate the premises.

Birthday Mystery

We pass the morning of Bill's thirty-first birthday piecing together a puzzle.

1. Yesterday I picked up a piece of chocolate candy and noticed the wrapper had been chewed through and the candy was notched with tiny nibble marks. I held the candy up to Bill's teeth, which were clearly too big to have made the marks. I looked at Maggie and immediately dismissed her as a suspect, for the simple reason that the candy and wrapper still existed. Bill and I figured a rodent had taken a taste of the candy while we had it out at a picnic table for lunch.

2. This morning, while tossing through our stuff looking for a change of clothes, we found Bill's towel and canvas jacket had been partially dismantled. They were frayed and shredded at several edges, the resulting fuzz distributed throughout the back.

3. Upon further inspection of the car we discovered a sparse blanket of fresh, black, rice-sized turds in the cubby hole and lying next to a discarded sunflower seed shell.

---

[76]USA! USA!

4. We also found half a roll of toilet paper, torn apart by tiny fastidious hands, in tatters around the remainder of the roll.

From this evidence we deduce the obvious: A mouse has joined our roadtrip.

We begin unpacking the whole car. Again.

"You know, if we had just listened to my mom and brought along that mangy cat from West Virginia we would probably not be in this position," I suggest to Bill.

"Yeah, hindsight," Bill says. "Also, if you hadn't spilled Cheez Doodles all over the car, it wouldn't smell like an all-inclusive Caribbean resort for rodents."

That makes me laugh thinking of a bunch of mice in red, green, and yellow hats dancing reggae all night while we are asleep in the tent. But then I am annoyed at the Rasta partiers for ruining Bill's birthday. He really loved that canvas jacket, and he really hates poop in our car.

The search continues but we find no culprit. If we're lucky, the stowaway may have stealthily vacated the premises while we were tearing apart the car.

To lift Bill's spirits, I make him a special lunch of macadamia nut pasta, white wine, and a birthday Ho Ho, which I had secretly bought a few days before and managed to keep secret from him, Maggie, and the mouse. Afterward, we leave behind our mystery and head for the Buckhorn Viewpoint of Hell's Canyon National Recreation Area in Oregon. The spot boasts a birds-eye vista of the confluence of three rivers—the Imnaha, the Salmon, and the Snake—and the canyons they have carved through the ages. Through most of the day, thick clouds and spotty rain showers have muted the land. But for a few moments, as we gaze out over the conjoined boundaries of Oregon, Washington, and Idaho, the clouds break to alight the misty green of the canyon slopes and the distant snowy peaks of the Wallowa Mountains.

After sunset, we set up camp in a dirt parking lot and retire to the tent. Sleep is hard to come by because all through the night, Maggie paces at the door of the tent and stares at the zipper, willing it to open. I wake periodically to find her obsessing over some unseen agitator that lies on the other side of the tent wall. I wonder at her strange behavior but am feeling warm and lazy and unconcerned in my sleeping bag. Besides, if it were anything dangerous, she would be growling and/or quivering.

When morning comes, Bill rises while I stay in the tent and sleep for another couple of hours. Around 9:00 a.m., half asleep, I hear Bill patiently waiting for me outside the tent. After another fifteen minutes have passed, he loses patience.

"When are you going to get up?" he asks from outside the tent.

"I don't know," I answer.

"Come on, Maggie is freaking out over something."

"Still?"

I can hear her whining and her little feet skittering this way and that. Finally, I give up on my desire to return to dreamland and open the tent door to see Maggie frantically pacing around the car, now and then sticking her nose up into the undercarriage. Bill hunches down under the hood, trying to discover the origin of her disturbance. I join him and we strain our eyes searching the engine until Bill spots what Maggie has been pointing at with her sniffling nose. A tiny trembling chipmunk has crammed itself into one of the slots of the motor's fan. It appears terrified and clearly has no intention of moving.

Really? Did we have a chipmunk living in our car for the last week, or more? Or is this a second hop-on?

We try prodding it with a stick. That doesn't seem to alleviate its fears or encourage it to budge. We try talking to it in gentle voices, saying things like, "Come on little buddy, come on out of there."

It doesn't trust us.

Maggie is not helping. She has grown even more excited now that the three of us are working as a team. We decide her barking and snorting are not lending any credibility to our sweet-talking approach, so we put her in the car and close the windows.

"Come on, little guy. Mean drooling dog is gone, you can come out now. We're vegetarians."

"No. I do not think so," the chipmunk says back to us decisively with a blink of its tremulous bulging eyes.

Then Bill has the idea to take a more persuasive approach. He grabs a bottle of water and pours it on the fan. I watch the bottom of the car to see if the chipmunk flees. I see nothing leave the vicinity but when we inspect the fan we find that the chipmunk has disappeared. I fear it has retreated further into the mechanism so that we can't see it and debate the possibility with Bill when he wants to turn the car on.

"What if it's in there?" I say.

"It had to have left. Besides, we can't stay here all day wondering," Bill responds.

He is right about that, but neither of us wants to mutilate a chipmunk, even if it did shred Bill's beloved jacket. We stand around looking for the creature for another ten minutes, then decide to start the car. As he turns the key, I hold my fingers in my ears and squeeze my eyes shut. Nothing happens aside from the soft drumming of the engine, so apparently the chipmunk has escaped or returned to the back to rebuild the fluffy nest we disposed of the day before.

Buckle up, little chipmunk, we're headed to Yellowstone.

57

When we arrive in Yellowstone, Bill and I head straight to the pinnacle of National Park clichés, Old Faithful. I have heard of this place since I was a child, seen photos, postcards, cartoons with bears and picnics. But this place defies expectation. Clichés are predictable. This landscape? Full of surprises.

We walk the length of the geyser basin where hot springs flow over flame-orange growth that blankets the scalded ground; aquamarine pools boil and bubble in anguished bursts of steam and pressure; and clouds of energy erupt from the earth, an upending manifestation of explosive beauty. Here the earth pulls back her cloak to expose the violent creative rage forever boiling within the planetary body; the business of vital organs is boldly visible, intestines absorbing, lungs inflating and deflating, stomach bubbling and churning. In the human body, the business of internal organs is to facilitate the chemical reactions that build cells for hair and fingernails and flesh and blood. In the earth, these same types of energy transfers, enacted on a monumental scale, forge and transform rocks and volcanoes, mountains and rivers, the flesh and blood of the planet.

In Yellowstone, where the earth's agitated innards are exposed, the rhythm of a pulsing heart can be intuited from atop the earth's thick mantle of skin. It is a rumbling beat that quivers through the ground with a volatile vulnerability. And amid all this creative angst walk a profusion of wild creatures unlike any place I have ever been: elk, bear, birds, bison, deer, moose, beaver all living out their own stories on a paradisiacal landscape.

Yellowstone does not disappoint. But it does for me present an emotional conundrum, making words of description stop and start in aggravating indecision in my brain. I am divided in my reactions, between unburdened appreciation of its beauty and weighty contemplation over what it represents. Like the Everglades, Yellowstone offers a glimpse into what once was. There are just enough wild animals left to inspire me to mourn the number there used to be before humans made a long string of destructive decisions. We rode the back of our fortune, rode it hard, and when we were done (or rather half-done, as our ultimate end has yet to be determined), twenty million American bison had been reduced to a few hundred, many millions of birds had been reduced to a relative handful, whale species were driven to extinction, water was poisoned, air poisoned, our own bodies poisoned by the byproducts of our reckless accumulation of comfort and convenience.

In the Genesis story, God creates human beings because He is lonely and has no one to share His beautiful creation with. In Yellowstone I am struck with sadness for this Genesis *God*, who must now be filled with the deepest of grief, for instead of creating a being who would appreciate His magnificent creation, He got one that would destroy it. Tree by tree, species by species, river by poisoned river.

Yellowstone provides a bittersweet return to paradise. Aside from the scenes that Yellowstone's bison and elk herds inspire in the imagination, the only way to envision what this country once was like is through some trick of a Hollywood camera or computer animation. We have doomed ourselves to simulations of the wondrous natural world. Fallen from graceful paradise, fallen into facsimile.

But in Yellowstone, perhaps above all, there *is* hope.

At dawn I rise for a walk along a bank of the Madison River, leaving Bill and Maggie sleeping in the tent. A group of several dozen bison suddenly catches my attention strolling through the heart of our campground. I hold my breath as I see one mammoth bull step gingerly around the tent that Bill lies sleeping in. If it were me in there, I'd be sitting bolt upright from the vibrations of the ground as the herd passed by. Bill most certainly has not even stirred, though Maggie has quite possibly shat herself[77] upon my sleeping bag. The bison continue traveling in my direction and my heart begins to quicken.

I am, to a two-thousand-pound bison, what a squirrel is to me. They appear to be constructed of a city block of steel sinew. And though they have little need of noticing a creature the size of myself, if stalked or harassed by camera-toting humans they have been known to dispense with our presence. At the Yellowstone visitor's center we saw a cautionary video of a man sneaking too close to a bison, provoking the animal to chase him around a tree. When the bison caught the man it lowered its head under the tourist's terrified ass and jerked its great five-hundred-pound head of muscle, flipping the man up into a tree like a deflated bike tire.

---

[77]Again.

Bison were once a keystone of the continent's prairies, as elemental to the ecology as fire and drought. Due to their sheer numbers and their perfect integration into the landscape, they were continually shaped by and shaping the very essence of the ecosystem—from managing the length and health of the grasses through grazing, to fertilizing the ground with their manure. Since they were removed, the land has never been the same.

But in their small pockets, they continue to behave as they have for millennia, and one day, if we can figure out ourselves and our relation to the planet, maybe we can help return them to their rightful place as caretakers of the prairie.

I look around from behind the meager camouflage of my tripod at the bison herd moving toward me. I take a few steps backward with my gear. They are within fifteen feet but taking no notice as they stroll and graze along the riverside. The problem as I see it, is that I am between them and their river. What if they want a drink? They look thirsty. I can feel the blood moving through my neck and temples, trying to get oxygen to my brain so that I can either think my way out of such close proximity to these giants or draw a halt to my rising panic. I opt for the second option and freeze where I am—directly between the heart of the herd and their beverage. The leading bison begins to veer toward the river, and fifty thousand pounds of muscle and skull-crushing bone follow the leader. I step slowly sideways as they pause to nibble but I don't get far before they again approach the bank ten feet in front of me. This is too close . . . too close!

My panic is unfounded; they pay zero attention to me—not a turned head or a shifted eye. I inch carefully away and out of their path and begin to breathe normally again. I am nothing to them, a moth, a varmint, beneath notice. But they have given me back my life, pressed paddles to my heart and (clear!) drummed me with electric shock. I have not been so alive for years, perhaps never.

And at this moment, on a Yellowstone morning in the company of bison utterly uninterested in me or my internal musings, I return again to my time with the creosote of Joshua Tree. Having found some liberation from self-pity at the knee of the world's oldest living thing, a pitiless survivor of every hardship life can conceive, I find here in Yellowstone, a future. If the bison can hold on and hold fast to his work on the landscape until the landscape itself is returned to him, then maybe I can rebound from hopelessness by helping him try to get there—however I can.

58

As the sun sinks, its last stretch of light falls on the Devil's Tower National Monument. This unique geologic feature sits so oddly on its earthen base that many have, over the ages, conjectured or mythologized about how it came to exist.

The Kiowa people said the tower was once a great tree stump which rose into the sky in order to lift seven sisters out of reach of a pursuing bear. The bear, intent on eating the sisters, scored the bark of the tree leaving the vertical indentations upon the surface of Devil's Tower.

There have been many scientific hypotheses to explain the tower. At the current time, scientists believe that subterranean magma percolated nearly to the surface of the earth long ago but stopped short of erupting through the ground. The magma then cooled and hardened into rock. As years passed the surrounding earth eroded away, leaving the more indestructible rock formation as an isolated stony mass towering above the plains. So, though the mighty tower gives the impression that it rose triumphantly from the ground in one earth-shaking push, it more likely resulted from an obstinate resistance to the weathering forces of time—a stubbornness that resulted in it becoming the first national monument in 1906.

Mount Rushmore is a bit easier to explain and it has all the kitsch of an amusement park and the price tag to go with it. Ticket booths, gift shops, flags, granite parking garages—all supported by the twenty-one dollar camp fee and eight dollar parking fee. Just who do they think we are, the royal family? The unexpected costs have thrown our budget off and a good bit of bickering has ensued.

After visiting Rushmore this morning, we stop at a mini-mart and I pick up a can of Pringles and head to the cash register.

From across the store Bill spies me, Pringles in hand and a determined look on my face. He beelines to my side—eyebrows knitted and lips pursed—and interjects his opinion of my intended purchase. "Those are $1.59! Can't you wait until they're on sale?"

"Nope," I answer.

Normally I would have hesitated, probably even put them back. Bill's strict adherence to budget has kept us on the road for many months. But he has arrested my dream of Pringles one too many times of late. Back in Oregon we found a 99-cent sale on the dehydrated potato carcass that we love so much. Since then, Bill has considered the delicacy off-limits unless that price is matched. Unreasonable. Unacceptable.

I carry my extravagant snack to the car and pull the vacuum-sealed top from the tin. Ooohhhhhh that wholly-unnatural, lab-fabricated scent tickles my salivary glands . . . I have to restrain myself. Generally, I eat something in short supply very slowly, so as to make it last.[78] Following this fashion, I begin to indulge in my long denied and debated booty. I eat one Pringle, put the can down, and munch slowly. Bill, seeing the can down at my side, picks it up, grabs a stack of potato product and shoves it all in his mouth at once. That happens three times before I put the can on the other side of me, out of Bill's reach.

"What are you doing?" Bill says when the can has disappeared.

"Let's save some for later," I say.

Later arrives about ten minutes hence, when Bill gets out of the car to use a pay phone to call his mom. I watch him, about ten feet from me, chatting with his mom, sufficiently distracted from my activity. Then I pull out the Pringles and begin to savor. Bill must sense the pleasure vibe emitting from the car window or perhaps he smells the sodium in the air. His eyes grow wide with fear, then narrow as they scan the car. Our eyes meet. I return his steely glare and, without blinking, ever-so-slowly lift another Pringle to my lips. *Crunch!* Every sinew in Bill's body tightens and he clenches the phone receiver as he tries to hurriedly end the conversation with his mom. He clumsily hangs up the phone then races back to the car, opens the passenger door where I sit, and grabs the can of Pringles from my hands.

---

[78]Though I have grown understandably wary of this strategy after living in a car with Maggie.

"They're almost gone!" he shrieks, shoveling the final handful in his mouth lest he be outsmarted again. "How could you?!" he says heartbrokenly through a mouthful of crumbs.

"You had just as many as me, you just ate them all at once. Besides you didn't want to get them in the first place."

"I did *not* have as many as you," he retorts.

"Did too."

"Did not."

. . . This exchange lasts in some form or another for the duration of our drive to Wind Cave National Park and through half of our tour through the cave . . .

"Did too."

"Did not."

As we are still debating the ratio of Bill's stack of chips to my more frequent single Pringle, we hear some young girls on the tour with us bickering incessantly over who would get to ride in the front seat on the drive back to the campground.

Really. I shake my head at the obnoxious children. I see Bill is making the same show of disapproval.

"That would get old," I comment.

"Yeah, I don't know if I could deal with kids," Bill agrees.

Badlands

Fierce South Dakota wind throttles the cottonwood tree that towers above our tent in Badlands National Park. During the day we had felt clever for finding the rare shady site to cool us in the harsh Badlands heat. We regret our cleverness all night long.

Because of the heat and a desire to see the South Dakota night sky through the mesh tent ceiling, we had not attached the rain fly, expecting the arrival of rain would wake us in time to don the cover. And shortly after falling asleep, awakened I am, but not by rain. An angry windstorm has begun ravaging the campground. The unimpeded prairie wind pursues our lonely tree through the night, setting its branches and leaves into relentless bouts of psychotic thrashing. I wake again and again thinking a storm is pelting the tent with rain, only to find that the noise of a downpour is not accompanied by any wetness. When the wind rests momentarily, so do I. But before long the air rises again to battle our tree and I wake with the same panic of rain. Again rain does not fall and I stare into the possessed tree as its convulsing leaves laugh at me. Unable to sleep I watch the tormented leaves above lashing about; they cackle and shake and spin until the sun rises.

When daylight charms the wind into serenity and our tree has quieted itself, I wake Bill and we set out on the landscape for a view of the morning calm. But there is no real calm in the Badlands. This landscape conjures drama on the quietest of dawns. The eroded earth speaks ceaselessly. A mound of smooth, bone-colored earth whispers to a russet, gravel-pocked spire, which murmurs in turn to a gray-grooved eroded earthen sail, which croons to a razor sharp ochre hillside, which bellows to the blue-blazing sky. And the sun answers back, throwing showers of light and shadow upon the restless land.

This conversation is acted out in different languages all over the earth's natural landscape. And it will continue almost anywhere the sun and wind and water and wild things, unburdened by concrete and steel, have freedom to play upon the earth.

But it occurs to me, as I watch the Badlands morning rise, it's time for me to go home—or, somewhere like that. I have been considering the thing for a few weeks now. Every day brings something new, and always something I am thankful for seeing, but road fatigue has worn on me. I know I have found what I was looking for out here, but I now need some time to figure out exactly what that was, to sit for a long while and think about what I've learned and what happens next. I can't do that when we are continually moving and searching. I've tried to put it off because I know Bill wants to keep going. I see the better part of joy—that shy emotion so often glued in the forgotten amber of childhood—halo his eyes every time he sets out on a trail. I could almost continue just for that. But I can't, not right now. And from what I have learned of him over the past eleven months, I know he will understand.

As the gentle drama of the dawn light on the South Dakota landscape grows harsher in the rising sun, Bill and I seek a shady spot for a snack and some rest.

As we sit down, I begin clumsily, "Um, Bill."

"Hmmm," he says, half listening it seems.

"I think maybe we need to stop now," I say.

He looks at me, then puts his arm around me as he turns back to the landscape. "I know."

We sit silently, eating the last of our snack and enjoying our last moments as wanderers on a land that has given us both back our lives.

As we walk back to camp, I ask Bill, "What now?"

"Well, we'll go back to Chicago and stay with family, then we'll figure out our next adventure together. Right?"

"Right," I say.

59

We camp our last night in a rest stop on Interstate 90 and wake before dawn to visit nearby Effigy Mounds National Monument. This monument preserves a series of mysterious burial mounds, built roughly 1,500 years ago. From the ground, the mounded monuments appear simply as formless, grass-covered hills. But from the air, they form shapes—some circular and others in the form of an enormous bear or bird. Archeologists are uncertain as to the exact significance of the mounds, but one theory suggests they derived from communal burial ceremonies. Perhaps, after separating for the winter, different clans would gather together in spring from the far reaches of the territory. They would bring the remains of those they had lost since the past spring and when they united their dead with the dead of the clan at large, a communal burial would take place.

We take a long, leisurely walk in the woodlands that shelter the mounds and later as we drive away toward Chicago, I consider the practice of those ancient peoples. It seems likely that the clans only made the long trek to a central gathering place once a year and perhaps specifically for the purpose of properly honoring their dead. Death connects us all over the ages, connects us to family and friends, to the world at large, to the origins and history of humanity, to the beginnings of life on this planet. Natural law guided the evolution of Earth's creatures and no matter how far we may distance ourselves from the natural world, one law will always govern us. Death pulls us together under a mandatory ritual that dwells in perpetual mystery, one that has forever inspired our deepest emotions of fear and grief. Death sends us searching and returns us to our homes. It pulls at our will to live even as we rage against life's ending. It causes us to distance ourselves from nature and wilderness, because within the natural world death is near and untamed, it has no positive or negative implications—it is simply a force within this grand, graceful Earth, as necessary as birth to creation and the progression of time.

Why fight what we are and where we are headed?

Perhaps because pain is an exquisitely unpleasant partner.

60

Bill and I never really spoke of the future in specifics, but we had over the past year, even through all the turmoil we weathered, decided each on our own that wherever we went following the trip, we would go together. There had developed a measure of understanding between us that no amount of car-cramped suffocation or world-weary sadness could destroy. We had been through our own torment and through some of the most soul-widening and eye-watering beauty the world can conjure, and something very important inside us both had been welded together.

We returned to Chicago in mid-June and began the daunting task of establishing a semi-stationary existence. I told Bill about my realization that morning with the Yellowstone bison herd, that I had discovered a passion for environmental conservation that I was sure could help bridge my discord with the past. That sounded just about right to him so we began sorting through our photos from the trip and working on starting a freelance nature photography and writing business with the hope of perhaps, just maybe, giving a little something back for all the wild has given us.

While we worked on the startup of the business, we stayed in Chicago, where Bill's sister and my brother lived. The end of the trip signaled a return to time, which had in many ways been suspended while we traveled. And, in order to return to a life that leaned toward a future, I had to face two emotional impediments that I had previously chosen to avoid. One of those trials was the burial of Daniel's ashes, which I managed with much care from family and friends. The other was the establishing of a new home, one without Daniel, which I did by returning to Washington, DC, with Bill and Maggie that winter.

I had avoided both of those events because as long as they remained undone, I felt I could forestall the reality of a life without Daniel, or a life with him as a memory.

Strange that only long after the trip did I realize that Bill and Maggie were not the only ones traveling in the Saturn with me those many months. In my journal entries I see Daniel's name or feel his spirit in my words. I recognize the momentum that pushed me forward when I wanted to lay down and sleep was always entwined with Daniel and my need to honor his life by finding a way to continue mine.

When Daniel died it seemed that the world became instantaneously uninhabitable, shrunk to a singularity floating out of time and space. But where there is an ending, there must also be a beginning.

As a pupil of wild things, I have come to understand that life must continue despite the cruelty of the climate. Lack of sunlight does not defeat the albino Indian pipe; scarcity of water does not destroy the creosote. Survival depends on evolution and evolution on a determined will to adapt.

Over the years, I have learned to find sustenance where there is scarcity. In the bend of dune grass under an ocean breeze. A solid rock for a luncheon rest on a sunny peak. The wings of a heron reflected in low flight over the Anacostia River. The forlorn cry of a loon echoing through the silent fog of Little Tupper Lake. The rare glimpse of a grizzly bear free upon a Yellowstone meadow. Bill's hand in mine on a trail in a hushed forest. The sound of Daniel's laughter visiting me in my dreams.

These are my needs, all else is adaptation.

Epilogue

Looking back I see that one reason for leaving on this journey in the first place was to gain some clarity. In fleeing the city and the site of my experiences with Daniel, I had hoped the heat and pollution haze that smothers Washington, DC, on hot summer days would lift from my skin and the crisp whip of mountain air and flutter of leaves in lands of trees would pull the shadow from my eyes, and then maybe I could see clearly just what I had lost.

And it has. I can see that along with losing Daniel, the landscape of my life, and myself for a while, I lost a romantic view of life, the naiveté that there is a threshold for how cruel life can be. In fact, life can throw knives in eyes that are searching for a reason to keep believing. And life makes no apologies. The very nature of life demands unsympathetically that you redefine beauty to include pain. We are the students—life and death are the masters. The only control we have is the will to see and be affected.

As humans we are predisposed to rail against this reality and seek shelter from pain above all else. Still, we are drawn away from safety and intrigued by wildness. But in a world where we have dominated, destroyed, or domesticated so much of the wild world, an experience of wildness has become rare. And when people encounter wild animals, the urge is often to tame. We want to feed them so we can pet them and they'll be safe for us to be around. But if a wild animal is amenable to being tamed, and we succeed, then we have lost the very thing that attracted us to it in the first place. We cannot have everything; there must be sacrifice. If we want wildness, we have to be willing to let go our death-grip on security. If we want total safety, we will be closing the door on nature altogether.

We have to ask ourselves, if safety and comfort are the prize we make them out to be, why are so many people in this country so unhappy?

In the *Seven Pillars of Wisdom,* T.E. Lawrence (a.k.a. Lawrence of Arabia), describes the life of the Bedouin, polar opposite of the modern-day American.

> *The Bedouin of the desert, born and grown up in it, had embraced with all his soul this nakedness too harsh for volunteers, for the reason, felt but inarticulate, that there he found himself indubitably free. He lost material ties, comforts, all superfluities and other complications to achieve a personal liberty which haunted starvation and death.*

Well, we can't all be Bedouins. But perhaps the only way we can be truly free from fear and death and fear of death is to plant ourselves square in the middle of these troubling perplexities, open our eyes wide, and go on living. Some people have this by virtue of their birth. Others, including many pampered Westerners, have to seek it out.

In this enterprise, I was not a volunteer, but a draftee. Unsought pain can torturously scrape the crust of comfort from one's skin, as it did for me, catapulting me into this journey. Beyond that, there is only consciousness and a vigilant life-long pursuit of this peculiar truth: if you seek to experience the sublime in life, the force of a beauty so terrible and powerful it rends your soul a weeping wound and then a cataclysmic giggle, you have to be willing to walk where the wild things are, in the stillness between light and dark, between pain and comfort, between life and death.

It is there, where neither force devours the other that the amber glow of dusk rests upon this world. If only for a moment.

I count these spare moments of perfect balance as the greatest blessings of my life. As time wears on I take them where I can. I continue to find Daniel in the company of trees and cactus, in the curious gaze of a jackrabbit, the whisper of the wings of a dragonfly—and my work as a photographer and writer has given me lots of opportunities to do that. I have found him as well in an infinite darkness made brilliant by a billion infinitesimal pinpricks of universal memory cast in millennia-old light trails. And I have found him in the shared company of a small friend who barfed in my car and ate my Amish cheese. For a time.

Maggie's body began to falter around the age of fourteen. We three managed for a while but there came a time when the goodness in her life was overshadowed by the pain. I came to accept this reality one night, one especially difficult night for Maggie. As she was sniffing around the backyard with the limp she had acquired by then, I thought of all the years we had shared. Maggie was with me when I got my first job, she pooped all over the first yard I ever owned, climbed over the first fence I ever built. and uprooted and shredded the first tree I ever planted. She was the first being that depended on me for her very life and the first I gave over my life and independence to. She was standing at our apartment door waiting for us to come home the night Daniel was diagnosed with cancer. A few months later, when the first round of chemo seemed successful and we celebrated, she was there. Just like she was there when the cancer came back within a month and when it put Daniel in a wheelchair and when all hope had faded a year from his first diagnosis and I sat on the edge of his hospice bed in our condo, holding his hand, begging for his pain to stop.

She traveled with Bill and me across the country and back, and moved into our first shared home together, where she pooped on the floor. She was my faithful friend for longer than any other creature in my adult life. As I looked at Maggie, limping slowly around the yard, I knew it was time to let her go. In the morning Bill drove us to the animal hospital. I held Maggie in my arms and pressed my lips to her soft little head, and said, "We've lived a great universe together." I think she would agree, with the exception that there should have been more bacon and cheese, much, much more.

That night, Bill and I sat together in the bay window that looks out onto the backyard of our house and tried to begin the transition into a world without Maggie. I looked out into the dark sky and immediately spotted Sirius shining brightly in the east, as brightly as I'd ever seen in DC. I looked to her side to find Orion, right where he always was.

"Look," I said to Bill. "It's Canis Major and Orion."

He looked out into the sky, eyes sad but a small smile on his face. He squeezed my hand and said, "A boy and his dog."

As Bill looked up to our friends, I looked at him and thought, how lucky I am to have his friendship and love. Healing is a process and I still feel broken and incapable of faith in continuity. But when I look at him, I think, maybe, just maybe I could believe.

It is an internal argument that I may wage my entire life. Are all things meant to end or can there be a thread of permanence that remains even after all evidence of it is gone? As star-stuff we must be as enduring as any celestial matter, with trails of remnant light that glow for millennia. But as animals we are as momentary as a lightning bug, just on a different timeline. They have a summer to flicker and shine, we have twenty or thirty or seventy summers. It is all a quivering blink in time. My head knows we are not meant to last, we begin to whither physically from the moment we become fully-grown. And all through that time we are changing. Growing and withering, growing and growing and withering, finding endless avenues for rebirth and an infinity of deaths behind each corner turned. Life is, if nothing else, one long string of major and minor singularities, an ongoing process of small and big bangs, from the moment we rise from the dirt, to our final resting place within it.

Amidst all of this becoming and unraveling, I wonder, how can there be continuity? And yet I look at Bill, and think . . . maybe. It is the glimmering figures of Sirius and Orion that make me both certain that I will be disappointed and certain that my faith is well placed.

1215